WINNING THE

LONG
WAR

Lessons from the Cold War for Defeating
Terrorism and Preserving Freedom

WINNING THE LONG WAR

Lessons from the Cold War for Defeating Terrorism and Preserving Freedom

To Polley

thnks for your service
to the nation

James Jay Carafano & Paul Rosenzweig

Published by HERITAGE BOOKS
an activity of
The Heritage Foundation
214 Massachusetts Avenue, NE
Washington, DC 20002-4999
(202) 546-4400 • heritage.org

Library of Congress Control Number:
200920780

Printed in the United States of America

Distributed to the Trade by
National Book Network
Lanham, Maryland

ISBN 0-9743665-4-4

Cover design by Elizabeth Brewer
Book design by Alex Adrianson

Front cover photo: Stephanie Sinclair/Corbis
Back cover photo: Photo by Photographer's Mate Chief
Eric J. Tilford, USN

For George F. Kennan—citizen, scholar,
diplomat, historian, patriot,
American

Contents

Appendices

Foreword

Everyone knows the tragic story. On September 11, 2001, al-Qaeda transformed passenger airlines into missiles, targeting our nation's financial, political, and military centers, but also intending to reduce the American people's confidence in their government and in their own commitment to freedom at home and abroad. Nineteen hijackers attacked icons of America's public and private sectors, and inflicted a catastrophic loss of innocent human life.

The terrorists developed a network across 60 countries to attack a U.S. government that was not networked. They knew more about our world than we did about theirs. As the 9/11 Commission made clear, they defeated America's intelligence system—both our advanced technical collection capabilities and our worldwide human resources. Our elaborate immigration processes and our layered security systems—all of which should have defeated them—barely slowed them down.

There is no longer any doubt that America has a new mortal enemy. This enemy has no fixed address, but has global access to information, finance, and weapons. Defeating this enemy will require a new U.S. counterterrorism strategy—one that coordinates our military, diplomatic, and intelligence resources through better intelligence, more integrated analysis, greater interagency interoperability and collaboration, and broader application of existing and new technologies. The goals of this new strategy are to stop terrorists before they can strike, to frustrate their attacks by hardening our critical infrastructure, and to be prepared to respond and recover if another attack is successful in spite of these efforts.

The long-term threat posed by international terrorists is alarming, because eventually they will have access to weapons of mass destruction (WMD). Yet this is hardly the first time the United States has faced a strategic threat from an adversary with WMD. In the Cold War, as James Carafano and Paul Rosenzweig remind us, dealing with the Soviet Union required a comprehensive strategy including explicit military, diplomatic, and intelligence elements. The U.S. government was structured to win that long war—and did so. Americans, confronted with the threat of nuclear annihilation, were forced to define and defend their values as a free people—and did so. This Cold War experience, despite the many differences between the twentieth century Soviet threat and the twenty-first century terrorist threat, has valuable lessons for us. We are the same free people, and our challenge is to preserve our democratic way of life.

Our national, state, and local governments have made dramatic changes since 9/11. The private sector, firefighters, police officers, emergency medical professionals, and public works employees have all emerged as new stakeholders in U.S. national security.

Nine days after the terrorist attacks, President George W. Bush created a new White House Office of Homeland Security. On March 1, 2003, Secretary Tom Ridge took the helm at the Department of Homeland Security, the largest reorganization of the executive branch since the Department of Defense was created in 1947. Congress passed the USA Patriot Act to give intelligence and law enforcement better tools to combat terrorism. In January 2003, Congress established the House Select Committee on Homeland Security, which I chaired, to oversee what was already the fourth-largest Cabinet department. In the 109th Congress, that committee has been made permanent, and I will be proud to serve as its chairman.

Our nation has used its military force to launch a strong offensive against terrorists. President Bush, applying the lessons of past just wars, pursued al-Qaeda, its leaders, and its enablers throughout the world. This aggressive hunt for terrorists abroad destroyed the al-Qaeda infrastructure in Afghanistan and drove Iraq's Saddam Hussein from power. The message to terrorists is now clear: If you attack America, we will come after you—wherever you run and however long it takes.

Despite setbacks suffered at the hands of America and her allies, terrorists continue to threaten us, and will do so for the foreseeable future. They expect that our nation will become paralyzed by fear. They seek to force upon us a defensive response that will weaken our economy, erode our freedoms, and force an American retreat from global leadership.

The terrorist threat is dynamic and continuously adapts to our counter-measures. Therefore, we must constantly adjust and strengthen our security. In this long-term struggle to stay ahead of the enemy, we must focus on the intersection of our greatest vulnerabilities and the terrorists' most serious threats. At the same time, we must live within spending boundaries that are sustainable, protect our civil liberties, and give priority to security measures that also contribute to our productivity and our economic growth. Dr. Carafano and Mr. Rosenzweig help to stimulate discussion on the correct issues to get us to that point.

Serious work remains. Early in 2004, for example, the Department of Homeland Security unveiled a series of bottom-line goals as part of its strategic plan. The House Homeland Security Committee pointed out that a strategic plan must go beyond mere aspirations: It must include clear-cut objectives (supported by specific steps toward their attainment) to be completed within unambiguous timelines. The President himself has, over the past two years, issued a definitive homeland security strategy, several homeland security policy directives, and a number of sector-specific strategic documents. It will fall to the Department of Homeland Security to realize the objectives identified in each of these, even as it completes the merger process from which it was created.

Although we should applaud the Department of Homeland Security for its significant accomplishments, we must also focus on improving its functionality. The Department of Homeland Security must integrate and serve all the homeland stakeholders—including state, local, and private entities—and do so in a manner that does not repeat the decades of bureaucratic torpor experienced by the Department of Defense in the decades following its creation.

In the long war against terrorism to which we are now committed, federal, state, and local officials must be equal players. The notion that the federal government is the source of everything worth knowing is no longer just an annoyance—it is a dangerous fallacy, which, if indulged, will kill us. Federal agencies must learn to listen. State and local governments, as well as private businesses, are sources of key information. They are also, now, among the intelligence community's key customers. Serving them well is largely the responsibility of the Department of Homeland Security and the FBI. It is not an act of largesse for the federal government to share threat-related information with state and local officials: It is essential—and the Homeland Security Act requires it.

The 9/11 attacks showed that the failure to share information among federal, state, local, and private sector entities is an exploitable vulnerability. That information gap enabled al-Qaeda terrorists to defeat our law enforcement, intelligence, immigration, and airport security systems at multiple levels. It was a tragic irony that valuable information that our tax dollars had procured—often at considerable risk to those who obtained it—was not analyzed comprehensively in context and shared quickly with those who needed it to help protect us.

Eliminating this vulnerability requires that we discard the common assumption that the most important information is classified. In this new world, it may not be. The long-haul trucker in the small hours of the night may be the only one who sees the critical, anomalous act that indicates a possible terrorist attack. That information may be the critical, missing piece of a complex puzzle. Likewise, sharing classified information with state and local officials can no longer be considered some grand gesture of noblesse oblige by a privileged coterie of federal agencies. State and local law enforcement and first responders need access to classified information in order to protect us. They must have it—period.

Mere presidential speeches or congressional mandates, however, will not be enough to ensure that this kind of information sharing actually occurs. Dr. Carafano recognizes that rigorous, focused, and relentless congressional attention will also be necessary. He has repeatedly stressed the importance of a homeland security committee with primary legislative and oversight jurisdiction of the Department of Homeland Security. This is necessary, he realized, if both the department and the broader homeland security mission are to succeed.

The diffusion of legislative jurisdiction over the Department of Homeland Security in its early days weakened the ability of Congress to perform these needed oversight and law-making functions. Again and again, Dr. Carafano encouraged the congressional leadership to establish a permanent Committee on Homeland Security. When the Speaker of the House decided to do exactly that in late 2004, Dr. Carafano stressed the need to give the new committee the legislative jurisdiction necessary to do its job. This meant, he said, that legislative authority and responsibility should not be diffused among many committees primarily concerned with other matters. Here again, he hit the nail precisely on the head.

"Homeland security" describes a myriad set of elements at the intersection of domestic and foreign policy, law enforcement and intelligence, government and the economy that supports it, and professional specialties ranging from warfighting to medicine to computer technology to counterproliferation. These many ingredients of our national response to terrorism must be integrated explicitly in our consideration of a great many public and private policy questions that previously have been deemed unrelated. Therefore, for example, immigration can no longer be a question only of our social, economic, and foreign policies—it is now a component of our national security. We must now recognize that the failure to enforce our immigration laws will, over time, have a growing impact on the security of the American people in their own territory. However, this is not to say that homeland security lacks discrete boundaries. For our nation to become adept in this wide-ranging new discipline means not that one Cabinet department or congressional committee will henceforth be responsible for all aspects of our domestic, foreign, and security policies, but rather that there needs to be a deliberate focus on the many connected elements that cut across traditional boundaries.

The twenty-first century tool that will prove most useful in transcending these boundaries—real and imagined—is technology. Terrorists who prey upon America are using modern technology to further their efforts against us. Yet our society—the private sector and our government—has an insurmountable technological lead over any terrorists, if only we will exploit it. The information technology revolution that has transformed our economy has also given us the tools, infrastructure, and commercial capabilities to maintain a constant advantage over our terrorist enemies. The consequences of not exploiting that advantage were seen on 9/11. It is almost certain that if then-available information technology tools had been employed, some of the terrorists would have been detained, and some of the plots would possibly have been foiled.

Technology has revolutionized the economy with dramatic productivity improvements. That same technology (e.g., wireless data networks, encryption, powerful miniature computer chips, the global Internet, data mining software, and biosensors) can likewise make our counterterrorism efforts vastly more productive. Nor must our investment in homeland security technology, apart from the protection it provides, be nothing but dead weight economic loss. It is possible that, just as technology investments during the Cold War gave birth to the economic and technological boom of the 1990s, the investments we make today might yield significant economic, health, and public safety benefits.

Indeed, we can ensure this result if we are judicious in our homeland security technology investments. The threshold test for deploying any new security technology at airports and seaports, in the financial sector, in commerce, in agriculture, or in our critical infrastructure should be whether it can also make a positive contribution to the performance of those areas of our economy. The airport security measures hastily contrived after 9/11 clearly fail this test. Yet more recent security investments in electric power infrastructure offer improved reliability, as well as greater protection from terrorist attack. Likewise, technology tools now being employed to track overseas shipments throughout the supply chain will also benefit customers who need real-time data about the location and condition of their cargo. In the future, well-designed security technology will pay for itself by improving the efficiency of the productive systems of which it is a part.

Perhaps the most important point that the authors make is that increased security must not come at the expense of our civil liberties. We must use new technologies and improved information sharing not as a trade off for civil liberties, but to protect those liberties that are the foundation of American life. Congress and the President recognized this imperative when they created the Department of Homeland Security, putting the protection of Americans' civil rights at the very core of the department's mission. The Homeland Security Act establishes within the top of department's management the Officer for Civil Rights and Civil Liberties—a unique position within the federal government. No other federal department has a senior official who is appointed by the President, answers directly to the Secretary, and focuses solely on shaping policy in ways that enhance civil liberties.

Because the war against terrorism has no immediately foreseeable end, neither unsustainable spending in its support nor intrusions on our civil rights can be justified as emergency measures that will eventually lapse. Americans will have to live with the policies we adopt to wage the war on terrorism for many years. Sacrificing our economy or our liberties in the name of homeland security, therefore, can only be self-defeating. Indeed, to do this would be to concede gratuitously to Osama bin Laden what he is seeking to accomplish by way of violence. His stated aim is to destroy our economy and our freedom. Defeating him means securing both.

Finally, Dr. Carafano and Mr. Rosenzweig argue that communicating the language of freedom across the globe is an essential aspect of a homeland security strategy, one that is necessarily reliant on support within the international community, and especially on support within the Islamic world. This point is of vital importance because modern-day terrorism is not an accidental occurrence: It is bred. Free people must challenge those who see the deliberate murder of innocents as the preferred instrument of "God's will" on earth.

America today is not engaged in a clash of civilizations. Rather, we are challenged as never before to extend the dialogue of freedom across a rapidly shrinking world in which technology is providing small bands of terrorists with destructive capabilities previously restricted to nation-states. The true conflict is between the billions of people who together comprise civilization, and the relatively tiny, but lethal, portion of humanity that would annihilate us all. Civilization will win, if only we will marshal our superior energies and resources. In that case, our victory is assured because we are more numerous; because we have superior technology, tools, weapons, and information; and most important of all, because we embrace the essential dignity of man, the nobility of the human spirit, and the ideal of liberty—which, unrestrained, is the most powerful force on earth.

The Honorable Christopher Cox
Chairman,
Committee on Homeland Security
U.S. House of Representatives

Prologue

The Long Shadow of the Long Telegram

Eight thousand words scribbled in the drafty apartments of the U.S. embassy in Moscow could be the secret to winning the war against global terrorism. Their author was George F. Kennan, an ambitious, erudite Foreign Service officer with Victorian principles and a penchant for controversy.

In 1946, when Kennan penned what became known as the "Long Telegram," few Americans had ever heard of him or his advice to the State Department about how to deal with the Soviet Union. In the pageant of history, however, Kennan's missive has become one of those dramatic, movie-like moments—a turn of fate when an obscure government bureaucrat crafted the kernel of an idea that led to winning the Cold War.

The truth about the importance of the Long Telegram lies somewhere on the dividing line between myth and fact. Historians will continue to write books and build careers debating the point.[1] For us, the Long Telegram has more immediate relevance, for what cannot be debated is that within the final three paragraphs—a mere three hundred and fifty words—is America's survival guide for dealing with the security challenges of the twenty-first century.

In View of Recent Events

No winter in Moscow is enjoyable. February 1946 was doubly miserable. The cold, windblown, and cheerless Soviet capital hunkered under a crust of blackened snow. U.S.–Soviet postwar relations were as sour as the weather. To make matters worse, Kennan, the minister-counselor for the American embassy, was horribly sick. He had a cold, a fever, and a toothache. After taking sulfa drugs to combat an infection, he became even sicker.

Kennan could not have been more miserable. The U.S. wartime ambassador, Averell Harriman, had left the country, leaving the minister-counselor (largely an administrator responsible for managing the sprawling U.S. compound) in charge of everything. There was Kennan, dragging himself from his sickbed to answer the endless daily queries from Washington, including a despairing note stating that the Soviets were unwilling to participate in the World Bank and the International Monetary Fund—envisioned by the White House as two key instruments for stimulating global postwar economic growth. Awful as he felt, Kennan decided to use his response as an opportunity to critique U.S.–Soviet policy. (See Appendix 1.)

The minister-counselor began his reply with an unpretentious introduction, appropriate to his modest station: "In view of recent events, the following remarks will be of interest." Even though he was the number two man in Moscow, Kennan's anonymity and lack of influence were not surprising. Generals were the rock stars of World War II. Diplomats were note takers. That was the way President Franklin D. Roosevelt wanted it.

President Roosevelt had intended to personally craft postwar relations with the Soviet Union. He had a plan.[2] Roosevelt believed he could ameliorate Soviet behavior by establishing "open spheres" of influence for the great powers, in which each could control security policies over adjacent territories, but with trade, people, and ideas flowing freely back and forth. In this manner, Roosevelt believed that Stalin's Russia would be gradually seduced and disarmed.

There were only two problems. Roosevelt shared the totality of his vision with no one—least of all Stalin. Then he died.

Achieving Roosevelt's postwar hopes would have been difficult, even had he lived. After all, the Soviet Union was—as President Ronald Reagan famously declared decades later—an "Evil Empire." America's wartime ally against the Axis powers had much to account for. Joseph Stalin killed more innocents than Hitler. His nation was guided by a soulless ideology that choked the hope of freedom for hundreds of millions. Security was sought by enslaving a ring of nations from Europe to Asia and making trouble around the world. Taming the Russian bear would be no easy task.

Although he has been treated kindly by historians (perhaps in part because of the grave handicap under which he began his presidency), Harry

East Berliner looks back to West Berlin, as Communist police seize him at border, August 1961. (COURTESY OF USIS/BAD GODESBERG)

Truman was hardly equal to the job he inherited upon FDR's death. Roosevelt had never explained his grand design to his Vice President. "You know," FDR once quipped, "I never let my right hand know what my left hand does...."[3] When Roosevelt died shortly before the end of combat in Europe, the man from Missouri assumed the duties of finishing the war against Japan and determining the course of postwar affairs with scant knowledge of FDR's plans or negotiations with wartime allies.

Bracing for the challenges ahead, Truman went so far as to appoint former Senator and Supreme Court Justice James F. "Jimmy" Byrnes as his Secretary of State. To placate the ambitious Byrnes, Roosevelt took him to the Yalta Conference at which FDR discussed postwar arrangements with Stalin and Winston Churchill. Impressed by Byrnes's presence at the meeting of the Big Three, and looking to eliminate a likely competitor for the Democratic presidential nomination, Truman selected Byrnes as the architect for U.S. foreign policy. But, in truth, Byrnes had been excluded from the most critical and sensitive discussions with Stalin and was scarcely better informed than Truman.[4] He was also largely a failure as Secretary of State: He resigned on January 7, 1947.

In practice, with or without Byrnes, Truman's approach to dealing with the Soviet Union was a mish-mash of half steps and half measures, unguided by a coherent idea beyond hoping for the best and reacting to the worst. The Truman Doctrine, a 1947 pronouncement that accompanied a request for

George F. Kennan in 1968, after winning the Pulitzer Prize. (Courtesy of the National Archives)

$400 million in military assistance to Greece and Turkey, contained a lot of rhetoric about helping free people everywhere. Yet the truth was that Truman had no clear conception for expanding support to other countries. Likewise, the Marshall Plan, an aid package for Western Europe launched in 1948, was more about speeding economic recovery than combating Soviet expansion.[5]

Truman's boldest move proved to be the drafting of NSC-68, a top-level review of policies for dealing with the Soviet Union that concluded the Bolshevik empire could only be stopped if it were confronted at every turn on a global scale. (See Appendix 2.) The President took one look at the price tag implied by the declaration and ordered it hidden away. Truman did not begin to make significant budgetary investments in national security until after the outbreak of the Korean War forced his hand.[6]

Kennan had not watched these events from the sidelines. He was in the eye of the storm. Shortly after the Long Telegram arrived at the cables office in the United States, copies made their way around Washington. Navy Secretary James Forrestal admired the analysis so much he had mimeograph duplicates sent to senior officers throughout the Pentagon. After his posting in Moscow, Kennan, with his newfound notoriety, was appointed Deputy for Foreign Affairs at the recently established National War College, located on a spit of land in downtown Washington at the confluence of the Potomac and Anacostia rivers. In May of 1947, he left the academy to become Director of the Policy Planning Staff for retired General George C. Marshall. Marshall, whose steady hand as the Army Chief helped direct World War II, had been tapped by Truman to replace the mercurial Jimmy Byrnes at the State Department.

While serving as Marshall's principal policy analyst, Kennan struggled mightily to influence the course of U.S. relations with the Soviet Union. His article in the influential journal *Foreign Affairs*, "The Sources of Soviet Conduct," published anonymously as "Mr. X," became the talk of the town.[7] Kennan argued for using American might to "contain" Soviet power until the Communist empire collapsed.

Sadly for Kennan, little of what was being said and done actually squared well with the ideas that he had first proposed in the Long Telegram. For example, he "anguished" over NSC-68. "We should make our plans for steady, consistent effort over a long period of time," Kennan countered, "and not for an imaginary 'peak' of danger."[8] NSC-68, he feared, overemphasized the challenge of military competition with the Soviets. At the same time, the notion of "containment"—trying to block the expansion of Soviet influence everywhere, all the time—was, Kennan believed, just silly, as well as wasteful and dangerous.

The use of American might, Kennan cautioned in the concluding paragraphs of the Long Telegram, had to be measured in two important respects. "Much depends," he wrote, "on [the] health and vigor of our own society." In addition, Kennan argued, "We must have the courage and self-confidence to cling to our own methods and conceptions of human society. After all, the greatest danger that can befall us…is that we shall allow ourselves to become like those with whom we are coping." At the root of Kennan's proposals were the essential concepts for prevailing in any long war—whether it be taking down a rival superpower or responding to the challenge of shadowy, transnational terrorist networks.

Soviet troops march in review in the international sector in Vienna, August 31, 1951. (Courtesy of the National Archives)

Most Cold War policy makers missed the subtlety of Kennan's message. In the five years following VE Day, the United States largely failed to put his prescription into practice in any coherent manner. That would be a task for the boy from Abilene.

Ike's Hidden Hand

Kennan's Long Telegram arrived in Washington on the anniversary of George Washington's birthday, February 22, 1946. On February 22, 1951, Dwight David Eisenhower, the former Supreme Commander of the Allied Expeditionary Force that had vanquished the Nazi armies from the beaches of Normandy to the Rhine river, was rousted from a comfortable stateroom aboard the *Queen Elizabeth* for an unexpected rendezvous in a damp, cavernous Cherbourg warehouse. Bleary-eyed and unshaven, Eisenhower found himself surrounded by an unruly mob. A glass of champagne was thrust into his hands, followed by a litany of toasts to mark the occasions of the birth of the Father of America and the return of the liberator of France.

An unexpected road had led Ike back to Normandy. After leaving the military, Eisenhower had accepted the presidency of Columbia University. Residence in the ivory tower and retirement both proved short-lived. First, Truman asked Ike to fill in as an informal chairman of the Joint Chiefs of Staff (JCS).

The creation of the JCS had been part of a massive government reorganization directed by the National Security Act of 1947. In addition to establishing the JCS—a body consisting of all the heads of the armed forces who would serve as statutory military advisors to the President—the act combined the armed forces under what later became the Department of Defense and created the Central Intelligence Agency. The following year saw the creation of the North Atlantic Treaty Organization (NATO). Eisenhower approved of these initiatives. Yet while he supported Truman in each step, even agreeing at the President's request to take command of the North Atlantic Alliance in 1951, in truth he disapproved of Truman's scattershot approach to dealing with the Soviets. Thus, even as he sipped champagne at the break of dawn in a clammy Norman warehouse, Ike was already contemplating a run for the White House.[9]

When Eisenhower assumed the presidency in 1953, many of the key weapons that would be used to fight the Cold War had already been created and were in the process of being fashioned into effective instruments for national security. Yet beyond the vague notion of containment codified in NSC-68, the nation still lacked a practical, coherent blueprint for fighting and winning a protracted confrontation with the Soviets. Eisenhower provided that lifeline of a guiding idea, and his vision proved not too unlike the closing lines of the Long Telegram.

Eisenhower has always been underrated. Some historians have derided Ike's World War II generalship, dismissing him as merely a good "political" officer, keeping Roosevelt and Churchill happy while simultaneously refereeing the scraps between testy field commanders. These criticisms are misplaced. In coalition warfare, political skill is the acme of generalship. When Carl von Clausewitz, the great nineteenth century military theorist, wrote "War is an extension of politics," he implied a double meaning. War was not only a tool of politics, it is *like* politics—a contest of action and counteraction between two determined foes. Eisenhower knew his Clausewitz. Fox Conner, Ike's mentor, made the young officer read Clausewitz's *On War* three times.[10]

Ike learned his lessons well. Eisenhower's genius was that he always understood that war was more than just winning battles. Global conflict engaged leaders, peoples, economies, and ideas as deeply and intimately as bayonets stabbing across the trench lines.

Eisenhower's contributions to setting the course of the Cold War have been largely unappreciated. Americans may have liked Ike; most presidential historians have not. While most scholars have offered Truman a pass, they have generally given the Eisenhower White House the back of the hand. In part, this was

President John F. Kennedy with former President Dwight D. Eisenhower, following a meeting at Camp David to discuss the 1962 Cuban Missile Crisis. (Courtesy of the National Archives)

because Eisenhower's leadership style did not lend itself to drawing attention to the Oval Office. Ike made policy with a "hidden hand." He ran the government much like he ran the allied armies. There would be meetings, briefings, discussions—perhaps even some cajoling, negotiation, and a bit of subterfuge—and then Ike would make a decision and send forth his generals to do battle.[11]

Although his presidency has garnered scant respect from many academics, what Eisenhower did to shape the course of the Cold War was subtle, simple, and profound. Like many of his most important decisions, Ike's influence was reflected less in public declarations, press conferences, and bold legislative proposals than in the reasoning behind administration policies and the understated manner in which they influenced virtually every national security program.

There was a guiding vision behind Ike's approach to the Cold War, a worldview far more powerful than the crude notion of simply containing the Soviet Union. Eisenhower, like Kennan, believed that this was war of a different kind. It would have a military dimension, perhaps even battles and campaigns, but it would not end in an inexorable march to Moscow and a victory parade. Nuclear standoff made a direct confrontation unthinkable. Lacking the capacity to come to grips with the enemy, the war would inevitably be a drawn-out contest, a long war. Ike, the general, knew that winning long wars required strategies of a different character.

The bloody lines of history are full of tales of long wars, from medieval times to the modern age. When long wars are fought badly, even winners can be losers. The least preferable option for a long war is a battle of attrition in which the enemies fight to exhaustion—for instance, ancient Sparta and Athens in the Peloponnesus or the bloody trench warfare of World War I.

The way to win a long war was to ensure that the nation flourished, that the victor grew stronger, while it hounded its enemies into the pages of the past. Eisenhower was determined to craft a way of war that left America stronger at the end of the conflict than it had been at the beginning. Ike built his approach to the Cold War on four pillars:

- **Provide Security.** It was important to take the initiative away from the enemy and to protect American citizens—therefore, the nation needed a strong mix of both offensive and defensive means. Nothing was to be gained, as Kennan had argued, by seeming weak and vulnerable in the eyes of the enemy.
- **Build a Strong Economy.** Economic power would be the taproot of strength, the source of power that would enable the

nation to compete over the long term and would better the lives of its citizens. Kennan had it right; much depended on the "health and vigor" of society. Maintaining a robust economy had to be a priority. In addition, the United States, intricately tied to worldwide networks of trade and exchange, had to be concerned about its place in the global economy.

- **Protect Civil Liberties.** Preserving a vibrant civil society and avoiding what Kennan called "the greatest danger"—the threat of sacrificing civil liberties in the name of security—was critical as well. Only a strong civil society would give the nation the will to persevere during the difficult days of a long war.

- **Win the Struggle of Ideas.** In the end, victory would be achieved because the enemy would abandon a corrupt, vacuous ideology that was destined to fail its people. In contrast, the West had a legitimate and credible alternative to offer. In Kennan's words, America needed to face its detractors with "courage and self-confidence."

Eisenhower's policies reflected the core of each of these principles. He supported strong defense spending, but not at the expense of expanding the economy. Ike demanded "guns and butter." He eschewed the excesses of McCarthyism and racial segregation, rejecting the notion that stability and security could be achieved by sacrificing human dignity. He launched a concerted effort to make the case for democracy and free-market capitalism. These were Ike's legacies and they served as a guiding star for America's future; from the harrowing days of the Cuban missile crisis through the tragedy of Vietnam to the renewal of the Reagan years—and on to victory.

Lessons from the Cold War

With the collapse of the Soviet Union, the past no longer seemed prologue. In the aftermath of the fall of the Berlin Wall, it became fashionable for politicians and pundits to deride every national security instrument as a legacy of the Cold War, irrelevant to the challenges of the twenty-first century. That is simply wrong. The most important lessons of the Cold War are worth remembering. We believe there are three valuable teachings that can be drawn from the global struggle with Communism that have relevance to any age.

Lesson 1: *The fundamentals of fighting a long war remain unchanged—sound security, economic growth, a strong civil society, and willingness to engage in a public battle of ideas.* All are important. One priority cannot be traded off for another. When a nation begins to make compromises, that nation becomes the servant of war, not its sovereign—and war is a jealous, greedy, insatiable master. Long wars usually centralize power in the state and in the long run diminish it by crushing innovation, stifling liberty, and inefficiently employing resources. Sprawling militaries are fielded. Industrial production is controlled. Taxes are exorbitant. Internal dissent is crushed. During the Cold War, the United States largely resisted these urges and established means to confront the Soviet Union that served America well.

Historian Aaron L. Freidberg has persuasively argued that by the close of the Eisenhower years, "despite some relatively minor changes, the broad outlines of both the internal and external aspects of U.S. policy would remain fixed for the remainder of the Cold War."[12] There were mistakes and miscalculations along the way, but none threatened the survival of the nation or its cause because America never strayed too far from its chosen path. In the end, the results were as Kennan predicted. We left the Soviet empire in the last chapter of history.

Lesson 2: *It takes time.* History argues for patience. The National Security Act of 1947 created America's premier Cold War weapons—what eventually became the Department of Defense (DoD) and the Central Intelligence Agency (CIA). Yet it still took about a decade to figure out how best to fight the Russian bear and develop instruments like NATO, nuclear deterrence, and international military assistance, as well as the right concepts to guide how those instruments would be used. It required years of trial and error, experimentation, and bitter lessons to get it right.

Lesson 3: *Now is the time to get it right.* If there is one constant, it is how Washington works. Once our government is set on a course, change is very difficult, usually impossible. Momentum is Washington's greatest industry. Thus, bad habits get carried into the future as determinedly as successful policies and programs.

Again, the struggle against the Soviets offers a case in point. One area in which Eisenhower failed to put his stamp on the American way during the Cold War was in how the Pentagon would be organized. In the debates about the 1947 act, and again as President, Eisenhower lobbied for more integration of the services. Based on the lessons of World War II, he argued for joint operations, in which Army, Navy, Marine, and Air Force assets would work closely together. He largely failed to overcome the political opposition and service parochialisms that blocked necessary reforms.

On reflection, Eisenhower concluded glumly, "Tradition won."[13] As a result, fundamental problems in joint operations went unaddressed until 1986, which saw the passage of the Goldwater–Nichols Act. Jim Locher's excellent account of the Goldwater–Nichols history pointed out the following:

> The inability of war hero Dwight Eisenhower—with his great prestige and influence in military affairs—to overcome opposition to reform convinced others not to challenge the unyielding alliance between the services and Congress. Although the service-dominated structure repeatedly demonstrated flaws over the next three decades, administrations studied, but did not propose, reforms.[14]

The message is clear. Fix it at the beginning or live with the mistakes for a long time.

We believe that the lessons of the Cold War are a checklist for how to win the long war.

- Organize to fight for the long term.
- Be patient and get it right.
- Do not put off getting it right: Once innovation ends, stagnation begins.

These three principles could serve well as a measure of how well prepared any nation is to stand the test of protracted conflict.

War By Any Name

This is not all just interesting history. *Winning the Long War* is about the future—not the past. The real issue is whether any of these lessons matter for the global war on terrorism. We think the answer to that question is emphatically yes.

Most of the "experts" in Washington have, not surprisingly, entirely missed the point. For a decade, they have trashed anything invented before 1989 as hardly worth our interest or consideration. Any look back earns the tired chestnut of "preparing to fight the last war" or "repeating the mistakes

U.S. Army troops deploy from McGuire Air Force Base, N.J., in support of the campaign against terrorism, September 21, 2001. (Photo by Carlos Cintron courtesy of the U.S. Air Force)

of the past." These witless criticisms confuse the trappings of the Cold War with the core concepts behind it. Mutual Assured Destruction, "duck and cover," red-baiting, and the idea of armored battles on the West German plain deserve to be left in the past: The secret of future victories does not.

The Cold War's real lessons are not how to fight the last war, but any long war. And no one should mistake the global war on terrorism as anything but a real, life-and-death struggle. It is a war by any name.

When President George W. Bush declared a war on global terrorism in the wake of the September 11, 2001, terrorist attacks on New York City and Washington, D.C., he sparked, among other things, a furious war of words about whether we should or even can be at war with terrorists.

It is true that no country can top the United States when it comes to metaphor mania. "War," in particular, is a staple of American political discourse. We have declared war on everything from abject poverty to overweight pets. Few terms are more overused—but perhaps not in this case.

Detractors' main objections to declaring war on terrorism are:

- First, there is no universal definition of terrorism, and thus no clear enemy.

Smoke plumes moments after the terrorist attack on the Pentagon, September 11, 2001. (Photo by Michael Garcia courtesy of the U.S. Department of Defense)

- Second, combating terrorists, whoever they are, is not primarily a military operation, but a matter of law enforcement and social, cultural, and economic conflict. It is not "traditional" war, as one U.S. defense analyst declared, in the sense understood by military professionals. Wars, he argues, are supposed to have "clear beginnings and ends...[and] clear standards for measuring success in the form of territory gained and enemy forces destroyed."[15]

Both arguments are wrongheaded.

Every country in the United Nations may not have signed on to the Webster's dictionary definition of terrorism, but that does not mean that it does not exist and does not present a terrible threat to world peace. After all, there is no universal definition of fascism, but that did not keep the Allies from declaring war on the Axis powers during World War II.

Nor do terrorists seem concerned about definitional nuances. They have decided they are most certainly at war with us, and they think they are in a war they can win. In an interview before the September 11 attacks, Osama bin Laden declared, "We no longer believe in the great powers.... [W]e have heard from our brothers who fought in Somalia, American soldiers are weak and cowardly.... [T]hey ran away."[16] Al-Qaeda's leader frequently cited such incidents as proof that the United States could be attacked directly and could be defeated if bloodied.[17]

Additionally, arguing that this is not a "traditional" war is mere semantics. What is a real war? Only in the history books are war and peace divided into discrete chapters with bombs and bugles separated in neat paragraphs from social, cultural, and economic strife. Real wars are a competition between two thinking, determined foes who may or may not elect to restrict themselves to traditional military instruments or to respect quaint notions such as law, sovereignty, borders, or governments.

America *is* at war. It is not a war that can hope to forestall every terrorist act, everywhere, but it is a war that can find victory in destroying the capacity of those who seek to transform transnational terrorism into a corporate global enterprise for the indiscriminate murder of innocents. It is also a war that can be won by discrediting the legitimacy of terrorists in the eyes of those who believe that their violent acts will somehow miraculously address political, social, religious, or economic injustice.

The global war on terrorism, like the struggle against the Soviet shadow, will be a protracted conflict. The Cold War was constrained by the threat of nuclear Armageddon. This war will be long because the enemy is dispersed and disparate. It will take years to root them out and discredit their ideas. Indeed, it may be years between major confrontations. We know now that five years of consultation and planning went into the September 11 attacks.[18] Today, in some back room could be brewing the genesis of a plot that might not appear for another five years.

The terrorism war is also a war, like the Cold War, that needs to be placed in perspective. Kennan feared equally that the Soviet threat would be overstated and ignored. The Soviets were, he pointed out in the Long Telegram, "by far the weaker force." Thus, Kennan argued that it was critical that the United States not overreach and unnecessarily diminish itself against an enemy that could not win in the long term.

Similarly, transnational terrorist groups have limited means. They cannot attack everywhere, all the time. There is no need to waste national treasure or abandon our way of life, values, and aspirations for the future in the course of defeating this determined, but vulnerable and beatable enemy.

On the other hand, like the Soviet Union, terrorists cannot be ignored. Although the Soviet empire was built on a shaky foundation of inefficiency,

An aerial view, days after the terrorist attacks on the World Trade Center, September 16, 2001. (Courtesy of SSGT Michelle Leonard, SAF Charleston Air Force Base, South Carolina)

repression, and corruption, it nevertheless had enough chemical, biological, and nuclear weapons to annihilate the world several times over.

Likewise, today it would be folly to ignore fanatical transnational terrorist groups with even a modicum of resources. The age when only great powers could bring great powers to their knees is over. As the September 11 attacks so vividly remind us, the global links that ferry goods, services, people, and ideas around the world in unprecedented volume and at unprecedented speed can also carry terrible threats. To this must be added the viable threat of chemical, biological, radiological, nuclear, or conventional high-explosive arms that, if used to their most deadly effect, might endanger tens of thousands of lives and cause hundreds of billions of dollars in damage.

The sad truth is that the twenty-first century could be a war of never-ending vigilance. After all, the threat did not begin with Osama bin Laden. Before al-Qaeda, there was Aum Shinrikyo, the Japanese religious cult that conducted the sarin gas attack on the Tokyo subway in 1995. At that time, the cult had $1 billion in resources at its disposal, which Aum Shinrikyo intended to use for triggering an apocalyptic war that only its members would survive. Plans included striking American cities with biological weapons. Documents seized during the process of investigating the cult and arresting its leaders also revealed members had an interest in buying nuclear weapons.[19] They failed only because of the ineptness of their operations and the poor quality of their weapons development programs.[20] The rise of Aum Shinrikyo is a cautionary tale. Even if al-Qaeda was destroyed tomorrow, that would be cold comfort. The modern world offers too many opportunities. There will be transnational terrorists after al-Qaeda.

If we can agree that the global war on terror is indeed a war, and likely to be a protracted one, then we must agree that ensuring we have the right approach to winning the long war is a compelling national imperative. Now is the time to ask the hard questions. That is why we have written *Winning the Long War*—to address what we believe are the most critical issues for all Americans.

The Lifeline of a Guiding Idea

Strategy matters. It matters not just for presidents and generals, but for the Congress, business leaders, the American Civil Liberties Union, the local Parent-Teacher Association, auto mechanics, Internet geeks, and soccer moms. That is the premise of this book. The strategy settled upon in the next few years will determine how we fight the global war on terrorism; how we decide to fight the terrorists will determine how we will live our lives.

Strategy consists of the ends, ways, and means of achieving national objectives. The *ends* define the goals of the strategy. *Ways* comprise the methods that are employed to achieve the ends. *Means* describe the resources that are available to accomplish the goals. National strategies involve more than just the use of the armed forces. They consider all of the economic, political, diplomatic, military, and informational instruments that might be used to promote a nation's interest or secure a state from its enemies.

Strategies are important because they are a call to action. The most influential strategies are those that make hard choices—allocating scarce resources, setting clear goals, or establishing priorities. U.S. strategy during World War II, which declared that the allies would "defeat Germany first," was one example. That simple declarative sentence drove a cascading series of decisions and actions that defined the conduct of the war. U.S. strategy for the global war on terrorism requires a similar clarity of focus if it is to serve as a focal point for national effort.

In the wake of the September 11 attacks, eight new national strategies were published; five were specifically developed to deal with the challenges of combating terrorism, while others were revised to account for the dangers of the post-9/11 world. The strategies break down into two basic components. The first is the global war on terrorism and the objective is to destroy global terrorist networks—to root out their sanctuaries, garner international cooperation in attacking their means and resources, and undercut their legitimacy and support in the global community. The second part of the strategy is to provide homeland security—layered protection consisting of a web of public and private measures at levels from the federal government to the individual.

The real issue is: How good are these strategies? There is no universal agreement about the necessary components of strategy for describing ends, ways, and means. An initial analysis of the national strategies by the U.S. Government Accountability Office (GAO) listed several useful criteria. The characteristics GAO identified are:

- purpose, scope, and methodology;
- problem definition and risk assessment;
- goals, subordinate objectives, activities, and performance measures;
- resources, investments, and risk management;
- organizational roles, responsibilities, and coordination; and
- integration and implementation.

(For the GAO's assessment of the national strategies, see Appendix 3.) By the GAO's count, the grades are mixed.

Winning the Long War takes a more holistic and less dogmatic approach to gauging where we are. The details of strategy are not to be minimized, but it is important to make sure that the first order questions—the fundamentals—are right. Have we learned the three lessons of the Cold War?

Our assessment of the first three years is generally encouraging. In fact, we argue that much of the hard thinking has been done and done right. The fundamental concepts argued by Kennan and embedded in U.S. policies by Eisenhower have already taken root in contemporary strategy.

Lesson 1: *Organize to fight for the long term.* We find, generally, that the United States is developing the right strategic approach for a protracted war, neglecting neither offense nor defense, focused on promoting continued economic growth, sincere in its desire to preserve the constitutional rights of its citizens, and mindful of the nation's responsibilities to set an example in the world.

Lesson 2: *Be patient and get it right.* It is also clear that the United States has tried to do more than simply throw money and the military at the problem. Efforts are underway to build long-term, sustainable security programs, measures that can protect Americans today, tomorrow, and ten years from now.

Lesson 3: *Do not put off getting it right: Once innovation ends, stagnation begins.* The area in which the assessments of *Winning the Long War* are less sanguine is on this third point. In virtually every key area of the strategy—security, the economy, civil liberties, and the war of ideas—there is more work to be done.

Thus, we find ourselves with a dual task.

First, we must convince Americans that they should believe in the diplomat from Princeton and the soldier from Abilene. There is a right way to win a long war. Americans must also believe in themselves: The United States is taking the right approach to the war on global terror.

Second, we are not there yet. There is more work to be done in building the basic weapons we will need for this war and it is essential that we forge these weapons now and get them right—or we will face the future with a flawed arsenal that will likely remain faulty for a long, long time.

Where We Are and Where We Need to Be

Our assessment of what has been accomplished and what remains undone follows in seven chapters, corresponding to the four cornerstones of long-war strategy. Chapters One and Two look at the issue of security. Chapter One examines "offensive" measures; the task of taking the battle to the terrorists. Here is one area in which the criticism of "preparing to fight the last war" does have some validity. The genius of fighting a long war is knowing how to set priorities—to know which national security instruments have to be replaced, refurbished, or replenished first. At the center of America's offensive means are three key capabilities: strategic intelligence, military force, and interagency operations. They are all in need of attention. They are the prerequisites. All the other instruments of a great power build on them. Equipping these three assets for the long war has to be a top priority.

Chapter Two looks at "defense," or what we now call "homeland security": protecting Americans from terrorist attacks. Here the third lesson of the Cold War seems least learned. There is still much to be done in establishing the right kinds of organizations and programs to serve the nation for the long term. Topping the list is reorganizing the Department of Homeland Security; fixing the shortfalls we have observed in its first few years of operation, before it, like the Pentagon, becomes set in concrete, unmovable for a generation. This chapter also considers the requirement for building a truly national homeland security "system of systems," which incorporates all appropriate public and private entities. Additionally, this chapter examines the lack of reform in congressional oversight for homeland security.

Chapters Three and Four look at the issue of civil liberties. They debunk the notion that in the twenty-first century we must have a stark choice between security and liberty. Chapter Three establishes the principles that should be guiding our efforts to fight terrorism through the adoption of new legal authorities, technologies, and programs that promise to provide both greater security and better protection of civil liberties.

Chapter Four offers practical recommendations for the kinds of domestic counterterrorism resources that are needed. In particular, it considers the role of the USA Patriot Act, controversial legislation intended to provide law enforcement with new tools for combating terrorism. This chapter also examines how we should legally detain terrorists when we "out" them before they have committed a crime. Finally, it looks at the role technology must play in providing a decisive edge in battling terrorists.

Chapters Five and Six examine the prospects for maintaining a strong economy while vigorously pursuing the war on terrorism. Chapter Five focuses on the domestic economy, concluding that it is not the cost of security that threatens the future of the nation, but other forms of discretionary and mandatory federal spending. It recommends the measures that have to be taken to ensure continued economic growth in the decades ahead—in particular, fixing a broken tax code that may be as a big a threat to U.S. security as the terrorists themselves.

Chapter Six looks at the U.S. role in the global economy. It is about the imperative of making international trade and travel both freer and safer. Free trade is essential to winning the long war. Additionally, while new security measures will make us safer, they also have the potential to stifle global growth, particularly in the developing world, which lacks the capacity to fully implement anti-terrorism measures designed to safeguard the flow of people and products. This chapter also examines efforts to clothe protectionist measures in the cloak of homeland security, false arguments that somehow by closing American markets, Americans will be more secure.

Chapter Seven examines the struggle of ideas. It finds that more must be done to discredit the ideologies that feed terrorism. At the same time, the United States must continually make the case that democracy and free markets offer a credible alternative to extremism and repression. Finally, the United States must make clear that it will never retrench or retreat. The "idea" offensive must destroy any glimmer of hope among the terrorists that we will ever let them prevail in their fascist schemes.

In the epilogue to *Winning the Long War*, we offer a new (albeit shorter) Long Telegram, a restatement of the ideas for ensuring national survival recrafted for the challenges of the twenty-first century. We could not hope to recapture the power and poetry of Kennan's writings or Eisenhower's breadth of vision, but in our own words we hope to rekindle the call to action, the courage and confidence in the rightness of America's cause, and the optimism that that this nation can—and will—not just prevail, but thrive and grow in the decades ahead.

Chapter 1

Taking the Offensive

After a long day of arduous negotiation in the midst of one of the many crises that erupted during the Cold War, U.S. Secretary of State Henry Kissinger and British Foreign Secretary James Callaghan engaged in the following exchange:

> KISSINGER: You know, one respect in which all the humanitarians and liberals and socialists were wrong in the last century was when they thought that mankind didn't like war....They love it.

> CALLAGHAN: Most of us like it for a day or two, but there is a handful who like [sic] it forever.

> KISSINGER: That's right. It doesn't mean that the humanitarians were wrong, it just means that life is harder than we thought....

> CALLAGHAN: I don't know what sort of an age we're passing through or going to pass through, but historians like yourself ought to give us a rundown on it sometime and tell us how you think this next half century is going to look.

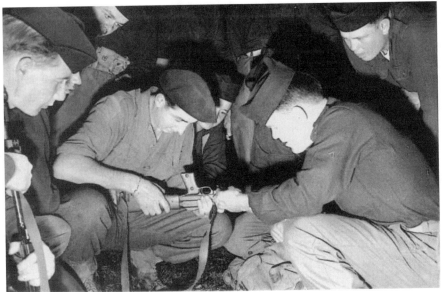

U.S. and French troops conducting joint training in the Austrian Alps, September 7, 1951. (COURTESY OF THE NATIONAL ARCHIVES)

> KISSINGER: I'll tell you ... I'm glad I'm not going to be running part of it. It's going to be brutal.[1]

Facing today's threat of global terrorism, these words seem all too prophetic; they provide another reminder that—in some fundamental ways—the security challenges of the twenty-first century are little changed from those of the twentieth century. Evil is still with us and likely always will be. We also face Kissinger's dilemma. Ignoring evil will not dissipate its force. Complacency will only allow it to grow. An enemy that is allowed to take the initiative uncontested will sooner or later find a way to win. Kissinger and Callaghan were right: The evil ones will often get the confrontation they want, because someone must stand and stop them.

The Cold War was a constant struggle that required, at times, taking the offensive. Yet taking the battle to the enemy was a chancy affair. The threat of nuclear war always made such decisions dangerous. However, even without the specter of mushroom clouds, such choices should never be taken lightly. Even in the best of times, they are always measured in national treasure sacrificed and young lives lost. Nevertheless, there are times when the battle must be joined. The lesson of the Cold War is that when you take the offensive, make sure you do it right.

Dr. Henry Kissinger, President Richard Nixon's adviser on National Security Affairs, on board Air Force One, January 18, 1973. (WHITE HOUSE PHOTO)

No one appreciated the challenge of the offensive better than the woolly-haired professor from Harvard with a baritone voice and German accent. Of all the warriors who wielded the weapons of the Cold War, none stand out more starkly than Henry Kissinger, President Richard M. Nixon's National Security Advisor and Secretary of State. Kissinger managed a unique achievement; he was vilified by both the far left and the radical right. "They broke the mold after Kissinger," President Ronald Reagan's Secretary of State, George Shultz, once quipped.[2] Most Kissinger haters would probably respond, "Well, thank God for that."

Most of the criticism directed at Kissinger concerned how and when to go on the offensive. Détente (the Nixon/Kissinger version of containment that looked suspiciously like a repackaged version of Roosevelt's "open spheres") was, according to Kissinger, "under attack by liberals for being excessively focused on military security...."[3] While the left assailed Kissinger as a warmonger, neoconservatives were unhappy as well: They wanted a more muscular response to engage the Soviet military head on.[4] Kissinger, in contrast, believed that the United States, exhausted after Vietnam, stood unready for major military confrontations. Instead, he felt if the Nixon Administration could turn the Cold War from a military arms race into competition over trade and ideas, the United States would outpace the Soviets and recapture the lead.

Perhaps he was right. Kissinger always argued that it was the strategic pause after Vietnam that laid the groundwork for U.S. resurgence during the Reagan years. It took eight years of rebuilding the military under Reagan to make the U.S. military a force to be reckoned with once again. It should come as no surprise that America turned the corner in the Cold War only after it recharged its batteries and went back on the offensive.

In part, Kissinger earned the ire of both the far right and the distant left because he refused to base his foreign policy on ideology alone. He stuck with an old-fashioned, pragmatic view of international affairs known as "realism."[5] In fact, John Gaddis, the distinguished American diplomatic historian, always found a whiff of Kennan's thinking, a marriage of Princeton and Harvard, in Kissinger's approach to the Cold War.[6] In Kissinger's world, power is all that matters. States remain in ceaseless competition. Conflict is inevitable. States collide because they are rational actors, constantly working to ensure their national security by maximizing power in relation to other states, driven by the unending quest for security. States not only want power, they *need* power before they can influence anything.

Scholars continue to debate how well Kissinger practiced the art of power politics.[7] Still, the core of his ideas—the cautionary reminder of the value and limits of power—is worth remembering for the long war. It is important to do what is right, but you can only do what is right when you have the means and will to prevail.

The Case for the Offensive Tool Kit

Few subjects regarding war engender more controversy than how to take the offensive. Sadly, these squabbles often reflect more passion than reason. True to form, the foreign policy debates about the next steps in the global war on terrorism center on style rather than substance. Arguments abound about whether the United States should rely on international organizations (like NATO) and accords (such as the nuclear weapons nonproliferation treaty), or preemptive measures[8] and unilateral action, or if we should depend on military troops, law enforcement, or diplomacy. These speculations are simply fodder for cable news pundits, editorial page writers, and candidate stump speeches. In truth, we will employ all of these means and try to use them when they best suit the task at hand—just as we did during the Cold War. That is one of the advantages of being a great power: You have options.

The complex nature of global security also demands multiple, flexible instruments. In honesty, America has a fair amount of potential enemies. The threat of transnational terrorism is clear enough. Bookstores are suffering from terrorist book overload, minutely detailing the dangers of the new terrorism.[9] This danger requires little elaboration. Yet states also matter, and dealing with foreign states in the twenty-first century will be no easy task. In the future, there will be three kinds of nations that cause the United States trouble: aggressors, enablers, and slackers.

Aggressors. Though the United States has an overwhelming preponderance of power, it cannot ignore the possibility of being the target of another state. An enemy unable to match conventional American military power might instead attack vulnerable targets on U.S. territory. For example, a state might strike the American homeland as part of an anti-access campaign, attacking or threatening targets within the homeland to prevent the deployment of U.S. forces. Indeed, a state might sponsor terrorists to undertake these acts.[10]

There are numerous historical examples in which weak states have inflicted defeat on more powerful adversaries.[11] In the future, as in the past, lesser states may perceive failings in a strong state that could be exploited at acceptable risk. Ever since the end of the Cold War, there has been much discussion about identifying and exploiting America's potential weaknesses.

All aggressors are not equal. Size matters. However, the danger from lesser states, even very weak ones, should not be underestimated. National security analyses tend to treat these lesser countries—which predominantly run in a band from central Asia through Africa—as invisible entities. They focus instead on regional powerbrokers.[12] Ignoring the threat of lesser states is shortsighted. In the current global system, even the poorest nations can be formidable international actors. Poor countries have demonstrated the potential for offensive action by focusing limited resources on military forces, state-sponsored terrorism, or the development of weapons of mass destruction. For example, Sudan, a very poor country, maintained an extensive chemical warfare program for many years.[13] Emigration also contributes to weak states' power. Ethnic diasporas create international networks that provide income, intelligence, and political activism.[14] All aggressors might not be equal, but they may all be dangerous.

Enablers. "Enablers" are countries willing to facilitate transnational terrorism, share intelligence, or proliferate weapons or weapon technologies to those who, in turn, might threaten the United States. Enablers might be driven by one, or a combination of several motivations. For example, they could be engaged in some form of regional competition with the United States, or they might support terrorism or weapons proliferation to further their own interests, such as selling ballistic missile technology to shore up a cash-strapped economy.

An enabler state could well be a country that elects to support strikes on America even when not engaged in a direct conflict of interest with the United States. In the 1980s, for example, Libya emerged as a hotbed for planning attacks against American interests, even though there was virtually no direct regional conflict between the two powers.[15] For over twenty years, Lebanon (with strong backing from Syria and Iran) has been the base for Hezbollah, which has both conducted and supported attacks against Americans.[16] From 1991–1994, the government of Sudan also allowed its territory to be used as a base for planning strikes against American targets.[17] Throughout the 1990s, Belarus continued to sell arms and provide training to Iraq.[18] After September 11, Liberia and Burkina Faso allegedly harbored al-Qaeda operatives for cash bribes.[19]

As with aggressor states, enabler nations do not necessarily have to possess great resources to represent a significant security risk. Only three years ago, few would have predicted that the United States would go to war in Afghanistan, one of the world's poorest nations. Al-Qaeda, however, with the cooperation of the Taliban government in Afghanistan, turned a virtually destitute country into an effective platform for directing attacks on the United States.[20]

Slackers. "Slacker" states are nations with lax laws or enforcement means which unintentionally allow transnational terrorist groups to operate within their borders or permit state (or non-state) groups to obtain weapons or support illicitly from the private sector. Even friends can aid enemies. Relaxed immigration laws and customs enforcement, lax enforcement of non-proliferation regimes, the illicit use of monetary instruments, and the transfer of dual-use technologies that have either commercial or weapons program uses are problems endemic to America's allies, as well as other nations.

Slacker states might be countries that lack the legal systems, oversight mechanisms, and law enforcement assets to combat terrorism or weapons proliferation. There is little evidence to suggest, however, that poverty alone breeds terrorists or weapons proliferators. There are, for example, many poor states that do not harbor transnational terrorist groups that might threaten the United States.[21] On the other hand, even nations with the resources to reduce global threats may leave security gaps unaddressed for a variety of cultural, religious, political, or diplomatic reasons. Canada, for example, has strong humanitarian traditions, which have led it to establish the most generous asylum system in the world. In turn, terrorist groups bound for the United States have infiltrated Canadian borders under the guise of legitimate refugees.[22]

In a future in which America will have to deal with an unpredictable witch's brew of transnational terrorists, aggressors, enablers, and slackers, it should come as no surprise that there is no cookie-cutter solution for taking the offensive. Many of the measures taken will fall far short of war. Different problems will need different solutions. The priority should now be making sure the toolbox is full, so that we have the options we need when we need them.

The genius of fighting a long war is the ability to prioritize—knowing which tools have to be replaced, refurbished, or replenished first. At the center of America's offensive means are three key capabilities—strategic intelligence, military force, and interagency operations. These are the prerequisites. All the other instruments of a great power build upon them. Equipping these three assets for the long war has to be a top priority.

Strategic Intelligence—The Case for Responsible Reform

Getting strategic intelligence wrong can have terrible consequences. Based on bad information and forged documents, an American President sent U.S. troops into harm's way in a distant land on a mission that had no hope of success. That President was Woodrow Wilson. Based on clumsily forged documents, Wilson, believing the Russian Revolution of 1918 was being directed by the German General Staff, ordered U.S. forces to seize the Siberian railway. The operation was a disaster. It was only in 1956 that a distinguished diplomatic scholar revealed the fraud that started it all. The scholar? George Kennan.[23]

We can do better—and we have to. Intelligence is America's first line of defense in the war on terrorism, but the current intelligence network is not the right instrument for the challenges of the twenty-first century. The U.S. needs intelligence agencies that are as facile in dealing with shadowy transnational gangs as they are in countering conventional enemies. The only problem is that this is simply not the kind of intelligence community that the United States has today.

The Cold War Shapes the Intelligence Community

When Kissinger traded a desk at Harvard for an office in the West Wing, U.S. intelligence focused on the threat of the Soviet Union, the possibility of war in Western Europe, and support for the ongoing conflict in Southeast Asia. These threats shaped the way in which information was collected and analyzed by the various members of the intelligence community (IC). (See Appendix 5.) After the early 1990s, the primary threat to the United States shifted from the Soviet Union to terrorism. However, the infrastructure of intelligence collection and analysis did not—and still has not—changed from its Cold War roots.

Two major developments shaped intelligence policy and infrastructure in the 1960s and 1970s. The first was the development of technical means of intelligence collection, such as U-2 spy planes and photoreconnaissance satellites such as CORONA.

Due to the successful use of technical platforms during the Cuban Missile Crisis, U.S. intelligence became increasingly focused on obtaining photographic "hard intelligence." Furthermore, technical means of intelligence collection were ideally suited to gathering information about large-scale troop movements, as well the location of military bases, industrial plants, and missile silos—the primary targets of Cold War intelligence. As a result, priority for national intelligence collection shifted toward satellites and other electronic collection means and away from more traditional agent-based human intelligence (HUMINT).

At the same time, resources dedicated to HUMINT were severely cut back. The most dramatic reductions were in the area of overt intelligence—material collected from open (unclassified) sources (often through State Department and other analysts at U.S. embassies around the world) by personnel knowledgeable in local language and conditions. These reports address not only military threats, but also a range of cultural, economic, political, and social issues.

The second major development during this period was the formation of a multi-agency IC. As the U.S. government shifted toward electronic and photographic intelligence collection technologies, new agencies emerged to manage them. Over time the number of intelligence agencies proliferated, and coordinating and integrating their activities became increasingly problematic.

Although the National Security Act of 1947 gave the Director of the CIA (in his role as Director of Central Intelligence, or DCI) the overall responsibility for coordination of U.S. intelligence, he was given no direct control over the resources, personnel, or budgets of other agencies. Juggling competing priorities, differing corporate cultures, and smoothing over the inevitable inter-agency rivalries was (and remains) a difficult task.

The Cold War offered enough lessons that U.S. strategic intelligence was, even then, a flawed instrument. For example, when the United States discontinued research and eliminated its capabilities in offensive biological warfare in the 1970s, Soviet offensive biological and chemical warfare efforts accelerated. Believing the United States was continuing a covert bio-weapons program, the Soviets developed an impressive arsenal of biological and chemical weapons—including diseases that could destroy crops and ballistic missiles tipped with smallpox-dispensing warheads capable of killing millions of people. Research and production involved virtually every component of the Soviet military-industrial complex. Though these weapons have since been destroyed, concerns remain that unaccounted seed stocks of pathogens (or the scientific knowledge used to produce these weapons) might become available to other enemies. An even bigger problem is that the Soviet Union, the number one target of U.S. strategic intelligence, established its bio-weapons and America never knew of their existence.[24]

The Threat of Terrorism

Even though terrorism, especially Soviet-sponsored terrorism, was a concern during the 1970s and 1980s, it remained a secondary priority for U.S. intelligence until after the collapse of Communism in the early 1990s.[25] The bombing of the World Trade Center in 1993 came as a surprise to the IC, which initially believed the bombing to be the work of an "ad hoc" terrorist group. However, soon after the bombing, the name Osama bin Laden began appearing in intelligence reports. Al-Qaeda was specifically recognized as a serious threat to U.S. national security as early as the 1998 embassy bombings in

Africa. While the threat of transnational terrorism was widely recognized by the IC and policymakers, virtually no initiatives were taken to address the deep-seated limitations of U.S. strategic intelligence that made it an inadequate instrument for meeting this threat.

Although the terrorist threat was known and understood in the 1990s, spending on national security went down during that decade, which affected both counterterrorism and intelligence. With limited resources, there were other intelligence failures, such as foreknowledge of the sarin gas attacks in Japan. At the time of the attack, the Aum Shinrikyo cult was "simply not on the radar" because there were not enough intelligence analysts to research potential Asian terrorism.

Post-Cold War Strategic Intelligence Successes and Failures

At the center of the shortfalls of the IC is a CIA that lacks the resources and organization to adequately perform its mission. It has long been the job of the CIA to do two things—steal secrets and analyze information. It is failing the nation on both counts. The CIA failed to provide accurate information on Iraq's weapons of mass destruction in both Gulf Wars, underestimating the threat in 1991 and overestimating it in 2003. The Directorate of Operations is locked into old business practices, focusing on the recruitment of agents by deskbound operatives in embassy offices and relying too much on intelligence (without independent corroboration) provided by foreign governments.

Concerning the analysis of information, the CIA's Directorate of Intelligence (DI) fails to produce analysts who are nationally and internationally recognized experts. The current system does not reward analytic expertise in a given field; rather, it recognizes management ability. The DI has placed too much emphasis on "competing with CNN," in that it focuses on small, tactical pieces of information, as opposed to looking at the broader picture.

Reforming the Intelligence Community

Prior to 1981, with few exceptions, attempts to "reform" the U.S. intelligence community (such as the Church Commission) were punitive measures used more to limit permissible activities than to improve the collection

U.S. troops dressed as the "enemy" during exercise FROSTY, 1953. (Courtesy of the National Archives)

and analysis of intelligence. These reform proposals usually came in the wake of ethically questionable, sometimes illegal, operations by members of the IC.

Executive Order 12333, signed by President Ronald Reagan, explicitly delineated the duties and responsibilities of the various members of the IC. For the first time, the roles and missions of agencies and individuals were clearly defined. However, EO 12333 did not resolve the long-standing problem of the DCI's inability to directly control other elements of national intelligence. The FBI, the Departments of State, Energy, and Treasury, the National Security Agency, and other Department of Defense (DoD) elements all maintained control over their own budgets, personnel, and resources.

Perhaps the most often proposed reform subsequent to EO 12333 has been the creation of a Director of National Intelligence (DNI) with direct control over the entire IC. Proponents argue that having a DNI would allow the Director of the CIA to concentrate on running his own agency and allow for greater integration and coordinated direction of the IC. Additionally, the DNI, acting as the President's principal intelligence advisor would be able to provide independent, unprejudiced assessments of the analysis conducted by the IC. This would help address the shortfalls cited by Congress in the collection of information about Iraq's weapons production programs throughout the 1990s.[26] Congress finally followed through and created the DNI in law in December 2004.

At the same time, it would be mistake to stop at just creating the DNI. There are also good arguments for consolidating the polyglot of 15 current agencies and restructuring organizations like the CIA in order to break down the cultural and institutional barriers that have prevented the effective sharing of information. In addition, the United States must rebuild its human capabilities to collect and analyze intelligence, as well as exploit cutting-edge technologies to gather, distribute, and evaluate information.[27]

Dark Secrets

Finally, at the same time, we will no doubt have to improve our ability to conduct counterintelligence—finding enemy spies within the ranks of our law enforcement and intelligence services. Anyone who thinks this is a trivial problem should remember Robert Hanssen. Hanssen was a model FBI agent, in charge of counterintelligence operations at the Bureau, finding out the identities of people who were spying on the United States. It was the most secret and sensitive work in the agency. Hanssen was considered an expert in the field. The only problem was that he was working for the other side. Arrested in February 2001, it was later determined that Hanssen had spied for the Soviet Union for well over a decade. As an authorized user of highly classified computer systems, Hanssen was able to employ various means for stealing sensitive data, including encrypted floppy disks, removable storage devices, and a Palm handheld device. The Soviet used some of the information to capture and kill American agents. Hanssen used part of his Soviet pay to buy presents for his stripper girlfriend.

The simple fact is that as we succeed in sharing information more effectively among federal, state, and local agencies, there will be more opportunities to steal, sell, trade, or give away America's secrets. Intelligence reform will have to think through better ways to protect what we know. The problem is that right now no one is really in charge. No one is ensuring that best practices and lessons learned are being shared. No one is looking at the gaps and vulnerabilities across the web of systems used to exchange information. This will require an organized national effort—not just a part-time job for a few agents at the FBI. It is a job that has to be done to the highest standards, respecting the legitimate privacy and liberties of American citizens, while not allowing the enemy to get away with murder.

Rethinking how we conduct counterintelligence, as well as rebuilding the human side of intelligence, using technology, and reorganizing the intelligence community all have to be on the table. Responsible intelligence reform cannot be reduced to a bumper sticker or a single initiative, such as creating a DNI. It will require years of focused effort to build the IC we need for the long struggle with terrorism.

The Military: Sharpening the Point of the Spear

War is not the answer. Sometimes, however, it is the best of bad choices. A great power that lacks the capacity to defend itself is not a great power. It is a target, an invitation to aggression. In large part, Kissinger embraced détente because the United States had poor options. The Nixon Administration took office at the nadir of America's military might, an unprecedented weakness matched perhaps only by the armed forces funded by Truman before the Korean War. On both occasions, America had a "hollow" force—insufficient resources to provide for sufficiently trained and experienced troops, new equipment, and ongoing operations.[28]

Dumb Ideas for Our Time

During the Cold War, American strategy fell short most often when it lacked the military capacity to back up its policies. That is a lesson worth remembering. The number one priority for the future must be ensuring that we provide the Pentagon sufficient resources to do the big three: maintain an adequate, trained and, ready force; purchase modern equipment; and conduct its tasks around the world. We are in danger of going back to the Kissinger-era hollow force if we don't get the balance of investments right.

Clearly, today's U.S. military is either under-resourced or incorrectly structured to handle the missions that are being asked of it. Here is an example: In the summer of 2004, America had about 3 million men and women in uniform. Yet we are having a tough time keeping 160,000 of them in Afghanistan and Iraq. You do the math.

The problem is not that the military is too small. It is simply structured to fight the last war in the last century. The result? Too many troops in the wrong uniform, in the wrong places, trained in the wrong skills, who are subsequently of questionable value to the war on terrorism.

Yes, our military is overstretched. Washington needs to do something about that. Yet many of the ideas being floated by pundits and policymakers are simply wrongheaded. Three particularly dumb ideas come to mind.

Dumb Idea No. 1: *Don't Depend on Citizen-Soldiers.* Ever since 9/11, the Pentagon has used the military reserves[29] in numbers unprecedented since the Korean War. Critics see this as a failure, viewing citizen-soldiers as the military equivalent of couch potatoes. "Dragging them off to war proves we don't have enough troops," the Pentagon's detractors argue.

They're wrong. Using the reserves really means that the system is working. We keep a large pool of reserves exactly for moments like this when we need to rapidly expand. We will likely need them again after the current crises abate. The future is more likely to resemble a sine curve (with the need for troops whipsawing up and down) than a steady-state straight line.

The problem is not that we are sending citizen-soldiers to fight our wars. The problem is that we can't send more. The Pentagon tapped only a portion of the reserves. Additional call-ups will be limited, at best, because few of the remaining units have the skills and equipment needed. Much of the reserve force was created during the Cold War to fight World War III. Therefore, we still have lots of armor and artillery units to fight pitched battles on the German plains, but few trained to chase bin Laden in the Afghan hills or police the streets of Iraq. If we had a more usable reserve force, we could rotate more troops overseas.

Dumb Idea No. 2: *Bring Back the Draft.* This idea is unsuitable for so many reasons it is hard not to conclude that it is suggested just to scare people. Conscription made sense during World War II. America had 10 million in uniform—almost the entire draft-age male population. There is no need anything near those numbers today. A draft would be little more than a lottery for the unlucky.

Worse, a conscript army with, say, two years of mandatory service would be less skilled, less cohesive, and more expensive, because the services would constantly be training and replacing the ranks. Germany has this kind of army, and Germans think it is totally unsuitable. They are exploring ways to create an all-volunteer force based on the U.S. model.

Dumb Idea No. 3: *Add More Troops.* Permanently swelling the ranks of the military by tens of thousands is not the answer. Permanent increases bring all the baggage of a 20-year career; big-ticket items like housing, medical care, and

Soldiers watch over a village in the Baghni Valley of Afghanistan, March 1, 2003. (PHOTO BY SERGEANT VERNELL HALL COURTESY OF THE U.S. ARMY)

retirement. When Iraq ramps down, the armed forces will have more troops than they need. If all those troops were "regulars," the Pentagon would either have to keep them all aboard—shouldering needless expense—or launch a disruptive and costly downsizing. Too large a military will take us right back to the hollow force, with too few resources to train, equip, and employ the available troops.

The Better Idea

There are better long-term solutions to ensuring the force we need for the long war. To bridge the capabilities gap, the United States should focus its military resources on missions that are vital to the nation. Specifically, it must field a force capable of: fighting the immediate war on terrorism; fighting with little or no warning in unanticipated places; maintaining adequate capability to deter aggression against America's interests and allies; and contributing to homeland security. This is what we should do.

Maintain Robust Defense Spending. Defense is not cheap. The 2004 defense budget weighed in at over $400 billion. That's about right. Some Members of Congress entertained the idea of either cutting defense (at least modestly) to help rein in ballooning federal spending or taking money from some important programs to fund other programs that are more popular. However, cutting defense spending now is both unnecessary and dangerous. According to estimates by the individual services, even with recent defense budget increases, the Pentagon has $12.2 billion in unfunded priorities.[30] Maintaining adequate funding is essential to avoiding the hollow force syndrome.

End Nonessential Deployments. At last count, the United States still had over 3,000 troops on peacekeeping missions in the Balkans. This translates into 9,000 persons dedicated to that mission. For every soldier deployed, one is recovering from deployment and one is preparing for deployment. Ending this unnecessary deployment would significantly reduce the stress on the force by adding 9,000 soldiers to the rotation base. Likewise, ending other nonessential missions would put more troops at the Pentagon's disposal for real missions.

Put More Troops in the Foxhole. The U.S. military maintains bases and forces overseas that are largely a legacy of the Cold War. Likewise, many of the active and reserve units here at home are governed by personnel and mobilization policies and arrayed in organizations that are, in fact, designed to fight the last war. The Pentagon has been trying to change. For instance, the generals in Washington acknowledge they could right-size our force structure in Europe and Northeast Asia by consolidating commands and bases, freeing as many as 40,000 soldiers. The Pentagon could hire civilians or contractors for more administrative positions. By some estimates, this change alone might put as many as 300,000 more troops in the field. Encouraging the Pentagon to follow through on initiatives that will make greater numbers of the force more usable is just good common sense.

Continue with Base Realignment and Closure (BRAC). BRAC is a process that requires the Department of Defense to identify unnecessary facilities that can be closed. It also requires the Administration and Congress to review and approve the recommendations. BRAC is important because closing unneeded bases will free resources and forces for higher priority uses.[31]

Transforming Transformation

Not only is it important to make sure we have the right size military for the long war, it is equally important that we have a military capable of doing the right tasks. The old adage "that every problem looks like a nail when all you have is hammer," pretty much says it all. The Cold War military was a hammer. This long war needs a lot more appliances.

Expanding the toolbox will be tough. "Transformation" was the Pentagon's new buzzword after the Cold War. No one agreed on what it meant, but every general and admiral wanted some.[32] At the most basic level, the term meant providing a new set of military capabilities fundamentally different from those used during the Cold War. The tough problem was deciding exactly what those capabilities would look like. Not surprisingly, the first answer from the services was that the stuff they were already thinking about was transformational—and it should probably be paid for at the expense of some other service's budget.

With more than a decade of the post-Cold War behind us, there does appear to be a shift in transformation rhetoric in the halls of the Pentagon; talk of moving away from change for the sake of change to transforming to the military needed for the many kinds of missions that will be required of our troops in the twenty-first century. Thus, appropriately, there is much effort going into things that do not fit a single service paradigm, such as ballistic missile defense, space operations, better information systems, more special operations forces, and unmanned aerial vehicles. These are all hallmarks of the new military coming out of the Pentagon—and the Pentagon needs to keep at it.

Still, there is cause for concern. There is one very big gap in the military's transformation plan. Its ability to perform post-conflict operations is deeply flawed. The difficulties that the U.S. military and other coalition forces have experienced in Afghanistan and Iraq, and the consternation expressed in the Western press and the court of public opinion should come as no surprise.

There is legitimate cause for complaint. The shortfalls in how the United States and its allies approached the challenges of post-conflict operations run deeper than the debate over policies, the justification for the war, the number of troops committed to the occupation,[33] and the resources available.[34] The truth is that the military is least good at the fight for peace.

Should we be able to do better? Yes. This not to argue that we need more military forces for peacekeeping or nation building. Given the global demand for U.S. forces, America should not be deeply involved in peacekeeping or peacemaking missions. We should save great power forces for great power missions.[35] Nation building should also be avoided. It is not an appropriate task for the military. It should come as no surprise that America's greatest contribution to nation building, the Marshall Plan, had no military component.[36]

Post-conflict operations are another matter. If the United States has to go in and rip out a terrorist sanctuary or rogue regime, we need to make sure when we are done the weeds do not grow back.

Rhythm of Habits

We may not conquer countries very often, but when we do, it is in our strategic interest to get it right. Yet if our military is consistent in any of its failures, it is in its incapacity to think deeply about anything other than winning battles. Winning battles is important, but winning wars is more important—and winning the peace is part of winning the war.

However, most generals don't get it. According to Antulio Echevarria, a well-respected Army historian and national security analyst, the American way of war rarely extends "beyond the winning of battles and campaigns to the gritty work of turning military victory into strategic success."[37] The troubles in Afghanistan and Iraq may merely offer the most recent cases in point.

Among the traditions, experiences, preconceptions, and routine practices that determine how the military wages the fight for peace, the most powerful force shaping its thinking is a "tradition of forgetting." The services—particularly the Army—have a long record of conducting various kinds of peace missions. Traditionally, however, the armed forces concentrate on warfighting and eschew the challenges of dealing with the battlefield after the battle. The Army's experience and knowledge about peace operations have never been incorporated into mainstream military thinking in any major, systematic way. For example, the official report about U.S. participation in the occupation of the Rhineland after World War I noted that "despite the precedents of military governments in Mexico, California, the Southern States, Cuba, Puerto Rico, Panama, China, the Philippines, and elsewhere, the lesson seemingly has not been learned."[38] When the military got ready for the occupations in Europe and Asia that marked the end of World War II and the beginning of the Cold War, they started over once again. One of the first acts was to dig out the report on the Rhineland occupation. The missive introducing the report that spoke of not learning lessons of the past must have come as cold comfort.

Despite their many failings, U.S. occupations in places like Germany and Japan eventually accomplished their missions, giving truth to Churchill's famous conclusion that after Americans have tried everything else they will do the right thing. So it was in the early Cold War years. However, the Pentagon then largely forgot the lessons once again and continued to reinvent solutions each time it faced a new peace operation: Fighting the battles of the Cold War remained the military's overwhelming preoccupation.

Arguably, America's military after the Cold War has a better appreciation for its post-conflict responsibilities. It could not forget these missions entirely because they had become a fact of life in the post-Cold World disorder. On average, the U.S. military has conducted an operation related to peacekeeping, peacemaking, or post-conflict occupation every two years since the end of the Cold War. With the Soviet menace gone, there was greater pressure to employ U.S. forces for a range of operations, which the Pentagon termed "military operations other than war."[39]

Yet it is not clear that the military internalized the requirements for post-conflict operations. In 1995, the Pentagon produced its first joint doctrine for military operations other than war.[40] The U.S. Army established a Peacekeeping Institute at its Army War College in Carlisle, Pennsylvania. These initiatives left much to be desired. They paid scant attention to specific post-conflict operations—arguably the most difficult and strategically important of all the peace activities that military forces might be called upon to undertake.[41] Even the term "operations other than war" was problematic, implying a range of military tasks less strategically important than warfighting and grouping post-conflict operations (essentially an extension of the warfighting mission) in with a plethora of tasks that included everything from peacekeeping to helping out after hurricanes.[42]

There was also little special recognition that the military's two most recent major postwar operations in Panama (after Operation Just Cause) and Kuwait (after the first Iraq War) were both deeply flawed.[43] For example, Lieutenant General John Yeosock, who was given initial responsibility for overseeing operations in Kuwait in 1991, recalled that he received virtually no assets or planning assistance for the task. Yeosock recalled that he had been handed a "dripping bag of manure" that no one else wanted.[44] Operations in Iraq today appear different only in scale and duration. Initial assessments of U.S. military operations in Iraq suggest that the military failed to follow its own doctrine or to learn from past experiences. Halting efforts at rebuilding Iraqi security forces and controlling arms in the country offer two examples of this.[45]

Rather than figure out how to best win the peace, the military always tried, insofar as possible, to make post-conflict missions mirror traditional military activities. For example, during World War II, the military staff planning process for military government operations was virtually identical to the procedures for planning battles. Today, the staff process for planning operations other than war remains very similar to the combat planning process, encouraging leaders to use very similar techniques and procedures. An approach to post-conflict activities that mirrors combat can result in the misapplication of resources, inappropriate tasks and goals, and ineffective operations.

The military also insisted on shoehorning combat units into postwar tasks. In post-World War II Europe, Army tank battalions and artillery brigades were ill-suited to the conduct of occupation duties. Most troops lacked training in many critical security tasks such as conducting investigations, arrest, detention, search and seizure, interrogation, negotiation, and crowd control. It was not until months after the occupation began that the Army began to field constabulary units that were better designed to conduct a range of security tasks.[46] The U.S. constabulary forces served successfully, but were soon disbanded and replaced by conventional military units more appropriate to the tasks of fighting Cold War battles. As result, when the military tried to conduct similar types of operations as part of their counterinsurgency efforts in Vietnam, the results were pretty abysmal until nearly the end of the U.S. involvement—when General Creighton Abrams restructured units and operations specifically for the tasks.[47]

Today, U.S. combat units are still structured in much the same manner as they were during World War II. The United States has no forces specifically organized and equipped for post-conflict missions. Although the U.S. military has developed training programs and tactics for postwar duties, these were mainly provided for follow-on forces. Much as during World War II, the initial occupation troops were the same forces that conducted the combat campaign and that had to learn the skills of occupation on the job.

New Military Capabilities and Competencies

If we agree that the military is poorly prepared to conduct post-conflict missions—and that these are important tasks to get right—then developing these capabilities must become part of the transformation plan. That will require a deliberate strategy on the part of the Pentagon.

Suitable post-conflict forces can come from three places. First, a nation can have allies with suitable units to conduct the mission for them. Second, nations can reorganize and retrain traditional combat forces as units better prepared to conduct occupation duties. Third, nations can maintain forces specifically designed to spearhead an occupation.

A great power should be able do all three, using its abundance of resources to gain maximum flexibility to approach post-conflict operations and tailor the best force for the mission. Thus, the United States should do more to build up the capacity of its allies. It should also do a much better job converting forces for post-conflict duties and learning the lessons of current operations. Finally, it should build organizations and supporting programs specifically designed to conduct post-conflict duties.

Meeting the third requirement is undoubtedly the most difficult. Creating the right set of capabilities will require a set of initiatives that cut across the armed forces' education processes, career professional development patterns, acquisition programs, and organizations. Therefore, the following might be added to the military's transformation plan.

Reform Military Education. The skills needed to conduct effective post-conflict tasks require the right combination of "hard power" (the means to provide security) and "soft power" (not only the capacity to understand other nations and cultures, but also the ability to work in a joint, interagency, and multinational environment). These are sophisticated leader and staff proficiencies, required at many levels of command.

In the present military education system, however, much of the edification relevant to building these attributes is provided, if at all, at war colleges to a relatively elite group being groomed for senior leader and joint duty positions. This model is wrong on two counts. First, these skills are needed by most leaders and staffs in both the active and reserve components, not just an elite group within the profession. Second, in the United States this education comes too late in an officer's career. Virtually every other career field provides "graduate level" education to members in their mid-20s to mid-30s. Only the military delays advanced education until its leaders are in their mid-40s. We need to educate more leaders, earlier in their careers.

The armed services also need special schools specifically designed to teach the operational concepts and practices relevant to post-conflict missions. The services already have advanced schools (such as the Marine Corps' School for Advanced Warfighting) for instruction in the operational arts at their staff colleges. These courses train the military's finest planners. The curriculum in these courses should be expanded to include post-conflict missions.

Restructure Commands. Overseas commands should be reorganized to include interagency staffs with specific responsibility for developing post-conflict contingency plans in the same manner that current operational staffs plan for warfighting contingencies. In the event of war, the post-conflict interagency group can be attached to the operation's joint force commander to provide the nucleus of an occupation staff.

In addition, the joint force command should include a general-officer deputy commander who would oversee the work of the planning group and assume command of the post-conflict occupation force. These staffs and command positions could provide a series of operational assignments for the career development of a cadre of officers specially skilled in post-conflict duties.

Establish New Organizations. Special post-conflict units could be assembled from existing National Guard and Reserve units, including security, medical, engineer, and public affairs commands. Since many of the responsibilities involved in postwar duties are similar in many ways to missions that might be required of homeland security units, these forces could perform double duty, having utility both overseas and at home.[48]

Rethink Equipment Needs. The military also needs a more robust and integrated acquisition program—a "systems" approach to post-conflict missions that includes more aggressive development of non-lethal technologies, capacities to rapidly equip and interface with domestic security forces, and support for the reconstruction and protection of governance and other critical infrastructure. Indeed, the military might consider establishing a "future security system" acquisition program under a lead-system integrator responsible for developing a range of technologies applicable to post-conflict and domestic support missions.

Beyond Goldwater–Nichols

Another persistent rhythm of habit is the armed forces' penchant for largely eschewing integrated interagency operations (activities involving more than one federal agency), as well as ignoring the role of non-governmental organizations (NGOs). The result is that most operations lack cohesion, flexibility, and responsiveness. During the Cold War occupations, the military closely followed its tradition (as much as possible) of divesting itself of non-combat tasks. Traditionally, the services preferred to establish a "firewall" between civilian and soldier activities to prevent civilian tasks from becoming an overwhelming drain on military resources.[49] As a result, there was scant cooperation between the Pentagon and other federal agencies or NGOs.[50]

Post-Cold War operations also reflected chronic difficulties in coordinating military activities with outside agencies.[51] Prospects for better performances in Iraq did not bode well. As a result of U.N. sanctions, NGOs had little presence in the country, no accurate assessments of needs, and no logistical or support base. Lacking good intelligence about the country's internal conditions, the CIA, the State Department, and the Department of Defense were at odds about how to best deal with political and humanitarian concerns. Without a coordinated, integrated planning effort, miscues, mistakes, and disputes seemed inevitable.

Official U.S. accounts of cooperation in Iraq and Afghanistan give little indication of the chronic tensions that have marred American operations in the past. It is not clear how candid these assessments might be.[52] It is perhaps too early to pass judgment on these operations, but persistent reports of disagreements between the Departments of State and Defense and complaints by the Red Cross that military authorities were unresponsive to the organization's findings about the treatment of Iraqi prisoners that offer cause for concern.

Interagency cooperation during post-conflict operations is not the only troubling trend. Nor is achieving cooperation between agencies just an issue for the Pentagon. The integration of U.S. activities overseas has always been problematic.[53] The obstacles to effectively getting agencies to work together are legion.[54]

The limitations of government cooperation might be acceptable in another long war, but not in this one. The global war on terrorism will require unprecedented integration of military, intelligence, law enforcement, diplomatic, and other international security instruments.

Additionally, the offensive component will need more than just cooperation inside the beltway. It will require working together in the field as well. That is a particular problem: Bureaucrats in Washington are always suspicious of cooperation among their underlings who are forced to work together in the far-flung corners of the world. They are concerned that on-the-scene decisions made by subordinates will set U.S. policies, rather than being mandated by the decision makers. Overcoming this paranoia and empowering our nation's representatives to work together must become an imperative.

The Unified Command Plan

The centerpiece for accomplishing this reform could be a radical restructuring of the Pentagon's Unified Command Plan (UCP). Established during the Cold War to allow the DoD to manage global military operations, the UCP has become another relic of the last war that we may no longer need. This is iron-ic, given that it took most of the Cold War to get it right. It was Eisenhower who insisted on establishing regional commands to manage far-flung military activities. In another defeat by the entrenched constituencies defending serv-ice prerogatives, the initial command setup did not allow the regional com-manders (called CINCs) to have much authority.[55] It was not until 1986 with the passage of the Goldwater–Nichols Act that the CINCs gained full author-ity over their commands. The law worked. In fact, by the end of the Cold War, CINCs (now called combatant commanders), became so powerful that some felt they began to overshadow all the other instruments of foreign policy.[56]

After the Cold War there was considerable discussion about reorganizing the UCP. A protracted debate ensued about how to shift the regional com-mands from countering Soviet power to providing global military support to a variety of missions in a systematic and coordinated manner.[57]

One proposal included creating an "Americas Command" that would place the entire Western hemisphere under a single regional command. As late as 2000, a report commissioned by DoD recommended establishing a separate command with oversight of North America. Both foreign policy and domestic issues caused the proposal to be shelved. There was concern that Mexico, which maintains a strict neutralist foreign policy while seeking close economic ties with the United States, might object to being included under a U.S. regional security umbrella. In addition, the Joint Chiefs of Staff (JCS) remained sensitive to domestic concerns that the new command could be perceived as impinging on civil rights, as well as on state and local govern-ment responsibilities for public safety.

Within a week of the September 11 terrorist attacks the proposal was back on the table. The Joint Chiefs recommended the establishment of the U.S. Northern Command (NORTHCOM). The emerging requirements to fight a global war on terrorism clearly overrode previous reservations. As cur-rently established, NORTHCOM is tasked with the land, aerospace, and maritime defense of the continental United States, Alaska, Canada, Mexico, Puerto Rico, the U.S. Virgin Islands, parts of the Caribbean, and the Atlantic and Pacific waters (out to 500 miles).

As a result, today the world is divided into five commands with regional responsibilities (North America, South America, Europe, the Middle East, and Asia), four functional commands that control special operations, space, nuclear, and transportation forces (as well as overseeing joint training and experimentation.)

Even after the creation of NORTHCOM, all the commands were given responsibilities in the war on terror. The Central Command (CENTCOM) is running support operations in Afghanistan and Iraq. The European Command (EUCOM), also responsible for parts of Africa, is supporting counterterrorism operations in the Horn of Africa. The Pacific Command (PACOM) is providing counterterrorism training and support to a number of countries, including the Philippines. PACOM also provides defense and civil support to Hawaii and U.S. territories. Southern Command (SOUTHCOM) conducts a variety of counterterrorism-related missions in Central and South America.

The functional commands also have counterterrorism and homeland security–related tasks. In the latest revision of the UCP, Strategic Command (STRATCOM) was tasked to integrate combatant command missile defense operations. According to recent press reports, while NORTHCOM will be responsible for directing missile defense operations in its area of responsibility, STRATCOM will act as the global integrator to ensure that activities of the theater commands support one another. STRATCOM, for example, would be responsible for ensuring the right combination of offensive and defensive means were employed to counter a missile threat that might be launched at the United States from the PACOM area of responsibility. In addition, STRATCOM provides space support (such as early warning of missile launches) to all theater commanders, including NORTHCOM. STRATCOM also has responsibility for information operations to protect computer systems from foreign attacks.

Special Operations Command (SOCOM) provides special operations forces to the regional commands for a range of missions—from direct action, to psychological operations and civil affairs, to combating terrorism. SOCOM can also conduct activities independent of the combat commands at the direction of the President and Secretary of Defense. SOCOM has always had some homeland defense tasks. It maintains a national response force to respond to special contingencies. Special operations forces have been used as "red teams" to test the security of certain installations. SOCOM has also supported designated national security events (such as the Olympics).

The Transportation Command (TRANSCOM) provides transportation and logistical support assets used by all the commands. For example, the combat aircraft flying combat air patrols over American cities after 9/11 received aerial refueling from TRANSCOM assets.

Joint Forces Command (JFCOM) provides conventional forces to the regional commands, including NORTHCOM. While some combatant commands had forces assigned directly to them, Army, Navy, Marine, and Air Force units within the United States remain a part of a pool of troops that can be dispatched to the regional commands as needed. JFCOM is also responsible for conducting joint force experimentation.

Beyond Commanding the World

With the exception of creating NORTHCOM—and even though the commands are already conducting some tasks in the global war on terrorism—these organizations are still structured to provide global command for the last war. In addition, although the geographic commands each contain within itself a joint interagency coordination group to organize regional activities, in practice the operations are not much better run than they were during the Cold War. Competing with each combatant commander is the ambassador within each country in the commander's area of responsibility. The ambassador is in charge of the country team, which incorporates all civilian, military, and intelligence personnel assigned to the embassy. Combatant commanders cannot even "marry up" with the State Department at the regional level, because the regional desks in Washington cover geographical areas that do not match up with the UCP.

Given its limitations, and the fact that the Soviet empire is gone and the United States no longer has to worry about fighting a global conventional war, it is worth asking if the UCP is still necessary—and the answer is probably not. It is time to replace the UCP with a structure that better supports the nation's national security needs. That organization should probably be based more on facilitating worldwide interagency operations rather than combat action. A new structure, the U.S. Engagement Plan (US-Plan), crafted at the direction of, and answering to, the National Security Council rather than the Pentagon, might look like the following.

Time to Replace the Plan

Combatant Commands. There is still a need for permanent military commands under the direction of the Pentagon; however, the number of combatant commands should be reduced to three. In Europe and Northeast Asia, the United States has important and enduring military alliances and there is a continuing need to integrate the U.S. military commands with them. To this end, EUCOM and PACOM should be replaced by a U.S.–NATO command and a U.S. Northeast Asia headquarters. In addition, NORTHCOM should remain as the military command responsible for the defense of the United States.

Joint Interagency Groups. In addition, three "Joint Interagency Groups" (InterGroups) should be established. Joint-Interagency Task Forces (JIATFs) have already been used very effectively on a small scale to conduct counternarcotics operations in Latin America, the Caribbean, and off the Pacific coast of the United States. They incorporate resources from multiple agencies under a single command structure for specific missions. There is no reason that this model could not be expanded in the form of InterGroups to cover larger geographical areas and more diverse mission sets.

The InterGroups within US-Plan should be established to link areas of concern related to national security missions, such as transnational terrorism, transnational crime (e.g., piracy and drug and human trafficking), weapons proliferation, and regional instability. The InterGroups should be established for Latin America, Africa and the Middle East, and South and Central Asia.

Each InterGroup would have a mission set specific to its area. The Latin America InterGroup should focus on drug, human, and arms trafficking; counterterrorism; civil–military relations; and trade liberalization. The Africa–Middle East InterGroup should focus on counterterrorism, weapons proliferation, economic development, fighting AIDS and other infectious diseases, peacekeeping training and support, transnational crime, and civil–military relations. Central and South Asia InterGroup should concentrate on counterterrorism, weapons proliferation, training police forces, anti-piracy measures, civil–military relations, transnational crime, and fighting AIDS and other infectious diseases.

Each InterGroup should include a military staff tasked with planning military engagements, warfighting, and post-conflict operations. In the event that military operations are required, the military staff could be detached from the InterGroup (along with any supporting staff from other agencies required) to become the nucleus of a standing Joint Task Force (JTF). Using this model, operations in Iraq and Afghanistan would have been commanded by a JTF.

Functional Commands. Under US-Plan, military operations of short duration and global importance should be directed from the United States by three reorganized functional commands. These commands should also be responsible for global logistical and transportation support. The new commands should be a Strike Command, an Operational Support Command, and a Logistics and Transportation Command. Because control of nuclear weapons is such a vital mission, reestablishing a separate strategic nuclear command might be considered.

Preparing for the Future. It will take time and resources to develop the commanders, people, organizations, education, and doctrine needed to support US-Plan. There will clearly be a need for a Goldwater–Nichols II Act to provide the legislative framework—laying out the requirements, legal authorities, and resources needed to restructure how America engages with the world. This legislation will be one of the most important steps taken in improving the nation's offensive posture. It will not only spark a dramatic change in how overseas activities are conducted, it will lay the foundation for a new kind of governance, a federal government that will be able to leverage the full capacity of its institutions through true collaborative effort; a government made up of an empowered work force that understands how to work together and has the trust, confidence, and capacity to produce better results.

The Right Tools for the Right War

In July 2004, the congressionally chartered National Commission on Terrorist Attacks Upon the United States (the 9/11 Commission) released its final report. Included in the report were recommendations about how to respond to the future threat of terrorism. The release of the report garnered widespread media attention. Little noted in the headlines and talk shows, however, was the report's implicit endorsement of the importance of an offensive component for the long war.[58]

Recognizing the need for offense is important. More important, however, is ensuring that the best tools are available to fight the long war. The United States needs better than it has. It is time to put that right.

Chapter 2

Protecting the Homeland

During his two terms of office, President Eisenhower struggled to formulate a long-term strategy to fight a two-front war—with the Soviets and with the Democrats.[1] Any effort Ike made to hold back defense spending earned shrill cries from the loyal opposition, which was trying to earn political capital by claiming that the President was being soft on Communists. One of Eisenhower's harshest critics was Paul H. Nitze. The antagonism between these two has much to tell us about the challenge of playing good defense in the long war.

Before 1952, Nitze had been a Republican, although he had served in a key staff position in the Truman Administration. Nitze had followed Kennan as the Director of the Policy Planning Staff in the State Department, and was one of the key authors of NSC-68. He felt that Kennan was simply naïve in his understanding of how much conventional military force was needed fight the Cold War. "Kennan believed that two high-quality Marine divisions would be sufficient to support the military requirements of U.S. containment policies," Nitze fumed. "I disagreed."[2] Nitze argued that military spending needed to be more than triple what Truman had budgeted—and he crafted NSC-68 to make the case.

Nitze's falling out with Eisenhower began during the 1952 presidential campaign. In fact, Nitze backed Ike's campaign, until, as he later recalled, "I got mad at him."[3] Nitze switched parties. Shortly after the election he was ousted from the Eisenhower Administration, but remained active as one of the foremost commentators about defense affairs. Then Nitze received an

Paul H. Nitze (center) at a disarmament meeting at the White House prior to the departure of the U.S. delegation for the Geneva Conference, March 9, 1962. (Courtesy of the National Archives)

unexpected to call to serve on the Gaither Commission—a blue ribbon commission assessing the need for a civil defense program.

After the Soviets exploded a nuclear device in 1949, Americans knew it was only a matter of time before they had to be afraid in their own beds. By Eisenhower's second term, the threat of nuclear holocaust had become something more than fodder for science fiction movies with cheap special affects taken from stock footage of nuclear tests in New Mexico. Americans were afraid. Eisenhower tapped H. Rowan Gaither, chairman of the Ford Foundation and the Rand Cooperation, to form a committee of private citizens to study the need for civil defenses.

Nitze was pleased to be asked to act as a consultant for the committee. After World War II, he had served as director of the Air Force's strategic bombing survey—which, among other tasks, had studied the nuclear strikes on Nagasaki and Hiroshima. The experience convinced him that the United States needed to prepare for nuclear attack—and that meant digging in. He tried to convince builder Robert Moses to construct bomb shelters in New York City. "Paul, you're mad, absolutely mad," Moses disparaged. "Nobody will pay attention to that."[4] The Gaither study not only gave Nitze another chance to make the case for civil defense, but also to renew the arguments for higher defense spending advanced in NSC-68.

History is often a cataloguing of coincidences. So it was with the Gaither Report. On October 1, 1957, shortly before the committee's report was due to be presented to the President, a flicker of light reached into the sky above the Baikonur cosmodrome in Kazakhstan. Aboard was 184 pounds of metal called "Sputnik." The Soviets had managed to launch the world's first satellite, although all it did was circle the globe and beep at the astonished world below. An American admiral belittled the achievement. It was, he declared, "a hunk of iron almost anybody could launch." Americans knew otherwise. If the Soviets could throw a satellite into space, they feared, the Russians could drop a nuclear-tipped missile on a U.S. city.

Sputnik hysteria set the stage for equally hysterical warnings from the Gaither committee. Based on flawed intelligence, the report vastly overestimated Soviet capabilities, leading it to call for a $32 billion civil defense program as well as a huge expansion of offensive capabilities. Though the report itself was classified, news leaks whipped up a nervous public. Presidential candidates like John F. Kennedy decried a U.S. missile gap that threatened to give the Soviets an insurmountable lead in nuclear competition.[5]

Eisenhower proved skeptical of the report's findings. He refused to endorse a national shelter-building program. Rejecting the significance of Sputnik and the dire predictions of the Gaither Report, Eisenhower decided not to change his fundamental strategic approach to the Cold War. When pressed to revamp his plans for space and missile development, Ike told his staff they would do just like they had done in World War II when the plan for defeating Germany was continually attacked by critics. "We never abandoned it," he reminded them. "It was a good plan, a long-range plan that

A Soviet ICBM at a military parade on Red Square, 1971. (Tass photo from Sovfoto)

had been carefully worked out. We went on and won."[6] Good strategy required a steady hand.

Ike felt the same way about his hopes for the Cold War. Robert Bowie, who followed Nitze as the director of the State Department's Policy Planning Staff under Eisenhower's Secretary of State, John Foster Dulles, agreed. Bowie was Nitze's mirror image—a Democrat, working for conservative Republicans. Politics aside, Bowie concluded that, "To a large extent, his [Eisenhower's] strategy established the guidelines for the long haul leading to the ultimate end of the cold war."[7]

Yet, as Bowie pointed out, it was "a long haul," and there were moments when America got lost along the way. After John F. Kennedy became President, U.S. intelligence confirmed there was a missile gap, but it was in the United States' favor. Too late—the United States had already announced an expansion of its nuclear arsenal. Fearful of being left behind, the Soviets smuggled missiles into Cuba, sparking a showdown with the Kennedy Administration, increasing distrust between the superpowers, and precipitating an escalating (and seemingly uncontrollable) nuclear arms race.

As for the national civil defense program, it never became a central tenet of protecting the homeland, even though there were brief spurts of activity. After the Cuban Missile Crisis in 1962, the national civil defense effort received renewed attention when the government initiated a nationwide nuclear fallout shelter system, but the program soon lapsed.

Nitze's career, however, was far from over. Although Eisenhower retired to his farm in Gettysburg, Nitze went to work for successive Democratic administrations. Kissinger later tapped him to lead the crown jewel of détente, the Strategic Arms Limitations Talks (SALT) with the Soviets. Thus, Nitze capped his career (again working for Republicans) trying the slow the arms race that he had helped to create.

Providing for the defense of American soil is no easy task because it is not about holding trench lines or parrying a cavalry charge; it is about protecting our children, our homes, and our neighbors. Ike understood the dilemma in a way that Nitze never appreciated.

Eisenhower was always keen to remember the human dimension of war. This, too, is perhaps something he gained from his reading of the great Prussian military thinker, Clausewitz. One of Clausewitz's most famous constructs is that a trinity (composed of the military, the nation's leaders, and the people) governs war. The military provides the muscle; the leaders provide the cool, rational decisions that guide military effort; and the people provide the passion and will to prevail. Governments, Clausewitz argued, that lose the support of the people cannot sustain their forces in the field. Ike knew that he could never forget the passion of the people in fighting in the Cold War, but he also knew that it was a bad idea to make policy by whipping up fear or giving in to fear's excesses.

Eisenhower understood that Americans were afraid and that their concerns had to be addressed, but he also realized that spending billions of dollars on bomb shelters and excessive missile arsenals would buy little real security. He knew when the furor over Sputnik died down that, upon sober reflection, most Americans would agree with him. Nitze's answer amounted to little more than throwing money at the problem and encouraging people to take counsel of their fears.

The Face of Homeland Security

Putting the right face on homeland security is perhaps the greatest public policy challenge of our times. The Eisenhower approach is to build an enduring security system that is prepared for the long war and takes reasonable measures to protect Americans. The alternative is to do anything to create the illusion of progress—e.g., spend money haphazardly on state and local programs,

U.S. citizens treated to a mobile bomb shelter display, April 22, 1961. (Courtesy of the National Archives)

turn U.S. ports into a twenty-first century Maginot line, profile Arab-Americans, seal our borders, ban immigration, or inspect every package coming into the United States—without any real sense of whether these measures will actually help stop terrorists or of the impact they might have on the U.S. economy or our liberties. There is more to homeland security than throwing money at the problem. Defending the homeland is a strategic problem—and at the strategic level, thought should always precede action.

How We Got Here from There

To the Bush Administration's credit, after 9/11 the President quickly surveyed the instruments the United States possessed to provide homeland security and found them wanting. It would, however, be wrong to argue that nothing had been done to protect the United States from terrorist threats prior to the 9/11 attacks. The United States had a number of agencies involved in the task of safeguarding the homeland. The FBI looked for terrorists. The Coast Guard patrolled U.S. waters. The Customs Service and the Immigration and Naturalization Service (INS) watched people and goods.

Successive administrations also noted the gathering terrorist threat and tried to do something about it. Funding for activities related to homeland security rose in the mid-1990s, spurred by the 1995 bombing of the Alfred P. Murrah Federal Building in Oklahoma City and the sarin gas attack on the Tokyo subway. Federal expenditures from 1995 to 2000 for domestic preparedness against weapons of mass destruction (WMD) accelerated from almost nothing to $1.5 billion.[8] Presidential Decision Directive 39 (released on June 21, 1995) called for giving "the highest priority to developing effective capabilities to detect, prevent, defeat and manage the consequences of nuclear, biological or chemical (NBC) materials or weapons used by terrorists."[9] In 1996 Congress passed the Nunn–Lugar–Domenici Domestic Preparedness Initiative, which enhanced the capabilities of first responders to deal with WMD. Reflecting a growing concern about terrorism and WMD, Congress held over 80 hearings on these and related issues between 1998 and 2000.[10]

Yet all this effort appeared more like the scattershot Truman approach to the emerging Cold War than a coherent approach to protecting America from terrorists. The first reactions to 9/11 were much the same—a patchwork of measures: a law creating the Transportation Security Administration to oversee passenger inspections at the air terminals; a bill to improve port and commercial shipping security; another bill on food safety; and the Patriot Act to provide more tools to law enforcement for fighting terrorism. What was lacking was the guiding lifeline of an idea.

The Bush Administration quickly recognized that the earnest efforts of legislators and bureaucrats were not enough. The nation was getting security without strategy, priorities, or a plan. Shortly after 9/11, the President established an Office of Homeland Security within the White House to craft an overall approach to protecting the homeland—although walking in the steps of Eisenhower would be no easy task.

Homeland security needed its George Kennan. One candidate for the historians to consider will be Richard Falkenrath. At 34, he had done well. A doctorate in war studies from King's College in London and an assistant professorship in public policy at Harvard's Kennedy School of Government were notable accomplishments. He was a published author as well, coauthoring a 1998 book—*America's Achilles' Heel: Nuclear, Biological, and Chemical Terrorism and Covert Attack*—long before the subject of transnational terrorism was fashionable.

Falkenrath was no stranger to Washington. In his eight years at Harvard, he frequently served as a consultant to DoD, the intelligence community, and Rand (an influential government think tank). Falkenrath was also no stranger to the White House. He had served as a member of the Bush–Cheney Transition Team for the National Security Council and had begun working at the NSC, coordinating policy on weapons proliferation. Then the world turned upside down. By December of 2001 Falkenrath had joined the homeland security office. From 6:30 in the morning until well past dinner, he was at his desk as Senior Advisor and Deputy Assistant to the President, reviewing budgets, coordinating policies, and helping to draft the nation's first strategy for homeland security. After six months of meetings, debates, arguments, and deliberation, the strategy was published.

Homeland Security as Strategy

The Office of Homeland Security released its national strategy in July 2002. Like any good strategy, it included the basics of ends, ways, and means. The ends (the goals of the strategy) were embedded in the definition of homeland security—"a concerted national effort to *prevent* terrorist attacks within the United States, *reduce* America's vulnerability to terrorism, and *minimize* the damage and recover from attacks that do occur." The strategy's ways (how the goals will be accomplished) could be described in a simple word or short phrase—"layered security"—a notion as concise as "containment" or "beat Germany first" and with as significant an import for providing a blueprint for action.

The strategy's approach to homeland security rightly eschews the notion that there is a single, "silver bullet" solution to stopping terrorism at America's doorstep. Rather, it argues for a multi-layered system that assumes no one security initiative will suffice. This strategy provides multiple opportunities to thwart or mitigate terrorist acts. Security is not provided by a single initiative, but by the cumulative effect of all the homeland security programs. For example, a terrorist might be discovered by an overseas intelligence operation while applying for a visa, during screening of an international flight manifest, during inspection at a port of entry, or during a domestic counterterrorism investigation. Likewise, if layers of defense failed to stop the terrorists, other initiatives would be undertaken to reduce vulnerabilities (such as beefing up security at nuclear power plants), making key targets less susceptible to attack or less likely to suffer. Finally, if these measures failed, the strategy wanted to make sure there were resources in place to adequately respond to various kinds of potential terrorist incidents. Thus, improving security requires ensuring that each layer of the system is sufficient to do its part of the job and that efforts are complementary.

America's homeland security strategy also makes a fundamental statement about the means and the resources that would be needed to get the job done. Homeland security, the strategy argued, had to be a shared responsibility. While the federal government focused on counterterrorism, states and local government were tasked with providing for public safety within their communities. The private sector, which controls over 85 percent of the nation's critical infrastructure (from the electrical power grid to telecommunications), also had significant responsibilities in protecting the nation from the threat of terrorism.[11]

Perhaps the most significant contribution of the strategy was its designation of the six principal tasks—the critical missions—comprising homeland security. These are:

- Intelligence and Early Warning;
- Border and Transportation Security;
- Domestic Counterterrorism;
- Protecting Critical Infrastructure and Key Assets;
- Defending Against Catastrophic Threats (i.e., research and development); and
- Emergency Preparedness and Response.

Establishing these critical missions was important because the strategy detailed the tasks that had to done to secure the nation from terrorism. Each task has a special role in turning the strategy into action.

Intelligence and Early Warning. This includes activities related to detecting terrorists and disseminating threat information and warning. It is about promoting intelligence sharing across the public and private sectors. Effective intelligence sharing is a prerequisite for exploiting the full potential of national capabilities to respond to potential terrorist threats.

Protecting Border and Transportation Systems. This task includes managing the hundreds of borders and ports of entry into the United States, ensuring aviation and maritime security, and developing guidelines and programs for protecting national transportation systems. Border and transportation security is about ensuring the adoption of a layered security system—a combination of effective, mutually supporting initiatives that simultaneously provide useful counterterrorism measures, protect civil liberties, and do not encumber the flow of travel and commerce.

Domestic Counterterrorism. This comprises law enforcement efforts, principally by the FBI and U.S. Immigration and Customs Enforcement (although it also includes other federal, state, and local agencies), to identify, thwart, and prosecute terrorists. This critical mission area is about adopting programs that expand the capacity to conduct counterterrorism operations without impinging on civil liberties or detracting from other law enforcement priorities.

Critical Infrastructure and Key Asset Protection. This task includes protecting agriculture and food, water, public health, emergency services, the defense industrial base, telecommunications, energy, transportation, banking and financing services, chemical industry and hazardous materials, and postal and shipping services. This critical mission also includes protecting key assets such as national monuments and icons, nuclear power plants, dams, government facilities, and selected commercial assets.[12]

Defending Against Catastrophic Threats. This calls for efforts to develop better sensors and procedures to detect smuggled nuclear, radiological, chemical, and biological weapons; improving decontamination and medical responses to such weapons; and harnessing scientific knowledge and tools for counterterrorism efforts. The goal of this effort is to focus funding on developing new means to prevent, respond to, and mitigate the unprecedented dangers posed by catastrophic threats.

Emergency Preparedness and Response. This task is about preparing for, responding to, and mitigating the effects of terrorist attacks. The strategy argues for concentrating federal resources on creating a true national preparedness system, not merely to supplement the needs of state and local governments.

The strategy not only defined the essential tasks of homeland security, it also provide a blueprint for assigning responsibilities and reorganizing the federal government. Four months later, on November 25, 2002, the Homeland Security Act of 2002 merged over 22 federal entities and 180,000 employees into a single department—the Department of Homeland Security. Indeed, the strategy served as a blueprint for creating the four directorates of the Department of Homeland Security: Border and Transportation Security, Information Analysis and Critical Infrastructure Protection, Emergency Preparedness and Response, and Science and Technology.

Thinking About the Next 9/11

Within two years of the September 11 attacks, the foundations for homeland security were firmly established. The yeoman's service had been done. More work, however, remained. It took a decade to turn the mandates of the

Volunteer firefighters walk toward Ground Zero in New York, September 16, 2001. (Photo by Photographer's Mate Chief Eric J. Tilford courtesy of the U.S. Navy)

National Security Act of 1947 into the right instruments for twentieth century national security. We should think before we change a course we have just begun, even if another attack soon follows.

Americans should carefully consider how the country might react to the next 9/11. A key first step is thinking through how we should respond to attacks beforehand. If and when the next attack occurs, there are four arguments we will undoubtedly hear. They are simple, clear-cut—and usually wrong. Here they are:

"Throw Money at the Problem." If another terrorist attack occurs, we will hear shrill cries that it's the government's fault. We will be told that the billions being spent on homeland security wasn't nearly enough.

Yet few problems can be solved by money alone. Spending too much, too fast on programs that aren't well thought out would be wasteful and counterproductive.

We know, for example, that we need to do a better job spending the money we've already allocated to emergency responders. A study cited in *Time* magazine found that most grants to state and local governments have been distributed "with no regard for the threats, vulnerabilities and potential consequences faced by each region."[13] We need a system that will spend our money efficiently and effectively.

"Trade Safety for Civil Liberties." Calls for new security measures that require temporary impositions on basic civil liberties will surely be heard. This argument is almost devoid of logic. During the Cold War, the United States managed for decades to endure a protracted struggle against a global superpower without trashing the Constitution and the Bill of Rights. It is hard to see how a small band of religious extremists merit suspension of the liberties that generations fought to preserve.

On the other hand, Americans should beware of hysterical claims that every government action to fight terrorism is a slap at the Constitution. The USA Patriot Act is a case in point. Its detractors have yet to identify a single abuse or prove that its provisions are broadly unconstitutional. The debate over the balance between civil liberties and security warrants thoughtful debate, not knee-jerk histrionics.

"America Is at Fault." If there's another attack, one explanation will be that we deserved it. Critics might offer any number of reasons, but we generally should dismiss these assertions out of hand. No nation is perfect, but our country strives to be a force for good in the world. Some may not like American politics or policy, but nothing the United States has done justifies terrorist acts aimed against innocent people.

Still, no one should be surprised if the blame for attacks on Americans is pinned on Americans. The "enemy is us" argument was a refrain heard more than once after 9/11. That is to be expected. Reflection, criticism, and reassessment are part of democracy. They are part of what makes for a strong and vibrant civil society—but we should not let them become an excuse for inaction, retrenchment, and retreat.

"We Are on the Wrong Course." In all wars we witness advances and setbacks, victories and casualties. Every incident is not a call for change. The United States succeeded during the Cold War because it held firm, stuck to a long-term strategy that invested in security, protected civil liberties, and promoted economic growth. After 9/11, the nation established a homeland security strategy that is attempting to follow a similar path: We should stick to it.

We can be sure more terrorist attacks on the United States are on their way. They may come quickly or occur years in the future. After all, we know it took some five years to perpetrate the September 11 attacks. The terrorists may be travelers from abroad or people who have been living here for years—perhaps even American citizens. But attacks will come.

No administration can guarantee it will stop every attack, everywhere. However, if we take the offensive, we can steal the initiative away from the terrorists, lessen their chances of success, mitigate the damage they cause—and one day live in a world in which terrorists are left in the pages of history. All that is required of us is courage and a constant heart. Admittedly, this is no simple task.

Washington's Greatest Industry

Eisenhower shrugged off the distractions of the Gaither Report and steered a steady course. We should do the same. There is, however, no room for complacency. When the National Security Act of 1947 consolidated the services into a single department, the new organization—a product of debate and compromise—left much to be desired. It was called the National Military Establishment, a title that pleased no one because its initials were the NME. Embarrassed department representatives would go into meetings confessing that they were representing the "*en-em-ee*." The department's name, however, was the least of its problems. In order to prop up the power of the services, the department secretary was given almost no authority and, as an institution, the Joint Chiefs of Staff (JCS) had virtually no responsibility.

Two years later, a subsequent law was required to fix the most grievous errors in the Pentagon's organization, but serious flaws in the department remained. However, once the wiring diagram was set, budgets divided, and congressional committees established, Washington's greatest industry—momentum—took over. After that, fixing flaws was soon crushed by the momentum of entrenched interests and parochial jurisdictions. Change became almost impossible. The Office of the Secretary of Defense remained weak until the 1960s. The JCS stood impotent until the Goldwater–Nichols Act in 1986. We can learn lessons from this history.

We live in crucial times; times in which strategy must be turned into reality, the hard slug of years in which prudent improvements have to made—all without being pulled off course. It will not be easy. Eisenhower had his Nitze. New Nitzes will appear in the years ahead.

Completing the task of turning strategy into a national homeland security requires important but difficult steps, easily as difficult as putting the Pentagon in order. There are four areas in which more work needs to be done: undertaking congressional reform, reorganizing the Homeland Security

Department, balancing federal responsibilities with those of state and local governments, and building a true national security system.

Congress, Reform Thyself

When President George W. Bush proposed the establishment of a Department of Homeland Security on June 6, 2002, Congress joined the debate with vigor, arguing about every aspect of the issue, except how they would manage oversight of the new agency. That is a big problem. Congress's homeland security and terrorism responsibilities transcended all aspects of its traditional committee authority.

The day the President proposed the Homeland Security Act to Congress, it was referred to 12 standing committees in the House alone. Indeed, the White House identified 88 committees and subcommittees that might be considered to exercise authority over homeland security policy. In the House, for example, at least 14 full committees and 25 separate subcommittees claim jurisdiction over some aspect of homeland security. When the bill was proposed, 10 of the 13 appropriations subcommittees laid claim to a portion of homeland security expenditures. Moreover, in some cases committee jurisdictions overlapped.

A Disjointed Committee System

The congressional debate about legislation to establish the department illustrated the cost of the disjointed committee system. The House recognized that its standing rules would dramatically slow passage of any legislation to establish the new department. It created a temporary Select Committee on Homeland Security to process the legislation and gave this committee sole authority for debating and amending the bill, which the full House would then vote on.

The House leadership allowed all other committees to hold hearings and amend the initial draft, but this process was only to advise the Select Committee prior to its deliberations. When the Select Committee met for markup, it reviewed the President's proposed legislation—not the opinions of the other committees. Adopting this process allowed the House to focus on homeland security issues that directly affect the proposed department and to move quickly to pass legislation acceptable to the President. It did so on June 26, 2002.

The Senate, on the other hand, relied on its existing committee system—with disastrous results. The Senate Governmental Affairs Committee was assigned responsibility for reviewing and amending the bill prior to floor debate. The committee did not finish this process until after the House had already passed its legislation. After two months of debate in the full Senate, the bill stalled.

Additionally, instead of focusing on the many issues directly related to homeland security or the operation of the new department, the Senate allowed the debate to become hijacked by union special interests and a protracted and unproductive debate about the civil service provisions in the act. In effect, while terrorists plotted against us, the Senate debated the importance of merit pay raises. After these issues were resolved, the law finally passed. The Department of Homeland Security was created. Concern about the dysfunctional oversight of Congress passed, but the problems this lack of oversight engendered did not.

Inconsistent Oversight

Every day another uneventful morning passes without a major terrorist incident on U.S. soil. That is cold comfort. We do not know what threats are now in the works and when they may come to fruition. We need homeland security that will serve for the long term, protecting Americans on holidays and unremarkable days for years to come.

No one understood the frustration of preparing for the future better than Chris Cox (R–CA). This veteran congressman knew how Washington worked. He had been on both sides, first as a staffer in the Reagan White House, then as representative from California. Cox had always had a strong interest in national security issues. On the morning of September 11, 2001, he was having breakfast at the Pentagon with Defense Secretary Donald Rumsfeld. Minutes after the news that the World Trade Center had been attacked, Cox was on his way back to Capitol Hill. Then word came that the Pentagon had been struck. Cox joined other members standing on the steps of the Capitol building.

With a reputation as a diplomatic, tactful negotiator, he was an obvious choice to head up the Select Homeland Security Committee, a fractious gathering of 27 Republicans and 23 Democrats. It was a job Cox wanted. After all, he pointed out to a reporter, protecting the American people was "the primary responsibility of the federal government."[14]

Much like Eisenhower, Cox soon found himself fighting a two-front war—one with the terrorists and one with his fellow legislators. Although Cox and his Democratic counterpart, Representative Jim Turner (D–TX) made a good faith effort to craft bipartisan legislation, virtually none of their work reached the floor of the House. Cox's committee included the chairmen of other committees that had jurisdiction over homeland security–related issues and it seemed they spent more time undercutting the Homeland Security Committee than they did helping to push new legislation forward. After a year of hard work, Cox had little to show for his effort.

After eighteen months, Cox and Turner, whose committee had extremely limited legislative authority, had authored and dropped one significant bill to redirect federal first-responder grants to the highest threat areas. (The bill was later incorporated into H.R. 10, the 9/11 Commission Recommendations Implementation Bill, but dropped in conference.) On oversight, they had succeeded in forcing the department to increase its investment in analysis, to accelerate the development of a National Plan for Critical Infrastructure Protection, and to make the Homeland Security Advisory System more sensitive to regions and sectors.

The Select Committee's major achievement, however was in demonstrating that, without real jurisdiction, it could not achieve its principal goal—the first-ever DHS authorization bill. Cox and Turner drafted a bill, again with impressive bipartisan cooperation, but the standing committee chairmen would simply not cooperate. Most of them failed to show up for a markup on the modest first effort. The Select Committee subsequently, on September 30, 2004, submitted its recommendation to the Rules Committee, with a large majority of Republicans and Democrats signing on, that a permanent standing committee with strong jurisdiction be established. On November 14, Speaker Dennis Hastert announced that he intended to make the committee permanent in the 109th Congress.

The fact that congressional politics have derailed efforts to provide effective oversight is more than a subject of gossip on the Hill. It is a matter of national security. There is no question that Congress still has a major role to play in establishing an effective homeland security regime. Although the Homeland Security Act of 2002 created a lead federal agency for many domestic security activities, this was only the first step. Building an effective department requires sound supporting policies, solid programs, personnel reforms, and integration of information technologies. Congressional oversight—led by committees and professional staffs with the experience and expertise to address difficult, complex issues—plays an important role in achieving these ends. To this point, the Congress has failed to provide sufficient leadership.

Both chambers have established subcommittees to handle appropriations for the new department, but supervision of the department's operations is still fragmented and incoherent. In the Senate, the Government Affairs Committee provides nominal oversight, while Cox's temporary select committee tries to focus efforts in the House. Nevertheless, jurisdiction over department activities remains split among dozens of committees and subcommittees in both houses. The result has been oversight overload. From January to June of 2004, department representatives testified at a staggering 126 hearings. That's an average of one-and-a-half testimonies for every day of the legislative session. In addition, a typical day for the department includes at least a dozen meetings or briefings to legislators and staff.

The amount of time spent preparing, participating, and responding to queries from the Hill is not the only issue. Beyond having to testify before multiple committees, department representatives must accept oversight from these committees. After all, many of the department's initiatives cut across the roles and missions of the federal government, and strong congressional input and feedback is necessary. Yet multiple committees, with multiple interests and multiple (and sometimes conflicting) priorities exacerbate the challenge of building a comprehensive, focused national security regime.

Congress needs to move from scattershot supervision of homeland security to responsible oversight. This will include establishing permanent committees in both chambers with full jurisdiction over the department, as well as a role in the oversight of all critical national homeland security programs. Until that is done, Congress will have failed in its constitutional responsibilities to provide proper checks and balances to the executive branch.

Reforming the Department

Perhaps the most difficult next step in the process of building better homeland security will be rethinking the organization that Congress has just created. It would be unrealistic to believe that Congress could create a perfect agency. Major merger and acquisitions in the private sector offer innumerable examples of the difficulties of building new organizations from old ones. Sometimes you just have to get something up and running to identify and work out the flaws. The problem can be waiting too long to fix them. Problems have a way of becoming the traditional and routine way of doing things and then they become very difficult to change.

There is a sweet spot on the curve of experience when an organization has been up and running long enough to separate the good from the bad; this is when it is worth changing things before they get any further along. The Department of Homeland Security is rapidly reaching that point. The department's operations, roles and responsibilities, resources, and organization deserve a thorough, nonpartisan review. Of the many areas that might be prime for rethinking, one might be the trouble with visas; another might be the challenge of sharing information.

On Terrorism's Front Line: The Trouble with Visas

In the global war waged by terrorists, visas can be deadly weapons. One ready means available to enemies wishing to enter the United States is the nonimmigrant visa, which can be obtained from any of the 211 American consulates around the world.[15] Travelers holding nonimmigrant visas represent the overwhelming majority of individuals entering the U.S. Nonimmigrant visas are ideal for supporting attacks that require brief or repeated trips to the United States. In fact, all of the 9/11 hijackers entered the United States in this manner. These 19 terrorists received a total of 23 visas from five different consular posts over a four-year period.[16]

Terrorists can also enter the United States through the permanent immigration system, obtaining a "green card" to live in the country or become a naturalized citizen. One study of 28 known terrorists found that 17 of them were in the country legally, either as permanent residents or as naturalized citizens.[17] The prevalent use of identity theft and false travel documents makes the current system particularly vulnerable to abuse. In 2001, officials at border crossing points seized over 100,000 falsified documents. Over 50 percent of these documents were border crossing cards, alien registration cards, and fraudulent visas and passports.[18]

Terrorists have used such materials. For example, one of the perpetrators of the 1993 World Trade Center bombing entered the country with a doctored passport.[19] Thus, intelligence is critical, not only to keep suspected terrorists from legitimately obtaining and using passports, but also to prevent them from easily using falsified documents to travel into the United States.

Given that the issuance and monitoring of visas is so important to homeland security, you would think the President of the United States would be able to turn to one person in the federal government and say, "Don't screw this up!" Unfortunately, he can't. Although the Homeland Security Act of 2002 gave the Secretary of the Homeland Security Department exclusive authority to issue regulations and administer the visa program, consular officers remained a part of the Department of State. This was a mistake. Today, when legitimate travelers or terrorists walk into a U.S. embassy to apply for a visa or submit to an interview, we have no guarantee that those overseeing the issuance of these precious documents, which open the gates to America, will act with one voice.

Nor is the concern about visa issuance and monitoring simply a question of doing a better job of catching terrorists. It is all about maintaining America's lifeline to the world. The decline in the number of students and travelers visiting the United States is at historic levels. In Poland—a U.S. ally in Iraq and a member of NATO, but not a participant in the visa-waiver program—it requires, on average, one month's salary to apply for a visa. It takes one day of waiting in a long line for an interview. After this, however, there is no guarantee that at the end of the grueling process that a visa will appear—and if the visa application is unsuccessful, there is no refund. Many are frustrated. They deserve better, and so do we. We need a government that not only stops terrorists, but also serves our citizens and our friends.

For the Department of Homeland Security to fulfill its responsibilities in the visa process—and because of the national security aspect of visa approvals—the Bureau of Consular Affairs Office of Visa Services should be placed under the Homeland Security Department. Moving the visa office to Homeland Security would enable the department to focus on tightening, improving, and more broadly utilizing the visa function to meet the exigencies of homeland security.[20]

Information Sharing: Who's in Charge?

One of the mantras for further homeland security reform has been the call to improve information sharing between the intelligence and law enforcement communities. To its credit, in the years immediately after 9/11, the Bush Administration has undertaken several major initiatives for improving the current system. The first is the establishment of the Terrorism Threat Integration Center (TTIC) on May 1, 2003. The TTIC was designed to be a central location in which all terrorist-related intelligence, both foreign and domestic, is gathered, coordinated, and assessed. It is composed of elements of the FBI, CIA, Department of Defense, Department of Homeland Security, Department of State, and other intelligence agencies. According to the Administration, the TTIC would:

- Optimize the use of terrorist threat-related information, expertise, and capabilities to conduct threat analysis and inform collection strategies;
- Create a structure that ensures information sharing across agency lines;
- Integrate terrorist-related information collected domestically and abroad in order to form the most comprehensive threat picture possible; and
- Provide terrorist threat assessments for the national leadership.[21]

At the urging of the 9/11 Commission, the President created a National Counter Terrorism Center (NCTC) under the DCI. This center has taken over the management of the TTIC.

The second initiative was creation of the Terrorist Screening Center (TSC) under the FBI to consolidate all terrorist watch lists into a single function and give around-the-clock access to local, state, and federal authorities. The TSC will bring together databases that include the State Department's TIPOFF (a declassified file of likely terrorist information),[22] the FBI's Violent Gang and Terrorist Organization File, and DHS's many transportation security lists. The TSC will make it easier for consular officers to determine whether a visa applicant is a potential terrorist. The main source of TSC's information is TTIC. As part of these new initiatives, TIPOFF's database portion has been moved into TTIC, while the support functions for consular offices will move to TSC. TTIC will forward all terrorist-related information from the intelligence community to TSC.

Also noteworthy is the establishment of the intelligence arm of the Department of Homeland Security—the Information Analysis and Infrastructure Protection (IAIP) directorate. This directorate includes the Homeland Security Operations Center (HSOC). Nestled on the second floor of a nondescript building at the department's headquarters on Nebraska Avenue, the center is responsible for consolidating information and putting out warnings. This consolidation has been long overdue and contributes to the Department of Homeland Security's ability to see the "big picture," as does HSOC's Homeland Security Information

Network (HSIN). Creating the HSIN was also welcome news. HSIN links states, territories, and major urban areas to the HSOC. Collaborative tools like HSIN are essential for establishing the interactive communications necessary to effectively share information. With these tools today, the HSOC can monitor the Brooklyn Bridge, talk to a governor, alert a police department, and connect dots that could never before be connected.

Despite all the energy that went into creating these new (and necessary) organizations, their very creation sows the seeds of a problem. The Homeland Security Department was created to be the main center for data sharing and analysis for homeland security, but it has not been given the tools to exploit U.S. intelligence and law enforcement resources. TTIC and TSC stand outside of the department and in competition with IAIP. The result is an unintended war of alphabet organizations that have opened more gaps in our ability to share information. In the end, the current arrangement makes DHS little more than just another intelligence end-user, competing with other members of the national security community to ensure that its priority requirements are met.

Directors of both the FBI and CIA pledged to provide any support that the new agency requires. Yet such assurances, although well-intentioned, fail to address how agencies with competing demands and priorities will allocate scarce resources—particularly during periods of national crisis when the United States is engaged in active operations overseas and faces a significant terrorist threat at home. Placing TTIC and TSC outside DHS only exacerbates this problem.

The right answer is to group the entire alphabet (TTIC, TSC, and IAIP) under one boss—the Department of Homeland Security—so that the President can depend upon one person to get the right information to the right person at the right time.

Capping the Bottomless Barrel

In determining the right role of the Department of Homeland Security, no problem has become more contentious than how the federal government will assist state and local communities in establishing a national homeland security system. There is a danger, however, that the system set up after 9/11 (modeled on the way we distribute money to build bridges and schools) will turn a national security system into a national giveaway.

The amount of federal grants available for state and local government homeland security programs will never be enough to meet all of their needs.

Some would address the shortfalls in state and local capacity by throwing money at the problem. That is exactly the wrong approach. Spending a little bit of money on a lot of things does not achieve much of anything. The United States needs a strategic spending strategy that focuses on two goals that will make all Americans safer—creating a truly national preparedness and response system and expanding national capacity to respond to catastrophic terrorist attacks.

Anyone who wants to understand the scope of the challenge should ask Warren Rudman, a former senator from New Hampshire. Most Americans do not remember Rudman for his years in Congress or his efforts to rein in the federal budget. Instead, he is often remembered for a brief comment in the blue-ribbon Hart–Rudman Commission report. "A direct attack against American citizens on American soil," the commission concluded, "is likely over the next quarter century. The risk is not only death and destruction but also a demoralization that could undermine U.S. global leadership." The report came out in February 2001: Eight months later the Twin Towers collapsed.[23]

Just being right was never enough for Rudman, who led a task force sponsored by the Council on Foreign Relations to examine the requirements for improving U.S. security. One of its efforts, *The 2003 Independent Task Force Report, Emergency Responders: Drastically Underfunded, Dangerously Unprepared*, earned national headlines and garnered Rudman a grilling by Tim Russert on "Meet the Press."[24] The task force had concluded that nationwide, emergency responders needed over an additional $98 billion to be adequately prepared to respond to terrorist threats.[25]

Rudman, with a well-earned reputation as a fiscal conservative, had not thrown out that number lightly. He had not intended, however, to be the war on terrorism's Paul Nitze. Improving national preparedness did not mean that the federal government had to shell out $98 billion. What that number meant was that the United States faced a serious public policy issue that demanded a serious response and a serious strategy to make America safer.

Dollars and Sense

Admittedly, the process used to provide money to states and local governments in the first three years after 9/11 was not consistent with the national homeland security strategy. It was, however, consistent with typical congressional "pork-barrel" legislation. The formulas that drive the grant process are turning homeland security initiatives into state entitlement programs. Current funding formulas guarantee each state 0.75 percent of the funds available. As a result, 40 percent of funds are immediately tied up, leaving only 60 percent for discretionary allocations. In this manner, California, clearly a "target-rich environment" received only 7.95 percent of general grant monies—even though the state accounts for 12 percent of the nation's population. Wyoming, receiving 0.85 percent, accounts for only 0.17 percent of the population. This translates to $5.03 per capita in California and $37.94 per capita in Wyoming. Spending on U.S. territories is equally incongruous. In the 2003 round of grants, the U.S. Virgin Islands received $104.87 per capita; the North Mariana Islands $53.68 per capita; and American Samoa $37.32 per capita.

Within states, low density and rural areas often receive a disproportionate amount of money as well. For instance, in Iowa, the capital city of Des Moines (population 199,000) received $250,000. The less populous Sioux County (population of 31,600) received $299,000.

Other spending is curious, too. Reportedly, California distributes its federal grants in base amounts of $5,000 to each county—an amount so small that it is difficult to imagine how it could be used productively.

Even the Urban Area Security Initiative grants (monies targeted at major population areas that are also considered potential targets) produce some strange results. The three criteria used are population density (50 percent of the weight); presence of critical infrastructure (one-third of the weight); and finally, credible threats (about one-sixth of the weighting formula). Using this formula, San Francisco (with a population of 800,000) and Los Angeles (with a population of 4 million) get roughly the same amount of money. The inequities of the current distribution mechanism demonstrate its serious flaws. Washington's formula-based system needs to be replaced by strategy-directed spending.

Smart Spending

Much to the Bush Administration's credit, it significantly increased funding for homeland security to the point at which we are now spending more than two-and-a-half times as much as we were before 9/11—over $50 billion. In fact, it is not clear at present that more spending could be efficiently used, particularly in the area of improving emergency response. We are rapidly approaching the point of throwing money at the problem. Indeed, state and local governments are having difficulty absorbing and efficiently using the federal funds that are already available.[26]

The first and highest priority for federal spending must be investments that assist in creating a true national preparedness system, not merely supplementing the needs of state and local governments. Dollars that might be needed to equip every state and U.S. territory with sufficient resources to conduct each critical homeland security task could run into the hundreds of billions. Although the federal government has a responsibility to assist states and cities in providing for homeland security, it cannot service every one of their needs.

Federal funding should focus on programs that will make all Americans safer. That includes providing state and local governments with the capability to integrate their counterterrorism, preparedness, and response efforts into a national system. They should also be able to expand their capacity to coordinate support, share resources, and exchange and exploit information.

Performance-Based Budgeting

The U.S. needs broad national standards for emergency response, coupled with a method for evaluating risks and vulnerabilities. Without real standards, there is no way to determine the nation's most important unfunded needs. Standards are also essential for determining levels of readiness and are the only viable measure of how much spending is enough.

With a strategy and with real performance standards, the Bush Administration can move to performance-based budgeting for homeland security. This form of budgeting would set the performance goals that must be achieved without specifying exactly how to accomplish the mission, thus giving states and local governments maximum flexibility in determining how best to meet their unique security needs. It would also provide a basis for measuring what kind of emergency response capacity the federal government is buying and would allow Congress to focus on its proper role—overseeing how effectively the programs are meeting the nation's needs.

Performance and threat-based funding will direct most federal grants to where they are most needed, satisfying the greatest national priorities. At the same time, the effectiveness of state funding—monies to assist in establishing and maintaining emergency management centers, conducting planning and training, and participating in exercises—can be fairly evaluated to determine if we are getting appropriate value from these programs.

To the Bush Administration's credit, in December 2003, the President issued a directive requiring federal agencies to put a performance-based system into place. What is required now is for Congress and the states to work together in support of this initiative and for all of us to have the patience to let the system work—and resist the urge to turn national security in an entitlement for state and local governments.

System of Systems

Anyone who wonders whether it is worth it to try and do more than just throw money at the challenge of homeland security ought to talk to James Gilmore. Along with leaders like Falkenrath, Rudman, and other people who have helped shape the Administration's response to terrorism, few have more expertise and knowledge about what to do next.

The former Republican governor of Virginia was appointed by President Bill Clinton to chair the Congressional Advisory Panel to Assess Domestic Response Capabilities for Terrorism Involving Weapons of Mass Destruction. After producing an authoritative series of reports on both the threat of terrorism and how to respond to it, the commission was prepared to issue its last report—in September 2001. Gilmore's commission met its deadline, but at the cost of one of its own. Ray Downey, the Deputy Fire Chief of New York City, died trying to save lives in the Twin Towers.

What became popularly known as the Gilmore Commission was extended by Congress and the President to look at the nation's response to 9/11. The commission issued two more reports. Many of their findings foreshadowed the recommendations made by the 9/11 Commission.

The Gilmore Commission, however, included one critical finding that the 9/11 Commission missed. The Gilmore Commission concluded that the goal should be to provide "an enterprise-wide capacity to plan, equip, train, and exercise against measurable standards." Emphasis should be on efforts that enhance interoperable communications and information sharing, joint planning and exercises, leader and staff training, and mutual-support programs.[27] This recommendation was far bolder than proposals made by the 9/11 Commission—or by the Administration or Congress. Gilmore argued, and rightly so, that all individual efforts were going to need to be drawn together into one coherent program. Much like Eisenhower had argued that the Pentagon needed to be reformed—not to just get the services to talk to

Former Virginia Governor James Gilmore discussing recommendations of the "Gilmore Commission." (Photo from The Heritage Foundation collection)

each other, but to fuse their efforts into a single military instrument—Gilmore argued that the nation needed a "national" homeland security system, not just a patchwork of federal, state, and local programs.

The genius of Gilmore's recommendation was that it respected the Constitution of the United States. The structure of American governance plays a significant role in determining the manner in which the United States addresses homeland security missions. Under the U.S. federalist system, power is shared between federal and state governments. This division of responsibilities is largely defined by the U.S. Constitution. In turn, these divisions prescribe and proscribe duties for protecting the homeland. The federal government, for example, is charged by the Constitution with "providing for the common defense." Thus, keeping terrorists outside the United States from getting here and hurting us is Washington's job. In contrast, the Tenth Amendment to the Constitution reserves to the states and the people all power not specifically delegated to the federal government. As a result, responsibilities for homeland security, which include a broad range of activities undertaken by federal and state governments, local municipalities, the private sector (such as businesses and NGOs), and individual citizens, are shared.

Gilmore recognized that state governors had a key role to play in homeland security. They were responsible for state public safety programs that protected local communities. Thus, he rightly argued, governors should direct statewide programs and the funding of those programs.

Likewise, every mayor, county executive, and tribal leader had a role to play as well. After all, most of the first responders (fire, police, and emergency medical technicians) work for them, and in the event of a disaster the local community leader on the scene would be in charge.

The solution, Gilmore recognized, was not rethinking the Constitution, but using training, planning, and—above all—technology to make sure all levels of government could work together. This is sometimes called building a "system of systems." The scientific explanation of a system-of-systems approach sounds something like this. Network-centric operations generate increased operational effectiveness by networking activities, decision makers, and field officers to achieve shared awareness, increased speed of command, higher tempo of operations, greater efficiency, increased security, and a degree of self-synchronization. In essence, it means linking knowledgeable entities in an effort to coordinate a comprehensive national security plan. Such a system might produce significant efficiencies in terms of sharing skills, knowledge, and scarce high-value assets; building capacity and redundancy in the national security system; gaining the synergy of providing a common operating picture to all involved; and being able to readily share information.

Translating scientific jargon into English would render it thus: Building a system of systems means linking everything you have together so that you can get the right asset or information to the right person, at the right time, to do the right thing—or even more simply, knowing what the system knows.

What are the kinds of things a system of systems might do? For starters, it might take all the information available to federal, state, and local agencies and put it at the disposal of a first responder standing at the scene of a terrorist attack. It might provide:

- means to identify threat and critical infrastructure data that needed to be disseminated, where such information should go, and how the information should be delivered so that it is still at the required security classification;
- detection capabilities that can alert responders to suspicious objects and secondary devices, determine the location of agents after an attack, and recognize any downwind hazards;
- ability to know where other responders are in three dimensions and to be able to monitor the responders' physical and psychological status;
- standoff means to analyze biological, chemical, and radiological threats and to disseminate information about those threats; and
- capability to determine threats inside buildings and in underground infrastructure, including the ability to discriminate between responders, victims, and threats.

The issue before us should not be if we need a system of systems, but who should design it and pay for it. Those hard questions have already been answered. As part of the establishment of the Department of Homeland Security, the Bush Administration created a Science and Technology (S&T) Directorate. Currently, the directorate is focused on the here and now, getting commercial off-the-shelf equipment (that is already available) for use now. That is probably the right priority. Yet it is also time to think about what kind of homeland security system we want five, ten, or twenty years from now and to start building it. The S&T Directorate should be charged to work on this problem.

The issue of who should pay for it has also been answered by the strategy. All of us should pay. The federal, state, and local governments, as well as the private sector, should each do its part. We have a constitutional framework that lays out fairly well who should do what. Sharing the burden is not the right answer; it is the only answer. First, that is what the Constitution says. Second, it is the only answer that is sustainable. A flood of federal dollars might offer some quick fixes, but it will not do for the long term. States and local governments need to build sustainable programs that are affordable within their means, while the federal government provides them the "plugs" to engage with a national system that can provide appropriate additional resources as needed.

Bracing for a Very Long War

Overall, the strategy of layering security and sharing responsibilities makes so much sense it is hard to imagine doing anything else. No one measure will be adequate to defeat every terrorist threat and we need more tools that provide more options. More important, though, than insisting that every program is airtight and unbeatable—or demanding that Jackson Hole, Wyoming, have the same security as New York's giant Kennedy Airport—is ensuring that we have complementary layers of security implemented by people who cooperate and share information with one another.

It would be a mistake to abandon the course have set. We would be equally remiss if we avoided the difficult tasks of making what have better. Congressional reform, rethinking the organization of the Homeland Security Department, sensible aid to state and local governments, and building the systems we need to face the future are the right steps. We should, as the Long Telegram prompts, take these steps with "courage and confidence."

Chapter 3

Between Liberty and Order

Born in 1924 in Milwaukee, Wisconsin, William Hubbs Rehnquist served in the Army Air Corps during World War II, witnessed the birth of the Cold War, was nominated by President Ronald Reagan to be Chief Justice of the United States at its nadir, and subsequently ruled on some of the first issues presented to the Supreme Court at the dawn of the war on global terrorism. A veteran of real wars and legal wars, Rehnquist thought hard about the challenges of the long war. He wrote:

> In any civilized society the most important task is achieving a proper balance between freedom and order. In wartime, reason and history both suggest that this balance shifts in favor of order—in favor of the government's ability to deal with conditions that threaten the national well-being.[1]

Everyone does not share Chief Justice Rehnquist's vision of the balance between liberty and order. To be sure, Americans sometimes misperceive the nature of danger and err in their efforts to both protect liberty and secure order. This was, perhaps, one of the Cold War's most important lessons, a lesson taught by another famous judge from Wisconsin—"Red Hunter" Joe McCarthy.

When Joseph McCarthy, a former judge from Wisconsin's 10th Judicial District, became a U.S. Senator, he launched his anti-communist crusade.

Supreme Court Justice William H. Rehnquist. (Courtesy of the National Archives)

He was taking on an issue that was already in the forefront of concern for many Americans—the danger of Soviets spies and saboteurs freely walking American streets. Indeed, we know now that these fears were not unfounded. Soviet espionage and control over the American Communist Party were significant. These are facts confirmed by two sources: secret American Communist Party papers found in the Soviet archives after the Cold War, and the VENONA transcripts (decrypts of intercepts of KGB [the Soviets' version of the CIA] cables that had been hidden away in the vaults of the National Security Agency until the end of the Cold War).[2]

The danger of Soviet spying was all too real. High-placed agents in the Departments of State and Treasury gave away some of America's most precious secrets. Yet, as Ted Morgan writes, "McCarthy and his predecessors knew nothing of VENONA, and flayed about like blindfolded men in a room full of bats. The bats were there, but beyond their reach."[3] In fact, many of the biggest bats had flown, been captured, or died before McCarthy chaired his first congressional hearings.

Controversy still swirls around McCarthy's methods and motives and the controversial hearings he chaired about the alleged penetration of the Army by communist agents. What is incontrovertible is the hostility that erupted

Senator Joseph R. McCarthy of Wisconsin. (COURTESY OF THE NATIONAL ARCHIVES)

between Dwight D. Eisenhower and McCarthy. Eisenhower thought of McCarthy as little more than an ambitious fear-monger. "He wants to be president," Eisenhower fumed. "He's the last who'll ever get there if I have anything to say."[4] Ike was often taken to task for not criticizing McCarthy more openly, but the President considered dealing with McCarthy to be the Senate's job. (See Appendix 6.) "All of us on the staff, including the president," Press Secretary James Hagerty wrote, "will make it a point not to have any comment whatsoever on anything McCarthy says or does....The best treatment for McCarthy is to ignore him."[5] Eisenhower rejected the basic premise of McCarthyism—that security trumped civil liberties. Eisenhower believed that both had to be preserved in the long war.

Censured by the Senate, McCarthy died in office on May 2, 1957. By that time, however, he had ceased to be an influential figure on the national scene and the worst red-hunting excesses had subsided. "It's no longer McCarthy-ism," Ike quipped. "It's McCarthy*was*m."[6] Here, however, Eisenhower was wrong. While attacks on civil liberties and McCarthy's controversial role in them had come to an end, his name had lent itself to a fear. In American memory, McCarthyism will always be synonymous with the practice of making accusations without regard to evidence and using the power of government to suppress legitimate dissent and the right of free speech.

The Ghost from Wisconsin

Today, cries of McCarthyism are frequently raised by those concerned about the state of American civil liberties—and with some cause. We face a similar problem. Once again, there is an internal threat to safety and security. This time it is the threat of violent, mass terrorism against unprotected domestic targets. Additionally, today we also face the potential for over-balancing, for affording government too great a power to combat the perceived threat. The U.S. is in danger of doing exactly what George Kennan warned us against. "The greatest danger that can befall us…is that we shall allow ourselves to become like those with whom we are coping."

Much of the current debate's focus lies in discussions about the USA Patriot Act,[7] a law passed with overwhelming support in Congress immediately following the September 11 terrorist attacks.[8] The critics argue that the law tips the balance between liberty and order in the wrong direction. Criticism of the anti-terrorist campaign is not, however, limited to the Patriot Act: Many other aspects of the domestic response to terrorism have come under fire. Yet, the Patriot Act has come to serve as a symbol for all of the domestic anti-terrorist law enforcement actions. Indeed, the Patriot Act has become the poster child for criticism, a convenient shorthand for all questions about the alterations in the balance between civil liberty and national security that have occurred since 9/11.

The furor over the Patriot Act surprised no one more than a 36-year-old professor from Georgetown University, Viet Dinh. A Harvard graduate who had clerked for Supreme Court Justice Sandra Day O'Connor, Dinh preferred life in the academy to life in the courtroom. He served on the faculty at Georgetown University Law Center in downtown Washington. In March 2001, he was asked to join the Attorney General's office for two years to work on judicial nominations. After 9/11, he was drafted to work on the legislative reforms that became the Patriot Act.

War had stamped a lesson on Dinh's childhood about the struggle between liberty and order. At the age of seven, he witnessed the invasion of

South Vietnam and his father's detention in a "re-education" camp. Immigrating to America with his mother and five brothers and sisters, Dinh chose as his path a profession dedicated to safeguarding freedom and security. As one of the principal architects of the Patriot Act, Dinh believed the law served to preserve both.

While work on the act (and the subsequent congressional debate) were brief by Washington standards, the legal issues surrounding the bill—from authorities for wiretaps to examining business records—were hardly new: There was little uncharted ground. The critical portrayal of the bill came as some surprise. Frustrated by the critics' response to the law, Dinh concluded, "There has been a lot of hue and cry regarding specific provisions with USA Patriot Act that is predicated upon a misunderstanding....[T]he act has been mischaracterized and misunderstood and has engendered a lot of well-meaning and genuine fear, even if that fear is unfounded. The issue is not one of substance but one of perception. But perception is also very important because we do not want the people, however many of them, to fear the government when that fear is unfounded. "[9] Dinh understood that the problem was helping average Americans understand the difference between legitimate law enforcement tools and the excesses of McCarthyism. Looking at the complaints leveled at the Patriot Act (and other anti-terrorism tools), it is easy to understand why he saw it as a daunting challenge.

Why We Worry

There are three factors animating fears about the anti-terrorism campaign. First, critics frequently decry the expansion of executive authority in its own right. They generically equate the potential for abuse of executive branch authority with the existence of actual abuse. They argue that the growth in presidential power is a threat, whether or not the power has, in fact, been misused. These critics come from a long tradition of limited government, which fears any expansion of executive authority.

The second kind of criticism is stimulated by the "Luddite response"—a fear of technology. As the government begins to explore ways of taking advantage of America's superior capacity to manage data through new information technologies, there are rising concerns that it will use these means to dig into our personnel lives. Information equals power. With great efficiency comes more effective use of power. And with more power comes more abuse.

A third theme underlying criticism is more blatantly political. The Patriot Act, regardless of its true merits or flaws, is a great tool for raising money and energizing constituencies that are predisposed to be critical of the Administration's response to terrorism. Brand labeling has become a part of the political process.[10]

Fact and Fiction

Criticisms of the government's new anti-terrorism practices miss important distinctions and often blur potential and actuality. To be sure, many aspects of the Patriot Act (and other governmental initiatives) expand the power of the government to act. Americans should rightly be cautious about any expansion of government power. Yet, by and large, the potential for abuse of new executive powers has proven to be far less of a real danger than critics have presumed. For example, the Department of Justice's Inspector General (an independent investigative arm within the department) has reported that there have been no instances in which the Patriot Act has been used to infringe on civil rights or liberties.[11]

Where opponents of the Patriot Act are equally wrongheaded is that their belief in the potential for abuse stems from a misunderstanding of the new powers that the government has been given by Congress to combat terrorists. In many cases, provisions of the Patriot Act simply apply tools we have used to combat other crimes, such as drug trafficking, to fighting terrorism.

More fundamentally, those who fear the expansion of executive power in the war on terrorism offer a bad alternative: prohibition. While we could afford that solution in the face of traditional criminal conduct, we cannot accept that answer in combating terrorism. There is a better way. Vigilance and oversight (enforced through legal, organizational, and technical means) are the answer to deterring or preventing abuse. We must keep a watchful eye on controlling for the risk of excessive encroachment. Paying attention to the problem is the best way of preventing the erosion of civil liberties.

The answer to fighting terrorists while preserving civil liberties is simple. It is *not* debating which is more important: It is simply doing both. That, like in the other elements of fighting the long war, requires the lifeline of a guiding idea. As with the other elements of long-war strategy, the past can be prologue. It is no coincidence that the other judge from Wisconsin, William Rehnquist, is also a historian and that when he searched for answers to the question of how to preserve liberty and order in the present day, he found the answers in the past.

The Lessons of History

To a very real degree, how we think about the Patriot Act, and other instruments used in the war on terrorism, rests on context—how we view the history of American responses in times of war, the constitutional constraints imposed upon executive power, and whether, in the end, one believes the threat of terrorism should be treated as a law enforcement problem or a national security issue.

Discussions of history often begin with cautions against repeating past excesses. American history can be written as a series of painful lessons about over-reacting in the face of war. In this troubled story, responding to threats leads to a good faith, but overzealous response. McCarthyism is one example. There are other dark days as well.[12]

In 1798, the Napoleonic wars raged in Europe. President John Adams, a Federalist, effectively brought the United States (on the side of the British) into a state of undeclared war with France. Thomas Jefferson and the Democratic Republican party opposed these measures as being likely to provoke an unnecessary war. The Federalists, in turn, accused the Jeffersonians of treason.

To exacerbate the situation, the Federalist Congress enacted the Alien and Sedition Acts of 1798.[13] The Alien Act authorized the President to deport any non-citizen—without a hearing or the right to present evidence—that he judged dangerous to the peace and safety of the United States. The Sedition Act prohibited the publication of false, scandalous, and malicious writings against the government, the Congress, or the President with intent to bring them into contempt or disrepute. These were, in effect, aggressive efforts to suppress political criticism of Adams, his policies, and his Administration. After Jefferson succeeded Adams as President, he pardoned all those who were convicted under the act. Although never tested in the Supreme Court, these acts are widely regarded as having been unconstitutional and a stain on American liberty.

During the Civil War, President Abraham Lincoln suspended the writ of habeas corpus on eight occasions. The broadest such suspension declared that "all persons...guilty of any disloyal practice...shall be subject to court martial."[14] (See Appendix 7.) As many as 38,000 civilians were imprisoned by the military in reliance on this authority. [15] In 1866, a year after the war ended, the Supreme Court ruled that the President was not constitutionally empowered to suspend the writ of habeas corpus, even in time of war, if the ordinary civil courts were functioning.[16] Here again, the suspension is remembered by some as an excessive response to a crisis and has come to be regarded as an unfortunate wartime error.

In 1917, the United States entered World War I. During the war, federal authorities acting under the aegis of the Espionage Act[17] prosecuted more than 2,000 people for their opposition to the war. As a result, virtually all dissent with respect to the war was suppressed. Although the Supreme Court initially approved most federal actions in support of the war,[18] over the next fifty years, the Court overruled every one of its World War I decisions—effectively repudiating the excess of that wartime era.[19]

Finally, and most notoriously, on February 19, 1942, President Franklin D. Roosevelt signed Executive Order 9066,[20] which authorized the Army to "designate military areas" from which "any persons may be excluded." Over the next eight months, more than 110,000 people of Japanese descent were forced to leave their homes in California, Washington, Oregon, and Arizona. Although the Supreme Court upheld the President's action,[21] it has come to be recognized as a grave error. In 1988, President Ronald Reagan offered an official presidential apology and reparations to each of the Japanese-American internees.[22]

Making history during troubled times can lead to very different lessons. Noted legal scholar Geoffrey Stone concludes the worst. "In time of war—or, more precisely, in time of national crisis," he finds, "we respond too harshly in our restriction of civil liberties, and then, later regret our behavior."[23] He is right, of course. We should never disregard that caution. Yet reading too much into this history is a mistake.

First, history also reminds us that you cannot deal with enemies by doing nothing. Sometimes there is a necessity to act. As the late Supreme Court Justice Arthur Goldberg so famously said, "While the Constitution protects against invasions of individual rights, it is not a suicide pact."[24] Even though some of these reactions were plainly overreactions (nobody argues today that the internment of the Japanese served a useful military purpose)—others were not.

For example, Justice Rehnquist and others argue that Lincoln's suspension of the writ of *habeas corpus* was necessary to the prosecution of the war.[25] Lincoln certainly felt the necessity, believing suspension allowed for additional security measures that helped protect the troops, save Maryland for the

Union, and secure the safety of Washington, D.C. [26] Later in the Civil War, the anti-draft riots in New York (made cinematically famous in the movie *Gangs of New York*) threatened to deprive the Union army of conscripts.[27] Had that occurred, Lincoln feared a premature end to the war—leaving the United States divided and slavery ongoing. [28] Using the authority granted him by Congress in the Habeas Corpus Act,[29] Lincoln directed the draft boards to ignore writs of habeas corpus issued to them by state courts seeking release of the conscripts.[30] It is not unreasonable to argue that, however *de jure* improper Lincoln's acts were, they were *de facto* a justified necessity that ought, in retrospect, to be praised.

Perhaps, the lesson that we should take from history is not to be too harsh in our retrospective judgments. Hindsight is always 20/20. Indeed, examining past excesses, both real and imagined, suggests that our history should actually give us some comfort. Many who are concerned with current activities think that we are on a downward spiral toward diminished civil liberties. However, a better view of this history shows that the balance between liberty and security is more like a pendulum (that gets pushed off center by significant events, such as 9/11) than a spiral. Over time—after Americans have recovered from the understandable human reaction to catastrophe and after the threat recedes—the pendulum returns to center.

We have to acknowledge the historical reality that when the wartime crisis passes, the balance swings back in favor of freedom and liberty. Ever since World War II, our society has matured to the point that the scope of the pendulum's swing is not nearly as great as it has been in the past.

For example, whatever one may think of the detention of three Americans as enemy combatants, there can be little disagreement that the detention of three individual Americans (whose detention is based upon a quantum of individualized suspicion), is sufficiently different in degree from the wholesale detention of more than 100,000 Japanese-Americans (whose detention was ordered in the absence of any individualized suspicion): These incidents are different in kind.[31] As Chief Justice Rehnquist wrote:

> [T]here is every reason to think that the historic trend against the least justified of the curtailments of civil liberty in wartime will continue in the future. It is neither desirable nor is it remotely likely that civil liberty will occupy as favored a position in wartime as it does in peacetime. But it is both desirable and likely that more careful attention will

be paid by the courts to the basis for the government's claims
of necessity as a basis for curtailing civil liberty.[32]

Rehnquist's words are reassuring, as is the test of history. After all, there were
many casualties in the Cold War, but the Constitution was not one of them.

Times Have Changed

Looking to history for answers, however, is not enough. While we might look
to George Kennan or Dwight Eisenhower to describe the principles for fighting a long war, we would not want to take their ideas about how technology,
civil society, and government worked in the 1940s and apply them to running the war on terrorism in the twenty-first century.

The truth is that in some respects we may have less to fear from the power
of government than in the times of Lincoln or McCarthy. Things have
changed. Today, America has:

- **A more activist court.** The Supreme Court is far more willing to
  overturn executive branch action, acting as a limit on excessive
  power. Earlier times of crisis all occurred before the "rights revolution" of the 1960s and the growth of judicial power. Indeed,
  the current Rehnquist Court has invalidated more acts of Congress than any previous court,[33] exhibiting a high degree of
  involvement in curtailing authority.[34]
- **A more partisan Congress.** Though sometimes seen as a bad thing,
  the growth of partisanship has created at least one positive benefit—a growth in the "market" for oversight of the executive branch.
  Ever since the Watergate era, we have seen an increasing use of congressional investigative authority—sometimes for good, sometimes
  for ill. Yet the prospect of aggressive congressional oversight acts as
  a check on executive power, as even the prospect of public censure
  has the *in terrorem* effect of preventing abuse.
- **The "60 Minutes" factor.** Clearly, this is another change that
  has potential adverse consequences. Yet few can deny that the
  post-Watergate press serves an aggressively important public
  function: exposing activities that some might prefer to keep
  secret. No one can imagine a return to the days when the press

actively participated in concealing Roosevelt's injuries or Kennedy's dalliances. That means, equally, that the prospect of secret prosecutions and covert searches and seizures is—at best—minimal.

- **Public interest group proliferation.** At no other time in history did Americans organize themselves into public interest groups in the way they do now. No other era saw the existence, for example, of numerous public-interest litigation groups like the ACLU. These organizations, through their public information and litigation activities, act as an important check on the exercise of executive authority. They are, in effect, the "canary in the mineshaft," [35] serving as an early warning system of abuse.
- **An enabled citizenry.** Although technology offers assuredly greater opportunity for our government to monitor our activities, that same technology holds the promise of greater public accountability by enhancing the transparency of government functions.[36]
- **A public that is far more educated about civil liberties today than at any time in the past.** With the rise of the Information Age and the Internet, we are far more able to gather information necessary to make decisions and to organize a response to government power if one is deemed necessary. From the Ozzie and Harriet quiet of suburbia in the 1950s, we have come to a point at which many Americans are vitally concerned about freedom, liberty, and government action. They exercise their franchise with those concerns in mind.[37]

All this is good news. At the dawn of the twenty-first century, we have strengthened substantially our ability to examine, oversee, and correct abuses of executive power. The public is in a stronger position today than it ever has been before. That power of oversight gives us freedom—freedom to grant the government powers when the need arises, secure in the knowledge that we can restrain. History is not our master. We should not be utterly unwilling to adjust our response to liberty and security in today's crisis of terrorism. We have the capacity to manage that adjustment, and to readjust as necessary.

Crisis and the Constitution

Although a large portion of the debate about new law enforcement and intelligence measures focuses on perceived intrusions on civil liberties, Americans should keep in mind that the Constitution weighs heavily on both sides of the debate. The President and congressional policymakers must respect and defend the individual civil liberties guaranteed in the Constitution when they act.

But, as the Preamble to the Constitution acknowledges, the United States' government was established, in part, to provide for the common defense. The war powers were granted to Congress and the President with the solemn expectation that they would be used. Congress was also granted the power to "punish...Offenses against the Law of Nations," which include the international law of war, or terrorism.[38] In addition, serving as chief executive and commander in chief, the President has the duty to "take Care that the Laws be faithfully executed," including vigorously enforcing the national security and immigration laws.

Thus, as we assess questions of civil liberty, we cannot lose sight of the dual purpose of government—protecting personal and national security. So how do we square the circle? Here, contemporary interpretations of constitutional limitations are not much help.[39] Under settled modern Fourth Amendment jurisprudence, law enforcement may secure, without a warrant (through a subpoena), an individual's bank records, telephone toll records, and credit card records—to name just three of many sources of data. Other information in government databases, such as arrest records, entries to (and exits from) the country, and driver's licenses, may be accessed directly without even the need for a subpoena.

In 1967, the Supreme Court ruled that the Fourth Amendment protects only those things in which someone has a "reasonable expectation of privacy," and concurrently, that anything one exposes to the public (i.e., places in public view or gives to others outside of his own personal domain) is not something in which he has a "reasonable" expectation of privacy—that is, a legally enforceable right to prohibit others from accessing or using what one has exposed.[40] Therefore, federal agents need no warrant, subpoena, or court authorization to:

- have a cooperating witness tape a conversation with a third party (because the third party has exposed his words to the public);[41]
- attach a beeper to someone's car to track it (because the car's movements are exposed to the public);[42]
- fly a helicopter over a house to see what can be seen;[43] or
- search someone's garbage.[44]

The plain fact is that even before September 11, the government had the constitutional authority to do a lot of things already. Individuals' flight itineraries and charitable donations constitute information that the government may access because the individual has voluntarily provided it to a third party.[45] According to the Supreme Court, no one has any constitutionally based and enforceable expectation of privacy in them. The individual who is the original source of this information cannot complain when another entity gives it to the government. Nor does he have a constitutional right to notice of the inquiry.[46] Some legal scholars have criticized this line of cases, but it has been fairly well settled for decades.[47]

Congress, of course, may augment the protections that the Constitution provides, and it has with respect to certain information. There are privacy laws restricting the dissemination of data held by banks, credit companies, and the like.[48] Yet in almost all of these laws (the Census being a notable exception),[49] the privacy protections are good only against other private parties. They do not provide barriers to criminal, national security, and foreign intelligence investigations. Therefore, while both the strictures of the Constitution and the weight of history help point us toward our ultimate destination—a strong and secure civil society—they are not much help in telling us where to take the next turn.

The Reality of Terrorism

There are other reasons we have to deal with the world as it is, not as we might want it to be. The full extent of the terrorist threat to America is not fully known.[50] We do not even know how many terrorist operatives are in the United States.

The sad truth is that terrorism remains a potent threat to international security. The U.S. State Department has a list of over 100,000 names worldwide of suspected terrorists or people with contact to terrorists.[51] Before its camps in Afghanistan were shut down, al-Qaeda trained at least 70,000 people—and possibly tens of thousands more.[52] Al-Qaeda–linked Jemaah Islamiyah in Indonesia is estimated to have 3,000 members across Southeast Asia and is still growing.[53] Although the estimates of the number of al-Qaeda members, al-Qaeda wannabes, al-Qaeda look-alikes, and sons and daughters of al-Qaeda in the United States have varied since 9/11, the figure provided by the government in recent, supposedly confidential, briefings to policymakers is about 5,000.[54] This estimate may include many who are engaged in fundraising for terrorist organizations and others who were trained in some fashion to engage in a future attack, whether or not they are actively engaged in a terrorist cell.

All we know now is that no one can say with much certainty how many terrorists are in the United States. and that more may be coming, but we do not know how many. "[M]ore than 500 million people [are] admitted into the United States [annually], of which 330 million are non-citizens."[55] Of these non-citizens:

- Tens of millions arrive by plane and pass through immigration control stations, often with little or no examination.[56]
- 11.2 million trucks enter the United States each year.[57] Many more cars do as well: More than 8.5 million cars cross the Buffalo–Niagara bridges each year alone, and only about 1 percent of them are inspected.[58]
- According to the Department of Commerce, approximately 51 million foreigners vacationed in the United States last year, and this figure is expected to increase to 61 million in three years.[59]
- There are currently approximately 11 million illegal aliens living in the United States. Roughly 5 million entered legally and simply overstayed their lawful visit.[60]
- Over half a million foreign students are enrolled in American colleges, representing roughly 3.9 percent of total enrollment, including: (1) 8,644 students from Pakistan; (2) a total of 38,545 students from the Middle East, including 2,216 from Iran, 5,579 from Saudi Arabia, and 2,435 from Lebanon— where Hezbollah and other terrorist organizations train; and (3) about 40,000 additional students from North African and Central and Southeast Asian nations in which al-Qaeda and other radical organizations have a strong presence.[61]

Now very, very few of these people are a risk to the U.S., but hidden in their vast numbers are people we do have to worry about.

Virtually every terrorism expert in and out of the government believes there is a significant risk of another attack. Unlike during the Cold War, the threat of such an attack is "asymmetric." In the Cold War, threats were "symmetric." They had nuclear weapons. We had nuclear weapons. War meant we both lost. Asymmetric warfare means the two sides threaten each other with dissimilar means that do not line up well against one another. We have divisions. They have box cutters. What that means in practice is that it is difficult to deter attacks. Because of the terrorists' skillful use of low-tech capabilities, their capacity for harm is essentially limitless. Because they are dispersed, they are difficult to threaten with the preponderance of American power. The United States, therefore, faces the far more difficult task of discerning their intentions. Where the Soviets created "things" that could be observed, the terrorists create transactions that can only be sifted from the noise of everyday life with great difficulty. This is a different problem from the national security concerns we faced in the past. It reminds us, again, that the Cold War can teach us the principles of fighting the long war, but it cannot give us a "how to" manual. We are on our own.

The suppression of terrorism will not be accomplished by offense and defense alone. Rather, effective law enforcement and intelligence gathering are essential instruments. Recent events support this conclusion.[62] In fact, police have arrested more terrorists than military operations have captured or killed. Police in more than 100 countries have arrested more than 3,000 al-Qaeda–linked suspects,[63] while the military captured some 650 enemy combatants.[64] Equally important, it is policing of a different form—preventative rather than reactive, because there is less value in punishing terrorists after the fact when, in some instances, they are willing to perish in the attack.

An understanding of the nature of the terrorist threat helps to explain why the traditional law enforcement paradigm needs to be modified. The traditional law enforcement model is highly protective of civil liberty in preference to physical security. All lawyers have heard some form of the maxim, "It is better that ten guilty persons go free than that one innocent person be mistakenly punished."[65] This embodies a fundamentally moral judgment that when it comes to enforcing criminal law, American society effectively hates Type I errors (false positives, or accepting that in the process of catching all the bad guys, errors might be made that result in a few innocents being wrongfully or inadvertently punished) and would rather allow many more Type II errors (false negatives, or errors that let a few guilty escape rather than punish the innocent) than it actually does.[66]

America's preference for protecting the innocent over punishing the guilty arises from two interrelated beliefs: One is the historical distrust of government that animates many persons concerned about civil liberty. The other is simply a deeply held belief in how the scales of justice should tip. We value liberty sufficiently highly that we will not accept a Type I error (i.e. convicting the innocent). Additionally, although we realize that Type II errors free the guilty to return to the general population—thereby imposing additional social costs on society—we have a common sense understanding that those costs, while significant, are not so substantial that they threaten large numbers of citizens or core structural aspects of the American polity.

The post-9/11 world changes this calculus in two ways. First, and most obviously, it changes the "cost" of the Type II errors. Whatever the cost of freeing Mafia don John Gotti or Washington sniper John Muhammad might be, they are substantially less then the potentially horrific costs of failing to stop a terrorist assault that kills 3,000—or 3 million. The sad truth is that we simply cannot afford a rule that "better ten terrorists go free than that one innocent's conduct be mistakenly examined."[67]

We also need to rethink what kinds of Type I errors must be considered. In the traditional law enforcement paradigm, the liberty interest at stake is personal liberty—that is, freedom from the unjustified application of governmental force. The law focuses on things like arrests, the seizure of physical evidence, or searches. In the information age, in which we may employ new technologies to assist in tracking terrorists, the rules of the "physical world" (where we use the law to protect people and their homes from intrusion by the government) may not be as useful in helping us determine what kinds of law enforcement "mistakes" should be permissible.

We have to think about another conception of liberty: the liberty that comes from "anonymity."[68] Anonymity is a different, and possibly weaker, form of liberty. By and large, Americans recognize that they are not entitled to all anonymity, all the time. Even people who have not committed any criminal offense can have information on them collected for legitimate governmental purposes, although they are entitled to expect that their information is handled and safeguarded appropriately. Census data are collected in the aggregate and never disclosed. IRS tax data are collected on an individual basis, reported publicly in the aggregate, and only disclosed outside of the IRS with the approval of a federal judge based upon a showing of need.[69]

What these examples demonstrate is not so much that our conception of liberty is based upon absolute privacy expectations,[70] but rather that government impingement upon our liberty will occur only with good cause. In the context of a criminal or terrorist investigation, we expect that the spotlight of scrutiny will not turn upon us individually without some very good reason.

Finally, it bears noting that not all solutions necessarily trade off between Type I and Type II errors, and certainly not in equal measure. Some novel approaches to combating terrorism might, through technology, actually reduce the incidence of both types of error.

Where many critics of the Patriot Act and other governmental initiatives go wrong is in their absolutism: They refuse to admit of the possibility that we might need to accept an increase in the number of Type I errors. Yet that simply cannot be right—liberty is not an absolute value; it depends upon security (both personal and national) for its exercise. As Thomas Powers has written: "In a liberal republic, liberty presupposes security; the point of security is liberty."[71] The growth in danger from Type II errors necessitates altering our tolerance for Type I errors. More fundamentally, our goal should be to minimize both sorts of mistakes.

Principles for Preserving Security and Civil Liberties

What we need for the war on terrorism is a set of principles that work for this long war, principles that are consistent with the Constitution, mindful of the lessons of history, and that give us the tools we need to get the terrorists before they get us. Here is what a useful set of "first" principles might look like.

- No fundamental liberty guaranteed by the Constitution can be breached or infringed upon.
- Any new intrusion must be justified by a demonstration of its effectiveness in diminishing the threat. If the new system works poorly by, for example, creating a large number of false positives, it is suspect. Conversely, if there is a close "fit" between the technology and the threat (that is, if it is accurate and useful in predicting or thwarting terrorism), the technology should be more willingly embraced.
- The full extent and nature of the intrusion worked by the system must be understood and appropriately limited. Not all intrusions are justified simply because they are effective. Strip searches at airports would prevent people from boarding planes with weapons, but at too high a cost.
- Whatever the justification for the intrusion, if there are less intrusive means of achieving the same end (at a reasonably comparable cost), the less intrusive means ought to be preferred. There is no reason to erode Americans' privacy when equivalent results can be achieved without doing so.
- Any new system developed and implemented must be designed to be tolerable in the long term. The war against terrorism is one

with no immediately foreseeable end. Thus, excessive intrusions may not be justified as emergency measures that will lapse upon the termination of hostilities. Policymakers must be restrained in their actions; Americans might have to live with their consequences for a long time.

Rules for New Technologies

Because technology is going to be an important part of any set of counterterrorism tools, and because our lives in the Information Age are so dependent on many of the systems and databases where these technologies will look for information about terrorists, we also need a set of rules to guide how we implement the basic principles of long-war fighting in the electronic world. This is what these principles should look like:

- No new system should alter or contravene existing legal restrictions on the government's ability to access data about private individuals. Any new system should mirror and implement existing legal limitations on domestic or foreign activity.
- Similarly, no new system should alter existing operational system limitations. Development of new technology is not a basis for authorizing new government powers or new government capabilities. Any such expansion should be independently justified.
- No new system that materially affects citizens' privacy should be developed without specific authorization by the American people's representatives in Congress and without provisions for oversight of the system's operation.
- Any new system should be, to the maximum extent practical, tamper proof. To the extent the prevention of abuse is impossible, any new system should have built-in safeguards to ensure that abuse is both evident and traceable.
- Similarly, any new system should, to the maximum extent practical, be developed in a manner that incorporates technological improvements in the protection of American civil liberties.
- Finally, no new system should be implemented without the full panoply of protections against its abuse. As James Madison told the Virginia ratifying convention: "There are more instances of

the abridgment of the freedom of the people by gradual and silent encroachments of those in power than by violent and sudden usurpations."[72]

The Next Step

The fact that we can derive a set of principles and rules for the war on terrorism means they are more than just a set of guidelines for policies and programs. It means that the post-9/11 debates, which seem to offer a choice between security and civil liberties, are simply wrong. There are choices between McCarthyism and inaction. We can do better. It is not enough to condemn every governmental initiative. Nor is it wise to offer the government a blank check. We can have both liberty and order, but each program and proposal must be carefully assessed on its own individual merits.

Measured against these standards, the Patriot Act and related governmental programs hold up fairly well: By and large, they are of little practical threat to civil liberty and they hold the promise of significant benefit. The real question is: What should be next? What are the next steps that need to be taken to provide the right anti-terrorism tools for the long war? Can they be implemented within the guidelines and rules that demand both freedom and freedom from fear?

Chapter 4

After the Patriot Act

The cold truth is that we cannot always trust the people that work for us. For over fifty years, J. Edgar Hoover served as director of the FBI. He also spied on Americans for no good reason.

From the presidency of Calvin Coolidge to that of Richard Nixon, Hoover ran the chief U.S. agency responsible for fighting terrorism on American shores. From its inception, the FBI was always concerned about tracking down criminals and provocateurs. In 1918, one year after the Russian Revolution, fear about the threat of anarchists and Communists (the latter called the "Red Scare") grew after an attempted bomb attack against the U.S. Attorney General. Congress rushed through $500,000 in funding for a new anti-radical unit in the Department of Justice's Bureau of Investigation—led by a young official named J. Edgar Hoover.

In early 1920, federal agents conducted raids across the nation, taking thousands of suspected radicals—many of them immigrants—into custody and prompting an outcry from civil libertarians.[1] In 1939, the FBI used secret wiretaps, not only to keep tabs on Fifth Columnists, pro-Nazi groups, and Communists, but also to gather detailed political intelligence about President Roosevelt's anti-interventionist critics. The agency continued to pass on information about FDR's political enemies throughout the war.[2] However, the FBI's greatest abuses were saved for the Cold War when the agency pursued civil rights and anti-war activists under the guise of a counter-communist crusade. (See Appendix 8.)

After 55 years of searching for secrets, Hoover died in his bed on May 2, 1972. Until that time, he was still running the agency he founded: an agency that had taken on bootleggers and bank robbers, the mob and money launders, spies and saboteurs—and everyday Americans. President Nixon ordered a state funeral, even as Hoover's carefully cultivated image as the all-American "G-Man" was already under attack. In 1968, Congress passed a law requiring Senate confirmation of FBI directors and limiting their terms to 10 years. Meanwhile, as J. Edgar Hoover went to his final rest at Washington's Congressional Cemetery, Americans turned their attention to a crime the FBI had largely ignored—a burglary at the Watergate.

Although U.S. strategy during the Cold War often achieved all three of its priorities (adequate security, economic growth, and a strong civil society), it was far from perfect in execution. The excesses committed in the process of chasing the enemies hiding among us were a case in point. In the Cold War era, the legal structures designed to combat communism were, at times, effective, but were frequently overly intrusive. To enhance our ability to investigate potential domestic Communist influences, we too readily granted new investigative authority to the FBI and CIA—authority that was sometimes abused. To incapacitate domestic opponents we painted with a broad brush. At times, for example, communism was outlawed altogether. Meanwhile, neither Congress, the courts, nor the public paid much attention. The abuses of the executive branch ran unexamined and unchecked for over a decade. We can do better.

The answer is simple. We need enhanced investigative authorities, but none so broad as to become a license for abuse. We need a means of incapacitating those who would do injury to America, but in a manner that does not threaten cherished freedoms. We need to put into place an oversight mechanism that works—one that allows us to empower the executive to combat terrorism, while at the same time preventing abuse.

Looking for Mr. Terrorist

"Business as usual" will not stop twenty-first century terrorism. We need to do things differently. The first step that needs to be taken is to move forward on the successful initiatives that have already been undertaken.

During the well-publicized hearings of the 9/11 Commission, present and former government officials from both the Clinton and Bush Administrations,

President Lyndon B. Johnson speaks in denunciation of the Ku Klux Klan. At left: FBI Director J. Edgar Hoover. (Photo courtesy of the National Archives)

Republicans and Democrats, acknowledged that prior to 9/11 a "wall" of legal and regulatory policies prevented effective sharing of information between the intelligence and law enforcement communities. Attorney General John Ashcroft noted that in 1995 the Justice Department embraced legal reasoning that effectively excluded prosecutors from intelligence investigations. At times, for prudential reasons, Justice Department officials even raised the "wall" *higher* than was required by law, to avoid any appearance of "impermissibly" mixing law enforcement and intelligence activities.

Indeed, a very real wall existed. It was based on a standard that allowed the use of intelligence-gathering mechanisms only when foreign intelligence was the "primary purpose" of the activity. This old "primary purpose" standard derived from a series of court decisions. The standard was formally established in written Department of Justice guidelines in July 1995. Although information could be "thrown over the wall" from intelligence officials to prosecutors, the decision to do so always rested with national security personnel—even though law enforcement agents are in a better position to determine what evidence is pertinent to their cases.

FBI employee coding fingerprints. (Courtesy of the National Bureau of Standards)

The old legal rules discouraged coordination and created what the Foreign Intelligence Surveillance Court of Review calls "perverse organizational incentives."[3] The wall had some very negative real-world consequences. Former Department of Justice official Victoria Toensing tells of one: In the 1980s, terrorists hijacked an airplane, TWA Flight 847, which eventually landed in Lebanon. At the time that negotiations were ongoing, the FBI had the capacity to intercept communications between the hijackers on the plane and certain individuals in America. Negotiations did not, however, advance quickly enough and the terrorists killed an American, Robert Stethem, and dumped his body onto the airport tarmac on live TV. As a result, the Department of Justice announced its intention to capture and prosecute those responsible, which had the immediate effect of making the FBI's ongoing intercepts no longer for the "primary" purpose of foreign intelligence gathering: The "primary" purpose was now clearly prosecution. As a result, in the middle of a terrorist crisis, the FBI turned *off* its listening devices for fear of violating the rule against using intelligence-gathering techniques in a situation in which intelligence gathering was not the main purpose. It is difficult to conceive of a more wrongheaded course of conduct, yet the FBI, rightly, felt that it was legally required to act as it did.

Nor is this the only instance in which the artificial "wall" has deterred vital information sharing between the law enforcement and intelligence communities. Who can forget the testimony of FBI agent Coleen Rowley, who pointed to these very limitations as part of the reason the FBI was not able to "connect the dots" before 9/11. Instead, the culture against information sharing was so deeply ingrained that during the criminal prosecutions for the 1993 World Trade Center bombing, the Department of Justice actually raised the height of the artificial wall. Imposing requirements that went "beyond what is legally required," the Department instructed its FBI agents to "clearly separate" ongoing counterintelligence investigations from the criminal prosecution.[4] There is even some possibility that this wall may have been the contributing factor to our failure to prevent the 9/11 attacks.

Largely in response to these problems, Congress passed the USA Patriot Act subsequent to the September 11 attacks. As Viet Dinh (one of the act's principal authors) concluded, the law "makes the best use of the information we have, sharing information between law enforcement agencies to put the pieces of the puzzle together so we can look for the needle in the haystack."[5] Not only was the legislation needed, it has proved its worth in practice. The law has facilitated dozens of reported terrorist investigations by removing both real and imagined barriers that kept the people trying to protect us from working together. To date, as the Department of Justice Inspector General has reported, there has not been one single instance of abuse of the powers granted in the act.

Safeguarding the civil liberties of American citizens is vitally important, as important during war as during periods of peace. Yet so, too, is preserving our security. The Patriot Act preserves both. Hysterical criticisms that the act was unnecessary and is a threat to a healthy civil society have proven unfounded, and calls for repeal or significant revision are misguided.

Thus, we reject the broadest criticisms of the Patriot Act: that it was unnecessary, that it has added nothing to the efforts to avoid additional terrorist activities, and that it is little more than a "wish list" of law enforcement powers.

In particular, one aspect of the Patriot Act, embodied in Sections 203 and 218, was absolutely vital. (See Appendix 9.) Section 203 permits law enforcement information gathered through a grand jury investigation to be shared with intelligence agencies. Section 218 allows the use of intelligence information-gathering mechanisms whenever intelligence gathering is a "significant" purpose of an investigation—and it allows the information gathered to be shared with law enforcement. Taken together, these two sections effectively tear down the "wall" that existed between law enforcement and intelligence agencies and permit inter-agency cooperation.

Sections 203 and 218 empower federal agencies to share information on terrorist activity. This is an important, significant, and positive development. One of the principal criticisms made in virtually every review of our pre-September 11 actions is that we failed to "connect the dots." Indeed, as a congressional review panel noted: "Within the Intelligence Community, agencies did not share relevant counter-terrorism information, prior to September 11th. This breakdown in communications was the result of a number of factors, including differences in agencies' missions, legal authorities and cultures."[6]

In short, the Patriot Act changes (as a general principle) adopt the rule that *any information lawfully gathered during a foreign or domestic counterintelligence investigation or lawfully gathered during a domestic law enforcement investigation should be capable of being shared with other federal agencies.* The artificial limitations once imposed on such information sharing are the relics of a bygone era and, in light of the changed nature of the terrorist threat, are of substantially diminished value today.

We have already had at least one test case demonstrating the potential utility of enhanced information sharing between intelligence and law enforcement organizations: the indictment of Sami Al-Arian on charges of providing material support to several Palestinian terrorist organizations. The government's case against Al-Arian is apparently based on foreign counterintelligence wiretap intercepts that date back as far as 1993. According to the information in those wiretaps, Al-Arian is charged with having knowingly provided financing to a terrorist organization with the awareness that the funds he provided would be used to commit terrorist acts. That information has been in the possession of our intelligence organizations for at least the past seven years.

It was not until the passage of the Patriot Act and the ruling of the Foreign Intelligence Surveillance Court of Review (in November 2002) that the intelligence community felt it was legally allowed to provide that information to law enforcement officials. Only those changes allowed the government to file the charges pending against Al-Arian. As the Al-Arian case suggests, to the extent that the law removed longstanding statutory barriers to bringing information gathered in national security investigations into federal criminal courts, it is to be welcomed.

Nor can it be convincingly argued that these changes violate the Constitution. To the contrary, as the Court of Review made clear, a wall between intelligence and law enforcement is not constitutionally required. The change wrought by the Patriot Act "is a reasonable response based on a balance of the legitimate need of the government for foreign intelligence information to protect against national security threats with the protected rights of citizens."[7] The courts and Congress agree that appropriate information sharing is simply the right thing to do.

Roving Wiretaps

Other aspects of the Patriot Act are also worth preserving. Section 206, for example, authorizes the use of "roving wiretaps" in terrorist investigations— that is, wiretaps that follow an individual and are not tied to a specific telephone or location. America's original electronic surveillance laws (the Foreign Intelligence Surveillance Act and Title III of the Omnibus Crime Control Act of 1968) stem from a time when phones were the only means of electronic communications and all phones were connected by hard wires to a wall outlet.

Roving wiretaps have arisen over the past twenty years for use in the investigation of many crimes (e.g., drug transactions or organized crime activities) because modern technologies (cell phones, BlackBerries, and Internet telephony) allow those seeking to evade detection the ability to change communications devices and locations at will.

Here is an outline of the general structure of laws governing when law enforcement or intelligence agents may conduct electronic surveillance relating to suspected foreign intelligence or terrorism activity. Title III of the Omnibus Crime Control Act of 1968 (which governs electronic surveillance for domestic crime) allows a court to enter an order authorizing electronic surveillance if "there is probable cause for belief that an individual is committing, has committed or is about to commit" one of a list of several specified crimes.

The Foreign Intelligence Surveillance Act (or FISA—the statute governing intelligence and terrorism surveillance) has a parallel requirement: A warrant may be issued if there is probable cause to believe that the target of the surveillance is a foreign power or the agent of a foreign power. FISA also requires that the government establish probable cause to believe that "each of the facilities or places at which the surveillance is directed is being used, or is about to be used" by the foreign power or the agent of the foreign power who is the target of surveillance. Thus, FISA court warrants are issued by federal judges upon a showing of probable cause, and they describe the things to be seized with particularity—the traditional requirement contained in the Fourth Amendment.

Thus, no one can argue that these FISA warrants violate the Constitution. To the contrary, as the Foreign Intelligence Surveillance Court of Review recently made clear, the FISA warrant structure is "a reasonable response based on a balance of the legitimate need of the government for foreign intelligence information to protect against national security threats with the protected rights of citizens." This is so because, as the court recognized, there is a difference in the nature of "ordinary" criminal prosecution and that directed at foreign intelligence or terrorism crimes.

The main purpose of ordinary criminal law is twofold—to punish the wrongdoer and to deter other people from committing crimes. The government's concern with respect to foreign intelligence crimes, on the other hand, is overwhelmingly to stop or frustrate the immediate criminal activity before it happens.

Roving wiretaps (whether used in foreign intelligence or domestic criminal investigations) are a response to changing technologies. Phones are no longer fixed in one place and can move across state borders at the speed of flight. Sophisticated terrorists and criminals can change phones and communications devices constantly in an attempt to thwart interception.

In response to these changes in technology, in 1986 Congress authorized a change in the requirement for the investigation of drug offenses. Under the modified law, the authority to intercept an individual's electronic communication was tied to the individual who was the suspect of criminal activity (and who was attempting to "thwart" surveillance), rather than to a particular communications device.

Section 206 of the Patriot Act authorized the same techniques for foreign intelligence investigations. As the Department of Justice has noted: "This provision has enhanced the government's ability to monitor sophisticated international terrorists and intelligence officers, who are trained to thwart surveillance by rapidly changing hotels, cell phones, and internet accounts, just before important meetings or communications."

One important safeguard is that the FISA court may authorize such roving wiretaps *only* if it makes a finding as to the terrorist's actions—that "the actions of the target of the application may have the effect of thwarting the identification" of a terrorism suspect. With that safeguard, this tool (already in use for drug crime investigations) is perfectly appropriate for terrorism investigations as well.

"Sneak and Peek" Warrants

The same is true of another section of the Patriot Act that has engendered great criticism. Section 213 authorizes the issuance of delayed notification search warrants, which critics call "sneak and peek" warrants. Traditionally, when the courts have issued search warrants allowing the government's forcible entry into a citizen's home or office, they have required that the searching officers immediately notify the individual whose home or office has been entered. Prior to September 11, some courts permitted limited delays in notification to the owner when immediate notification would hinder the ongoing investigation. Section 213 codifies that common law tradition and extends it to terrorism investigations. Critics see this extension as an unwarranted expansion of authority. Yet here, too, the fears of abuse seem to outstrip reality.

Delayed notification warrants are a longstanding crime-fighting tool upheld by courts nationwide for decades in instances of organized crime, drug cases, and child pornography. For example, Mafia don Nicky Scarfo maintained the records of his various criminal activities on a personal computer, protected by a highly sophisticated encryption technology. Law enforcement knew where the information was—and thus had ample probable cause to seize the computer. Yet the seizure would have been useless without a way of breaking the encryption. Therefore, using a delayed notification warrant, the FBI secretly placed a keystroke logger on Scarfo's computer. The logger recorded Scarfo's password, which the FBI then used to examine Scarfo's records of various drug deals and murders. It would, of course, have been fruitless for the FBI to have secured a warrant to enter Scarfo's home and place a logger on his computer, if, at the same time, it had been required to notify Scarfo that it had done so.

The courts have approved this common law use of delayed notification. More than twenty years ago, the Supreme Court held that the Fourth Amendment does not require law enforcement to give immediate notice of the execution of a search warrant. The Court emphasized "that covert entries are constitutional in some circumstances, at least if they are made pursuant to a warrant." In fact, the Court stated that an argument to the contrary was "frivolous."[8] In an earlier case—the seminal case defining the scope of privacy in contemporary America—the Court said that "officers need not announce their purpose before conducting an otherwise [duly] authorized search if such an announcement would provoke the escape of the suspect or the destruction of critical evidence."[9]

Section 213 of the Patriot Act thus attempts to codify the common law authority given to law enforcement for decades. Now, under Section 213, courts can delay notice if there is "reasonable cause" to believe that immediate notification may have an adverse result, such as allowing a suspect to flee. The "reasonable cause" standard is consistent with pre-Patriot Act case law for delayed notice of warrants. The law goes further, narrowly defining "reasonable cause" for the issuance of a court order. Courts are, under Section 213, allowed to delay notice only when immediate notification may result in an individual's death or physical harm, flight from prosecution, evidence tampering, witness intimidation, or might otherwise seriously jeopardize an investigation.

In short, Section 213 is really no change at all: It merely clarifies that a single uniform standard applies and that terrorist offenses are included. Nor does Section 213 promise great abuse. As under common law, the officer seeking authority for delayed entry must get authorization for that action from a federal judge or magistrate—under the exact same standards and procedures that apply to getting a warrant to enter a building in the first place. The law makes clear that in all cases, law enforcement must ultimately give notice that property has been searched or seized. The only difference from a traditional search warrant is the temporary delay in providing notification. Here, the presence of oversight rules seems strong, certainly strong enough to prevent the abuse that some critics fear.

Nor can it be doubted that the delayed notification standards have performed a useful function and are a critical aspect of the strategy of prevention: detecting and incapacitating terrorists before they are able to strike.

One example of the use of delayed notification involves the indictment of Dr. Rafil Dhafir. A delayed notification warrant allowed the surreptitious search of an airmail envelope containing records of overseas bank accounts used to ship over $4 million to Iraq. Because Dhafir did not know of the search, he was unable to flee and he did not move the funds before they were seized. In another instance, the Justice Department described a hypothetical situation (based upon an actual case) in which the FBI secured access to the hard drive of terrorists who had sent their computer out for repair. In still another, they were able to plant a surveillance device in a building used by terrorists as a safe house. All of these are, with adequate safeguards, good uses of a new investigative authority.

Angry Librarians

Perhaps no provision of the Patriot Act has excited greater controversy than has Section 215, the so-called angry librarians provision.[10] This section allows the Foreign Intelligence Surveillance Court involved in a foreign intelligence investigation to issue an order directing the recipient to produce tangible things such as business records.

The revised statutory authority in Section 215 is not wholly new. Ever since its inception, FISA has had authority for securing some forms of business records. The new statute modifies FISA's original business records authority in two important respects.

First, it "expands the types of entities that can be compelled to disclose information. Under the old provision, the FISA court could order the production of records only from 'a common carrier, public accommodation facility, physical storage facility or vehicle rental facility.' The new provision contains no such restrictions."[11]

Second, the new law "expanded the types of items that can be requested. Under the old authority, the FBI could only seek 'records.' Now, the FBI can seek 'any tangible things (including books, records, papers, documents, and other items).'"[12]

Thus, the modifications made by Section 215 do not explicitly allow the production of library records. However, by its terms, it authorizes orders to require the production of virtually any business record. That might include library records, although it would also include such things as airline manifests, international banking transaction records, and purchase records of all kinds.

Like many parts of the Patriot Act, Section 215 mirrors (in the intelligence gathering context) the scope of authority that already exists in traditional law enforcement investigations. Obtaining business records is a longstanding law enforcement tactic. Ordinary grand juries have for years issued subpoenas to all manner of businesses—including libraries and bookstores—for records relevant to criminal inquiries.

For example, in the 1997 Gianni Versace murder case, a Florida grand jury subpoenaed records from public libraries in Miami Beach. Likewise, in the 1990 Zodiac gunman investigation, a New York grand jury subpoenaed records from a public library in Manhattan. Investigators believed that the gunman was inspired by a Scottish occult poet and wanted to learn who had checked out books by that poet. In the Unabomber investigation, law enforcement officials sought the records of various libraries, hoping to identify the Unabomber as a former student with particular reading interests.

Section 215 merely authorizes the FISA court to issue similar orders in national security investigations. It contains a number of safeguards that protect civil liberties.

First, Section 215 requires FBI agents to obtain a court order. Agents cannot compel any entity to turn over records unless judicial authority has been obtained. In this way, FISA orders are actually better than traditional grand jury subpoenas (which are requested without court supervision and are subject to challenge only after they have been issued).

Second, Section 215 has a narrow scope. It can be used only "to obtain foreign intelligence information not concerning a United States person" or "to protect against international terrorism or clandestine intelligence activities." It cannot be used to investigate ordinary crimes, or even domestic terrorism. Nor can it be used in any investigation premised solely upon "activities protected by the first amendment to the Constitution."[13]

This is narrower than the scope of traditional law enforcement investigations. Under general criminal law, the grand jury may seek the production of any relevant business records. The only limitation is that the subpoena may be quashed if the subpoena recipient can demonstrate that "there is no reasonable possibility that the category of materials the Government seeks will produce information relevant to the general subject of the grand jury's investigation."[14] There is no necessity of showing a connection to foreign intelligence activity, nor any limitation against investigation of United States persons. Thus, unlike under Section 215, the grand jury may inquire into potential violations of any federal crime with effectively limitless authority.

Critics make two particular criticisms of this Section 215: that the judicial review provision is a sham, and that the provision imposing secrecy on the recipients of subpoenas issued pursuant to this section imposes a "gag rule" that prevents oversight of the use of the section's authority. Neither criticism, however, withstands close scrutiny.

Section 215 provides for judicial review of the application for a subpoena for business records. The language provides, however, that upon application, the court "shall" issue the requested subpoena. From the use of the word "shall," critics infer that the obligation to issue the requested subpoena is mandatory and, thus, that the issuing court has no discretion to reject an application. This criticism misreads the statute, which, while saying that the subpoena "shall" issue, also says that it shall issue as sought or "as modified." Thus, the reviewing judge has explicit authority to alter the scope and nature of the request for documents—a power that cannot be exercised in the absence of substantive review of the subpoena request. The suggestion that the provisions of Section 215 prevent judicial review is simply mistaken. To the contrary, Section 215 authorizes judicial review and modification of the subpoena request that occurs prior to issuance of the subpoena. This is a substantial improvement over the situation in traditional grand jury investigations in which the subpoena is issued without judicial intervention and the review occurs at the end of the process—and then only if the subpoena is challenged.

Nor is judicial oversight the only mechanism by which the use of Section 215's authority is monitored. The section expressly commands that the Attorney General "fully inform" Congress how the section is being implemented. On October 17, 2002, the House Judiciary Committee, after reviewing the Attorney General's first report, indicated that it was satisfied with the Justice Department's use of Section 215: "The Committee's review of classified information related to FISA orders for tangible records, such as library records, has not given rise to any concern that the authority is being misused or abused."[15] If it were a problem (for example, if the Department were conducting investigations in violation of the First Amendment based upon the reading habits of suspects), we can be sure that Congress would have said so. That it has not demonstrates that, once again, critics' fears far outpace reality.

The second criticism—that Section 215 imposes an unwarranted gag rule—is equally unpersuasive. Section 215 does prohibit recipients of subpoenas from disclosing that fact, but this is a necessary precaution to avoid prematurely disclosing to the subjects of a terrorism investigation that they are subject to government scrutiny. It is also the same rule we apply in drug investigations, with no evidence of abuse. So long as the law is interpreted to allow judicial review, it poses no great danger.

Causes for Concern, Causes for Calm

There are parts of the Patriot Act that do warrant close scrutiny. For example, the "material support" provisions of the Patriot Act make providing material support to terrorists a crime. The problem here is that sometimes the line between legitimate public speech and actually helping terrorists can be hard to find. There is always the possibility that aggressive use of the law might jeopardize the fundamental right to openly criticize the government.

It could be argued that the actual language of the statute is pretty clear in what it means by material support. Yet it is also clear that an ill-minded government could seek to apply these "clear" words to protected First Amendment conduct. Thus, the concern is not with the body of the statute itself, but with a potentially broad application of the law. However, a simple change can limit the potential for abuse: construing the *scienter* (or intent) requirements in a manner that protects innocent actors. *Scienter* is an element of guilt that has to be proven in order to obtain a conviction. It requires that the accused person have knowledge of the illegality of his or her act. Thus, a person who unknowingly passes a counterfeit coin has not committed a crime. Someone who intentionally hands out fake twenty-dollar bills has. Likewise, an important part of the material support provision is proving that the accused is knowingly helping terrorists.[16]

Although the Patriot Act does not make clear what intent must be proven, it has begun to be interpreted by the courts in a restrictive manner. This demonstrates that we can grant the government additional powers to combat terrorism while reasonably anticipating that the checking mechanisms in place will restrain excessive use of those powers. In addition, juries will help sort this out. Our collective American experience is that juries are quite good at sorting out sham claims of innocence from legitimate ones. Although it appears that there may be sufficient provisions in place to keep abuses in check, we still need to keep an eye on how the material support provision is handled in practice—lest the ghost of Wisconsin slip under the door.

The right answer for addressing concerns over the material support provision (and other parts of the act, as well) is ensuring that we continue to provide the right supervision and control. Part of that supervision will be the judges. Nor are the courts the only oversight mechanism in place. The oversight function of Congress also acts as a direct restraint on executive abuse.

FBI Investigative Guidelines

Another set of law enforcement tools that bear watching are new FBI investigative guidelines[17] issued by the Attorney General in the wake of 9/11.[18] These guidelines are not laws; they are directions from the nation's chief law enforcement officer about how to enforce the laws. In short, the new rules authorize FBI agents to open up anti-terror investigations whenever information warrants. They have stirred controversy, at least in part, because the guidelines now allow FBI agents conducting such investigations to do so in any public forum—in effect, allowing agents to attend anti-war rallies or prayer at mosques. The FBI's critics wonder if the rules won't lead to a return of the "bad old days" during the Cold War when domestic intelligence became political spying.

Thus, there is a significant risk that even well-intentioned guidelines won't stop abusive operations that will impinge upon fundamental constitutional liberties. This does not mean that the risk of abuse requires abandoning new domestic investigations. However, fairly stringent steps are necessary to provide adequate safeguards. Those steps might include the following:

- The FBI's use of these new investigative guidelines should be subject to extensive, continuous congressional oversight. This should include more than the mere reporting of raw data and numbers. As a spot check, Congress should examine individual, closed cases (if necessary, using confidential procedures to maintain classified status) in order to assure itself that the investigative guidelines are not being misused.

- Authorization for "criminal intelligence" investigations under the FBI's guidelines should, in all circumstances, be in writing so that the FBI's internal system creates an "audit trail" for the authorization of investigations with potential First Amendment implications. Only through detailed record keeping can the use and/or abuse of investigative authority be reviewed.

- The FBI's new guidelines generally authorize the use of all lawful investigative techniques for both "general crimes" investigations and "criminal intelligence" investigations. There should be a special hesitancy, however, in using the undisclosed participation of an undercover agent or cooperating private individual to examine the conduct of organizations that are exercising core First Amendment rights. When an organization is avowedly political in nature (giving that phrase the broadest definition reasonable) and has as its sole mission the advocacy of a viewpoint or belief, we should be especially leery of ascribing to that organization criminal intent, absent compelling evidence to that effect.

- Additionally, there should be a hesitancy in visiting public places and events that are clearly intended to involve the exercise of core First Amendment rights, because the presence of official observers may chill expression. This is not to say that no such activity should ever be permitted. It is, however, to suggest the need for supervisory authorization and careful review before and after such steps are taken. Conversely, existing court consent decrees that expressly prohibit all such activity (as is currently the case in New York City[19]) should be revisited.
- No American should be the subject of a criminal investigation solely on the basis of his or her exercise of a constitutionally protected right to dissent. An indication of threat sufficient to warrant investigation should always be based upon significant intelligence suggesting actual criminal or terrorist behavior.

Finally, although the FBI's guidelines authorize preliminary inquiries through the use of public information resources, many Americans fear that these inquiries will result in the creation of personalized dossiers on dissenters. As it now appears, there are no explicit provisions in the guidelines for the destruction of records from preliminary inquiries that produce no evidence sufficient to warrant a full-scale investigation. An explicit provision providing for the destruction or archiving (with limited retrieval authority) of these documents might also be prudent.

It's the Technology, Stupid!

There is more to making sure the future is free and safe than the Patriot Act and the FBI's investigatory guidelines. We still need better tools than we have. One answer is technology. New twenty-first century technologies (ranging from data-mining,[20] to link analysis and data-integration, to biometrics,[21] to new encryption techniques) have much to offer in achieving the compelling national goal of preventing terrorism. At the same time, government access to and use of personal information raises concerns about the protection of civil liberties, privacy, and due process. Given the limited applicability of current privacy laws to the modern digital data environment, resolving this conflict will require the adoption of new policies for collection and access, use, disclosure and retention of information, and for redress and oversight.

It is appropriate to begin by asking a practical, concrete question: Can the new technologies be developed, deployed, implemented, and operated in a manner that allows them to be used as an effective anti-terrorism tool while ensuring that there is minimal risk that use of the tool-set will infringe upon American civil liberties?

Some believe this goal is unachievable. Civil libertarians argue that intelligence-gathering technology is a "Big Brother" project that ought to be abandoned. They begin with the truism that no technology is foolproof—every new technology will inevitably generate errors and mistakes will be made. As with the development of any new technology, risks exist for the misuse and abuse of the new tools being developed. From this, critics conclude that the risks of potential error or abuse are so great that development of many new technologies should be abandoned. To buttress the claim that these systems should be abandoned, these critics parade a host of unanswered questions. Among them: Who will operate the systems? What will the oversight be? What will be the collateral consequences for individuals identified as terrorist suspects?

These questions are posed as if they have no answers when all that is true is that for a system under development, they have no answers *yet*. The same is true of any new government program; thus, we know that these implementation issues are generally capable of being resolved.

Yet to hear civil libertarians ask these questions is to suppose that they believe there are no answers. In fact, there are a number of analogous oversight and implementation structures already in existence that can be borrowed and suitably modified to the new technologies. Thus, new enabling technologies can and should be developed if the technology proves usable. This can be done in a way that makes them effective, while posing minimal risks to American liberties, if the system is crafted carefully with built-in safeguards to check the possibilities of error or abuse. There are a number of things that can be done:

- Legislative authorization should be required before any new technology is deployed that would potentially infringe on civil liberties.
- New technologies should be "neutral"—that is, they should "build in" existing legal and policy limitations on access to individually identifiable information or third-party data and not be seen as a reason to alter existing legal regimes.

- New technologies should be used in a manner that ensures accountability of the executive branch to the legislative by, for example, requiring authorization by a publicly appointed and accountable official before the implementation or use of a new system.
- New technologies should minimize intrusiveness to the extent practical and consistent with achieving counter-terrorism objectives. Depending upon the context, this principle might mean:
  — Ensuring that entry of individual information into the system is voluntary;
  — Whether information entry is voluntary or involuntary, requiring that the use of any new system should be overt, rather than covert;
  — Using information technologies for the verification of information rather than as an independent source of identification;
  — Accessing information already in the possession of the government (which is more readily accepted than is access to information in the private domain);
  — Maintaining data and information in a distributed architecture as opposed to a centralized system in which a big central database is under government control;
  — When possible, making individually identifiable information anonymous (or rendered pseudononymous) and disaggregated so that individual activity is not routinely scrutinized; and
  — Further enhancing protection of individual anonymity by ensuring that individual identities are not tied to information about activities (such as purchases) without the approval of a neutral third-party decision maker (such as a federal judge).
- The consequence of identification by a new technology should not be presumptive. (Such identification is cause for additional investigation, not punitive government action.).
- Any new technology should have strong technological audit and oversight mechanisms to prevent against abuse built into it.
- There should be a robust legal mechanism for the correction of mistakes.

- There should be heightened accountability and oversight, including internal policy controls and training, executive branch administrative oversight, enhanced congressional oversight, and civil and criminal penalties for abuse.
- Finally, any new technology should be deployed with a recognition that many balances struck in the counter-terrorism context would be struck differently in the context of traditional law enforcement. To guard against "mission creep," we should be especially wary of the instinct to use new enabling technologies in non-terrorism contexts, such as chasing down deadbeat dads.

The Need for Preventive Detention

One of the most glaring shortfalls in the American response to the terrorist attacks of 9/11 is that we have not yet undertaken the difficult task of defining a legal regime in which actionable intelligence may, in fact, be acted upon. The hearings of the 9/11 Commission have, despite their sometimes rancorous tenor, made one thing clear: Prior to September 11, there were systematic problems that prevented appropriate coordination among various intelligence agencies and between the intelligence community and law enforcement.[22] Fixing that problem is a long and difficult task.

The simple fact is that a lot of good intelligence information has no place in a court of law. As those who are involved in intelligence collection know, much intelligence information, even the best and most accurate information that is directly actionable, is not suitable for use in our existing legal system. Consider:

- Highly accurate information may have been provided by a foreign government, but only on the condition that the information never be publicly disclosed, or indeed, that the fact of the government's cooperation with us never be disclosed. Using this information, even in the controlled setting of a criminal trial governed by the procedures of the Classified Information Procedures Act (CIPA),[23] would dry up the source of information for all future events.
- Information of unquestioned veracity may have been gathered through sources and methods that are not known to the public or to foreign powers and terrorists. Public disclosure that the

information is in the possession of the United States would compromise the source or method and render it useless.[24] There is some anecdotal evidence that this has already occurred. During the first World Trade Center bombing trial, the government disclosed that it had the capacity to intercept Osama bin Laden's satellite phone calls. It is reported that, naturally, he stopped using satellite phones.[25]

- Rules requiring disclosure of evidence can conflict with national security needs. One need only look at the difficulties created by the trial of Zacarias Moussaoui (the so-called twentieth hijacker) to recognize this problem. Criminal trial rules require that he have access to al-Qaeda operatives (reported to be Khalid Sheik Muhammad and Ramsi Binalshibh) as potential witnesses with allegedly favorable evidence. Yet allowing Moussaoui (or his lawyers) access to Muhammad and Binalshibh while they are still being interrogated would be a foolhardy compromise of vital intelligence assets.[26]

- The rules of evidence in a court of law strictly limit the admissibility of various bits of information. Documents and photographs must be authenticated. Hearsay is not allowed.[27] Yet often the best, most useful, intelligence information cannot meet these legal requirements. A stolen document (or one intercepted by electronic means) often cannot be authenticated. The individual who surreptitiously took a photograph may not be available in an American court to authenticate it. Sometimes the best oral intelligence ("At a meeting last week, Osama said ...") is rank hearsay.

- Finally, one must confront the new reality posed by the "problem" of interrogation. Virtually every practitioner of interrogation will tell you that one of the most successful means of productive interrogation is isolation. As the courts have said, interruption of the interrogation process may "have devastating effects on the ability to gather information" from those who have been captured.[28] Of course, the inability to gather information of this sort could well result in the failure to prevent future terrorist attacks. However, isolation of a terrorist suspect—that is, the denial of access to him by anyone—is inconsistent with existing practices, including rules relating to the provision of counsel.

These are but a few examples of the ways in which the intelligence-gathering function does not mesh with our conception of law enforcement and the legal system. Of course, not all intelligence information is as substantial as that required in the legal system. Certain intelligence may be enough to raise substantial suspicion, but it may fall far short of information that would establish someone's terrorist intents in a forum requiring proof beyond a reasonable doubt.

Thus the question: What do we do? If, indeed, our law enforcement and intelligence agencies have solid, actionable intelligence of a terrorist threat, and if that intelligence is sufficient to allow the identification of an individual or group of individuals, what should be our response? Under the existing legal system, as we have noted, it may be impossible to arrest suspected terrorists without unacceptable risks and costs. Yet detention outside the existing legal structures is also unacceptable. What then?

After 9/11

Our lack of a coherent answer to this question explains some of the most problematic and controversial actions taken by our government after September 11. The use of material witness warrants, the wholesale roundup of Arab immigrants in the aftermath of 9/11, and the detention of "enemy combatants" are all responses to this problem. On the merits, these policies have plausible legal grounds. They have engendered much controversy.

Our concern here is not, however, with their legal justification. Rather, it is that, examined objectively, the responses reflect a simple fact: We lack a legal system prepared for dealing with actionable intelligence. In other words, we lack a regularized process for preventive detention in lieu of criminal trial. As one observer has put it (albeit in a different context): "America was put off balance by September 11."[29] What we are doing now is trying to accommodate existing legal procedures to a new reality—in effect, squeezing a square peg into a round hole.

Material Witness Warrants

One of the first legal responses to the problem of actionable intelligence without a satisfactory legal structure was the use of material witness warrants.[30] Material witness warrants traditionally functioned exactly as their name implies—they were used to arrest and detain witnesses to criminal events when it was anticipated that the witnesses would flee the jurisdiction to avoid the obligation of giving testimony. Immediately after 9/11, a number of individuals suspected of involvement in terrorist activities were detained through the use of material witness warrants. Some detainees fit the traditional model (at least in part) because they were held pending their testimony before a grand jury. But the traditional rules were broken when the detention of some witnesses continued for a time despite their willingness to give testimony and have it preserved. It was further broken, to the extent that it was a constraint, when one material witness (Jose Padilla) initially held on a material witness warrant, was remanded to military custody as an "enemy combatant." The material witness provisions became, in effect, a proxy for a preventive detention program.

Challenges to this practice were swift in coming. Those opposing the use of material witness warrants in this manner challenged their use in pretrial investigations. Although the law had historically approved the use of material witness warrants for grand juries,[31] at least one court initially held that the post-9/11 jailing of witnesses pending investigation was a constitutional violation.[32] Eventually, however, the courts held that the material witness statute was applicable to pre-trial investigations, and that the government could lawfully detain a witness, notwithstanding the witness's willingness to have his or her testimony preserved, provided that the grounds for detention were subject to judicial review under the standard bail statutes.[33]

However, the approval of material witness warrants as a legal tool cannot obscure the practical reality that they were being used for a purpose different from that which Congress initially intended—the detention of witnesses despite the lack of any real need for their testimony. Because this legal structure is not designed to adjudicate issues for the long-term detention of suspected terrorists (rather than the short-term detention of potential witnesses), it lacks any number of legal checks on the exercise of executive authority. The burden of proof placed upon the government to justify its detention is ill-defined. There is only a limited opportunity for those detained to challenge their detention and secure the assistance of counsel. Additionally, because the use of material witness warrants occurs at the interstices of law and intelligence gathering, there is little, if any, sustained congressional oversight of the use of the power.

"Hold Until Cleared"

Immediately after 9/11, the FBI rounded up a number of Arab immigrants and detained them. In reviewing these detentions, the Inspector General of the Department of Justice concluded that approximately 762 aliens were arrested. The vast majority of those arrested were detained pursuant to civil immigration law for remaining in the United States after expiration of their entry visas or for entering the country illegally.[34] Despite the relatively unimportant nature of their wrongdoing, each of the detainees was held in the United States until such time as he or she was "cleared" by the FBI of any suspicion of terrorist connections.[35]

The Inspector General did not criticize this policy.[36] Moreover, he acknowledged that in all but one instance the detainees arrested were held on valid immigration charges.[37] It nonetheless remains the case that the implementation of the "hold until cleared" policy was overly inclusive and resulted far more in identifying immigration violations than it did in identifying individuals connected with terrorism.

Given the extremity of the times in which these detentions occurred (most arrests were in New York City or surrounding areas within three months of the attack), the reaction of government authorities was understandable. With the World Trade Center smoldering in lower Manhattan, a robust response was to be expected. In the end, however, immigration law served as a substitute for terrorist detentions—a substitution made necessary by the absence of any other viable legal mechanism.

Enemy Combatants

Many of the same observations can be made regarding the far more notorious cases involving the detention of Yasser Hamdi and Jose Padilla as "enemy combatants." Hamdi and Padilla were both American citizens, one caught on the field of battle in Afghanistan and the other detained as he entered the United States at Chicago's O'Hare airport. The government designated them as enemy combatants subject to special detention rules. These included, at least initially, a prohibition on contact with counsel and a contention that the detention decision was subject to limited judicial review.

Once again, the government's conduct was a response to a heartfelt perceived need. Although we should not take all of the government's concerns at unquestioned face value, there is certainly ample basis for thinking that the perception of the need was justified. Padilla, for example, may have planned significant terrorist activities in the United States.[38] Yet it is by no means clear that at the time of his initial detention Padilla could have been criminally charged, or that if charged, he would have been convicted. Thus the problem recurs again about how to treat those whom credible evidence suggests are engaged in terrorist activities, but for whom the legal system was not designed.

The Supreme Court has now concluded that detentions must be subject to more rigorous review than that initially afforded the detainees.[39] In doing so, the Court recognized that the capture and detention of those who would wage war against the United States was a universal historical practice. However, the Court recognized that the "war" in which we are currently engaged has unusual characteristics—not the least of which is that some aspects of the war have no foreseeable termination. In recognition of this, the Court determined that the Constitution required some form of process for reviewing detention claims, including notice of the factual basis for detention and an opportunity to rebut the factual assertion before a neutral decision maker. The Court left for another day more detailed questions about precisely what form this process would take, including questions about the admissibility of evidence, the burden of proof, and the identity of the decision maker.[40]

The Court's decision makes the case for congressional action in this area. The question remains: Exactly what sort of process ought to be provided?

What is needed is a new legal architecture to govern the detention of suspected terrorists. Any such system must provide a legitimate process by which we can decide whether those suspected of terrorism are really threats and a means of ensuring that the process is used appropriately—not abused. The challenge is an exceedingly difficult one—one that perhaps admits of no ideal solution. Yet the absence of any legal structure in current law has led to an unsatisfactory *ad hoc* approach. It is a near certainty that the detention powers we propose are a practical necessity. It is equally certain that the exercise of those powers is better constrained—and civil liberties better protected—when the exercise is regularized under the rule of law. Indeed, in the absence of any thoughtful effort to construct such a legal system *before* another terrorist attack on American soil, it is all too likely that the reaction will be similar. There is a need for a better answer.

An All-American Response

Plainly America needs a more thoughtful, comprehensive legal response to terrorism. It must "regain [its] balance"[41] and adopt a system of laws that truly regulate and constrain executive behavior, while simultaneously allowing the executive to respond effectively in those very narrow circumstances in which a response is necessary but the existing legal structures are inadequate. Here we outline what such new legal system might look like.[42]

First, the regime of preventive detention that we envision should be limited to cases of terrorism. This requires a narrow definition of terrorism—narrower than that used in current law. Detention will be appropriate only in situations involving individuals who:

- act or threaten to act in a manner that involves serious violence against a person or property and/or in a manner that risks the health and safety of the public; *and*
- does so to influence government policy or intimidate the public; *and*
- does so for the purpose of advancing a political, religious, or ideological cause.

In other words, the "gate" for the preventive detention system must be very narrow. Additionally:

- There must be a rigorous certification process at the front end. No individual should be subject to detention unless the U.S. Attorney General first certifies as to its necessity. The certification should affirm that credible evidence exists that: (a) the individual to be detained intends to commit a terrorist act; (b) the individual is affiliated with a terrorist organization; and (c) the existing criminal legal justice system cannot be applied to the individual without compromising national security.
- This certification should be subject to review in court. The preferred method of review is in an adversarial process in which the detained individual is represented by counsel. To allow assignment of counsel for proceedings in which classified materials are considered, the government should create a group of pre-cleared defense counsel (perhaps as part of the Federal Public Defender system) available for assignment to the detained individual(s).
- Proceedings to determine whether detention is appropriate, would have the following components (as required by the *Hamdi* decision): (a) Notice to the detainee of the factual basis for detention; (b) An opportunity to rebut the detention evidence; (c) A neutral decision maker. To regularize the process and insulate it

from executive influence, we would recommend the creation of a new adjudicative court like the Foreign Intelligence Surveillance Court; (d) Evidentiary rules would be relaxed with modified procedures to account for the need to use classified information, and rules would allow the presentation of evidence *in camera* (or in a form different from that in a traditional criminal trial); and (e) The government would bear the burden of proving the grounds for its detention decision by proof that meets the "clear and convincing evidence" standard—a standard more stringent than that currently used for pretrial detention in criminal cases.[43]

- In rare circumstances the government may have grounds for wishing to delay the detainee's appearance in court and access to counsel, so that ongoing interrogation can continue. The initial period of delay should be no more than 30 days and any extension of that time period should be periodically reviewed and justified (to the court) by a clear and convincing showing that a further delay is likely to provide additional intelligence.

- To ensure that the preventive detention authority is not abused, there should be routine, systematic oversight. Review of the general process should, of course, reside with the congressional intelligence committees. Beyond that, each individual detention decision should be independently reviewed and the subject of a public report. Possible entities for conducting the review might include the President's Intelligence Oversight Board or the Inspector General of the CIA.

In calling for Congress to enact legislation concerning this matter, we are not alone,[44] although there are some who will disagree with making the effort at all, who will say that Americans should never allow preventive detention in any form because it is an unwarranted threat to liberty.

The response to this criticism is threefold: First, it ignores reality. We already have incomplete and irregular forms of preventive detention. We advance liberty when we regularize the practice, cabin it to narrow circumstances, and use it sparingly. Second, other countries (such as the United Kingdom) have managed to adopt very limited forms of preventive detention without becoming noticeably "unfree" or "authoritarian." Adoption of similar legal forms in the United States will not render us an authoritarian regime either.

Finally, and most important, to reject preventive detention in those rare circumstances in which it is necessary is to exalt liberty at the expense of security.

The founding of the American republic was for the purpose of constructing a political system of ordered liberty. It simply cannot be right to unilaterally prefer liberty. Liberty is not an absolute value; it depends upon security (both personal and national) for its exercise. The growth in danger from the consequences of the failure to stop terrorism necessitates altering our tolerance for governmental order. More fundamentally, our goal should be to balance order and liberty.

We achieve order and liberty best, not by closing our eyes to the necessity of security nor by allowing security concerns to run rampant without oversight, but rather by taking appropriate steps to ensure that the powers given to the executive branch are exercised thoughtfully, with care, and subject to continual review and oversight by both the judiciary and the legislative branch. This concept of checks and balances was the fundamental insight of the framers of the Constitution—and is as applicable today as it was at the time of the founding.

Looking Over Our Shoulders

Perhaps the most important tool we need to develop for securing the future is our own vigilance. To allow us to guard against the abuse of power will require, among other things, knowledge of how that power is being exercised. That requires transparency in the acts of governance. After all, transparency is a vital aspect of democracy. Many of the powers that we need to provide the executive would be unacceptable if their implementation were conducted in secret. As James Madison wisely observed, democracy without information is "but prologue to a farce or a tragedy." Hoover's FBI was the embodiment of Madison's maxim. Unchecked by oversight from Congress, courts, or the public, abuses of public power continued unabated.

Yet transparency is not an absolute value. After all, Madison and others found it necessary to draft the Constitution in a convention whose proceedings were kept secret. Transparency, however, is necessary for oversight: It enables us to limit the executive exercise of authority. It also allows us to empower the executive. If we enhance transparency appropriately, we can also comfortably expand governmental authority, confident that our review of the use of that authority can prevent abuse.

In the post-9/11 world, the form of new oversight should vary depending upon the extent to which transparency and opacity are necessary to the new executive power. Legislation which exempts information supplied by businesses regarding potential terrorist attack risks from public disclosure offers a case in point. To be sure, there is a potential for abuse of that exemption: Businesses may over-disclose to the government as a means of concealing their operations from legitimate scrutiny by public interest groups. Yet surely, supplying this information to the government is vital to assure the protection of critical infrastructure. Disclosing such information is dangerous, as it risks use by terrorists. Thus, complete transparency will defeat the purpose of disclosure, while complete opacity permits misuse.

What is required is a concept of *calibrated transparency*, a measured, flexible, adaptable transparency suited to the needs of oversight without frustrating the legitimate interests in limiting disclosure. Calibrated transparency can take many forms. These might include enhanced judicial review (placing our trust in judges to oversee the executive branch for us). It also might employ legislative oversight as a proxy for public disclosure, having Congress checking to ensure the laws it passed are being implemented in the way it intended. In appropriate circumstances the transparency might be modified to allow review through closed proceedings. These proxy review mechanisms are substitutes for full transparency, and so the presumption should be in favor of full disclosure.

Transparency is actually enhanced if we recognize that it is not an absolute. In the scenario of infrastructure information, for example, one can readily conceive of calibrated transparency mechanisms (for example, random administrative and legislative auditing) that will guard against abuse, while acknowledging the value of limited disclosure. In short, Madison was not a hypocrite. Rather, opacity and transparency each have a place, in different measures dictated by circumstance. The wisdom of Madison's insight— that both are necessary—remains as true today as it was 220 years ago.

Therefore, as we proceed in providing additional authorities to the government as a means of combating terrorism, we must do so in a way that allows for oversight of the right forms. In some instances, this means a reformed and reinvigorated congressional oversight system. In others, it is judicial oversight. In still others, there must be public disclosure and debate.

Past Time for the Next Steps

When the Cold War began, it was more than ten years before the legal and structural systems that would sustain us through the fifty-year struggle were put in place. Even then, men like Hoover found ways to circumvent the rules when it served their purposes.

Screening passengers at the airport in Fargo, North Dakota after 9/11. (Photo by Noble Eagle Master Sergeant William J. Quinn courtesy of the U.S. Air Force/North Dakota Air National Guard)

We should get started now. We cannot, and should not, expect that at the start of this long struggle we will get it right the first time. As Michael Chertoff, the former Assistant Attorney General for the Criminal Division, has written:

> The balance [between liberty and the response to terror] was struck in the first flush of emergency. If history shows anything, however, it shows that we must be prepared to review and if necessary recalibrate that balance. We should get about doing so, in light of the experience of our fore-bears and the experience of our own time.[46]

Others have echoed that call.

The debate will continue. The courts and Congress are well positioned to fix any problem with additional legislation or more decisions interpreting the laws.

That is exactly as it should be. John Locke, the seventeenth-century philosopher who greatly influenced the Founding Fathers, was equally right when he wrote: "In all states of created beings, capable of laws, where there is no law there is no freedom. For liberty is to be free from the restraint and violence from others; which cannot be where there is no law; and is not, as we are told, a liberty for every man to do what he lists."[47]

Thus, the obligation of the government is a dual one: to protect civil safety and security against violence *and* to preserve civil liberty. Viet Dinh used almost the exact same argument to describe the government's role in fighting the war on terrorism: "The function of government is the security of its polity and the safety of its people. For without them there will be no structure so that liberty can survive. We see our work not as a balancing security and liberty," Dinh declared, "rather, we see it as securing liberty by assuring the conditions of true liberty." We can achieve that goal, but there is more work to done.

Chapter 5

Guns and Butter

When Eisenhower entered the Oval Office, the new President confronted "a ticking fiscal time bomb."[1] The federal government had more missions than money and no one was sure how Washington was going to pay its bills. Eisenhower was worried. Winning the long war required adequate security and a strong economy. America needed guns and butter, but all the future had to promise was an increasingly unsustainable budget deficit. Making government fiscally responsible, Ike believed, had to be high on his agenda.

The former commander of America's military legions had scant training in economic policy, but he had a strong dose of Midwestern common sense and he knew what he wanted; lower taxes, balanced budgets, and less government interference in the marketplace. As far as Eisenhower was concerned, Americans—not the government—understood best how to spend their money. On the other hand, an economy directed by Washington, Ike believed, would lead to "slavery."[2] Above all, Ike was determined to shake government from its wartime habits of centralized economic controls and high taxation. Such measures might be suitable for titanic, violent, armed struggles like World War II, but they did not suit strategies for long wars.

As in matters of national security, Eisenhower decided that the government's fiscal policy required presidential leadership. Ike might charge his Cabinet with implementing policies, but the policies would be made in the Oval Office: He would make them and they would be, if nothing else, fiscally sound. While temporary deficits might be necessary to fight a downturn in

Soviet Premier Nikita Khrushchev and President Dwight Eisenhower at Camp David. (Courtesy of the National Archives)

the business cycle or fight a short, hot war like the Korean conflict, Eisenhower believed they should not be a permanent government addiction.

Leaks from the Gaither Report proved to be one of the greatest challenges Eisenhower faced in trying to add fiscal responsibility to the congressional dictionary. From the beginning of his presidency, Ike had tried to reassure Americans that he took the Soviet threat seriously, but at the same time, remind them that the Soviets were not ten feet tall. America should not and did not have to spend itself into bankruptcy to fend off the threat of Communist expansion. The Gaither Report, much like NSC-68, challenged that logic—calling for $44 billion in additional spending within five years to slow the Soviet juggernaut.[3]

Eisenhower not only thought that Gaither's findings overstated the threat, but he complained that the report's prescriptions were simply unrealistic. How could damaging the U.S. economy help diminish the Soviets? Raising the kind of cash called for by the Gaither panel would have required new taxes, massive deficits, and probably wage and price controls to keep inflation in check. "This administration has gotten rid of controls as soon as it came into office," Eisenhower fumed, "because of a conviction that in the absence of controls the American economy would develop more rapidly. Are we now to advocate the re-introduction of controls?"[4] Eisenhower would simply not compromise good economic policies in the face of irrational fears.

The Balancing Act

The problem of balancing the competing demands for security and prosperity is reflected in the interdependent nature of military and economic power. In the short term, military power can be created more rapidly, but without economic power it is, as the Soviets discovered, ultimately unsustainable. By 1980, the Soviet Union had built a military behemoth equal to the United States', but it rested on a foundation as fragile as porcelain. By 1991, in the face of impending economic collapse, Soviet military capacity rapidly withered. The single-minded pursuit of either security or prosperity means failure in the long war. The necessity for maintaining security against immediate threats must be balanced against the long-term requirements for expanding prosperity.

Today, the challenge facing both the President and Congress is little different from the decisions faced by Eisenhower—defining the right policies to achieve security and economic growth. As in the coldest days of the Cold War, achieving both goals will require leadership that is steadfast and unswerving in its commitment to sound domestic economic policies. Part of winning the long war—a large part—is remaining a good steward to the world's premier economy.

No one understood the challenge better than R. Glenn Hubbard. On May 11, 2001, President George W. Bush appointed the Columbia University economics and finance professor to be the Chairman of the White House Council of Economic Advisers (CEA). Established in 1946 under the emerging shadow of the Cold War, the CEA drew its initial inspiration from the famed British economist John Maynard Keynes, who believed government spending could be used to fine-tune the economy and create full employment. In practice, the

Competing with the Soviet economy, Russian workers grind grain in a church. (PHOTO FROM THE NATIONAL ARCHIVES)

Glenn Hubbard explaining the need for tax cuts. (PHOTO FROM THE HERITAGE FOUNDATION COLLECTION)

CEA evolved into something far more academic and less threatening than a cabal of omnipotent technocrats trying to steer the national economy like a golf cart. In practice, for most of the Cold War, the CEA's role was fairly benign and its chairman was considered to be more a kibitzer than a player in White House economic policies. "CEA Chairmen," as Reagan's appointee Martin Feldstein noted, "have generally regarded their role as presenting professional advice on what is economically correct rather than on trying to balance economic and political considerations in determining the 'best' policy."[5] President Bush wanted something different from the CEA. So did Glenn Hubbard.

With a boyish face, sandy hair, wire-rim glasses, and a broad smile that seemed more reminiscent of Harry Potter than John Maynard Keynes, Hubbard nevertheless was an economist of the first order, with a Ph.D. from Harvard and a score of books to his credit. Unlike Keynes, however, Hubbard's view of the government's role in the economy was to get it out of the way. He believed that government's primary responsibility in setting economic policies was to do no harm.

Rather than offer dry analysis, Hubbard believed the CEA's job was to push for strong pro-growth policies—and that meant tax cuts. Although Hubbard's reasoning came from years of study and Eisenhower's from small town pragmatism, they both reached the same conclusion. Tax cuts make sense. They might create a short-term deficit, but they will unleash long-term growth that will more than offset near-term costs. As for federal spending, it simply had to be kept in check. Rapid growth in federal spending was anathema to pro-growth tax policies. Hubbard, like Eisenhower, knew that tax increases slowed economic growth and slow growth weakened the economy. An anemic economy cannot meet the expectations of its citizens and it cannot fight the long war.

Hubbard felt confident that his unabashed advocacy for disciplined federal spending and tax cuts would find favor with the new President. "I'm not a very political person," Hubbard confided, "but I have observed in this president a great concern about long-term growth. I think it's a credible...economic and political story to say you're concerned with long-term living standards. I think the American people are much smarter than many politicians give them credit for."[6] The President agreed: He had found his war economist.

Economics 101

Understanding the role of the economy in the long war begins with understanding the federal government's relationship with the domestic economy. That means appreciating that it is the total cost of government that is important, not just government activities related to security. The Soviet Union's economic collapse stemmed from more than just its government's insatiable appetite for military spending. It followed at least as much from the Kremlin's determination to control economic activity in the civilian sector while ignoring the enormous costs of imposing controls. The Soviet treatment of the economy is an object lesson in how *not* to fight the long war. Avoiding disaster means ensuring that the burden of government (in terms of spending, taxes and regulation) is not so high that it places an excessive burden upon the economy.

Preventing unnecessary tinkering with the economy is easier said than done. Politicians always want to do something. It is a condition Hubbard learned to understand well as he tried to shape the CEA's recommendations. As the jobs market in 2003 continued to languish, members of Congress felt compelled to show that they could do something to create jobs. Numerous bills were touted as "jobs bills" or cited for the jobs they would create, asserting that this would "grow" the economy. Most notable were the multi-billion dollar transportation and energy bills that were supposed to create employment and expand the economy through government spending.

All the rhetoric about government job creation had little prospect for actually creating economic growth. Even though Hubbard knew this, he encountered a great deal of flak from his critics and from Congress, in part because he always found himself fighting the ghost of John Maynard Keynes.

During the 1930s, in response to the trials of the great global depression, Keynes posited that government spending could be used to pump new money into the economy. He asserted that when the economy's total demand is lacking, government could act as a consumer and make purchases itself. Since the gross domestic product (GDP) is the sum of all purchases on final goods and services, these government purchases will add to GDP and the economy will grow.

Yet Keynes's version of fuzzy math raised the obvious question: Where does the government get the money that it pumps into the economy? The government does not have its own money, so every dollar the government pumps into the economy must first be taxed or borrowed.[7] This means that government spending does *not* create new income; it merely shifts existing income from one group of people to another.

To help explain exactly what Keynes was advocating, economists differentiate between two types of government spending: "transfer spending" and "direct purchasing." Transfer payments, such as Social Security and farm subsidies, tax or borrow money from one group and transfer it to another group. Even Keynesian economists acknowledge that transfer payments only move existing income and do not affect GDP.

Direct purchasing simply means buying things. For example, the Defense Department buys fighter jets from Boeing, and Medicare buys health care services from doctors. Keynesians believe these purchases expand

GDP. However, the money spent on them had to be first taxed or borrowed from people who otherwise would have spent the money themselves. Consequently, these government purchases merely displace private purchases, leaving total economic activity unchanged.

In either case, the reality is simply that every dollar government injects into the economy must first be taken from the economy. *The Wall Street Journal*'s Robert Bartley called this "Government Budget Restraint" (GBR).[8] GBR highlights the futility of government "pump-priming." The government is not priming anything: It is just moving wealth around, and probably far less efficiently than people could do it themselves.

This does not necessarily mean that government spending can never help the economy. Under certain circumstances, the right government spending could add to the economy's long-term *supply side*. A growing economy requires not only consumers and investors willing to spend money; it also requires businesses that are willing and able to supply goods and services.

There is some government spending that is unavoidable. At the most basic level, businesses and consumers require government spending for defense and justice to enforce the property rights and rule of law necessary for markets to function. Sustained economic growth also requires consistent investment in public infrastructure (such as roads), private capital (to expand businesses and technologies), and human capital (such as education and a motivated workforce). These investments create economic growth by helping businesses to produce and sell more goods and services more efficiently.

On the other hand, government spending is not the real engine behind economic growth. The private sector, motivated by profit, funds most investment needs by itself. If private investment falls short for some reason, governments could tax consumers to fund investment—although excessive taxes would harm investment and worker motivation, negating the policy's effects. Investment expands the economy *not* because the government pumps new money into it, but because structural changes increase its long-run capacity for growth. These structural changes can take years, therefore, government spending does not provide adequate short-run economic stimulus.

Bad Spending Habits

GBR means government spending will have a neutral effect on demand. In fact, government spending (beyond the necessary investments, such as defense and public goods) can actually harm the economy's supply side and impede economic growth.[9] Here are the reasons why:

1. Diminishing Effectiveness. Empowered by the opportunities for economic growth provided by defense, law enforcement, and basic public goods, governments often mistakenly conclude that they can solve any problem. Consequently, they tend to expand their efforts into services that the market is better equipped to provide, such as education, housing, food, and pensions. With each expansion, the government not only blocks the market from functioning, but also becomes less effective itself, until it ultimately becomes a barrier to economic growth.

2. Politics. Markets use the profit motive to ensure that resources are allocated efficiently. Businesses seeking profits must consistently respond to consumer demand with quality products at low prices. Governments, by contrast, are monopolies with no real profit motive or incentive to spend money efficiently. Therefore policymakers make re-election their "profit" and consequently allocate resources to even the most wasteful programs if it will help to ensure their return to office. Although innovation and "evolving with the times" are required for businesses to survive, they represent an unnecessary risk for politicians who are guaranteed re-election as long as they do not interrupt the flow of government funds to their districts. Hence, while markets helped the evolution of the Model T into the Porsche and the Apple IIe into the supercomputer, the federal government continues to run many of the same federal agencies—now obsolete—that it established as far back as the 1800s.

3. High Taxes. Increased government spending makes it difficult for working families to make ends meet. Even when the government funds itself by borrowing money, repaying those loans will eventually require higher taxes. Those higher taxes will leave families with less income to spend on necessities such as health insurance, retirement, housing, and education. Regrettably, many people praise government spending on families without acknowledging that families first had to be taxed—and that the burden of those taxes often outweighs the benefits of the government programs.[10] In addition to their high cost, taxes hurt the economy by distorting incentives. Families and businesses work, save, and invest because they expect a financial reward. These productive behaviors also make the rest of the nation wealthier by creating additional economic activity. Yet burdensome tax rates reduce the financial reward for being productive. Consequently, families and businesses cut back their productive behavior to escape taxes, and the entire economy slows down.

To see the consequences of excessive spending and taxation, one need look no further than Western Europe, where politicians have promised to provide for all of their citizens' needs in exchange for higher taxes and bigger government. Western Europeans have incomes 40 percent below Americans' and unemployment rates twice as high. They also pay 50 percent of their income in taxes.

The lesson of Economics 101 is that excessive government spending and other controls are bad for all economies. They are, however, especially deadly to countries fighting the long war. *In the long war, a growing economy is not just essential for prosperity. It is essential for survival.* Long wars are not lost on the battlefield, but in the hearts and minds of men and women—and often in their pocketbooks as well.

Budget Priorities

Avoiding excessive spending is a challenge both for homemakers and for nations—differing only by degree. Budgets are about setting priorities. Budget writers must juggle a finite supply of dollars and an endless demand for spending. The first task, then, is to rank budget priorities and separate necessities from unaffordable luxuries.

Most Americans would likely agree that the top priority of government is providing for the common defense and safety. Thus, defense, homeland security, and law enforcement must be sufficiently funded. Most Americans would also likely agree that the second priority of government is maintaining a healthy economy that creates jobs and raises incomes. History has shown that free-market economies create substantially more jobs and higher incomes than socialist economies and welfare states. Because government spending beyond security and public goods often reduces economic growth and incomes, lawmakers should reduce spending for lower-priority programs in order to reduce the tax burden and keep money in the productive private sector.

Some people focus obsessively on balanced budgets as the sole criterion for good government. Although balanced budgets are indeed desirable, they are not as high a priority as national security and a healthy economy. About national security, few would argue that the nation should not have fought World War II or the Cold War out of a reflexive fear of the budget deficits they required. Even Eisenhower, perhaps the nation's most balanced-budget phobic President in history, recognized that deficits had their time and place.

Economic growth and the increased prosperity and higher incomes that come with it is a higher priority, not only because it has a larger positive effect on people's lives than balanced budgets, but also because a larger economy can better repay its deficit debt in the future. Budget deficits themselves do not harm short-run economic growth, as they have not been shown to significantly raise interest rates.[11] The main long-run cost to budget deficits is the high future taxes required to finance and repay this borrowing and the negative economic effect of those taxes. Therefore, lawmakers should aim to minimize long-term budget deficits without sacrificing security and economic growth. Specifically, this means funding defense and homeland security and reducing wasteful spending in order to maintain low taxes and minimal deficits.

Although it is easy to argue that defense and homeland security must be funded first, that is a difficult prescription to put in to practice. Setting priorities, writing a budget, and getting it passed is Washington's version of the Twelve Labors of Hercules. That is because every budget carries with it the dead weight of history—and that history makes for heavy lifting.

History of Federal Spending

The federal government has expanded substantially during the past century. One of the best measures of the burden that the federal government, as a whole, imposes on the national economy through its spending policies is the percentage of GDP taken up by outlays. During the nation's first 140 years, the federal government rarely consumed more than 5 percent of the GDP. In accordance with the U.S. Constitution, Washington focused on defense and certain public goods while leaving most other functions to the states or the people themselves.

The Great Depression brought about President Franklin Roosevelt's New Deal, a program that expanded government in an attempt to relieve poverty and revive the economy. President Roosevelt created the Social Security program in 1935 and also created dozens of new agencies and public works programs. Although the economy remained mired in depression, the federal government's share of the GDP reached 10 percent by 1940.[12]

World War II pushed the United States into the largest war mobilization effort the world has ever seen. From 1940 through 1943, the federal government more than quadrupled in size—from 10 percent of GDP to 44 percent.

The enormity of this government expansion cannot be understated: An equivalent expansion today would cost $3.9 trillion, or $37,000 per household (compared with $2.1 trillion or $20,000 per household in 2003). Even with a top income tax rate of 91 percent, the nation could not fund World War II on tax revenues alone. The nation ended the war with a national debt larger than the GDP (which is three times the size of today's national debt).

Following the war, Washington's share of the economy fell back to 12 percent of GDP in 1948. Among the many ways this time changed America was by making its citizens more comfortable with expanded federal powers. The Supreme Court, under threats from President Roosevelt, had upheld these new federal powers by broadly interpreting the Constitution's Interstate Commerce Clause. From 12 percent of GDP in 1948, federal spending began a 35-year growth spurt that finally reached a peacetime record of 24 percent of GDP in 1983.

In the long decades of federal expansion from the end of World War II to President Ronald Reagan's election, Washington expanded into several new policy areas, creating the Departments of Health, Education and Welfare (in 1953; eventually becoming Health and Human Services), Housing and Urban Development (in 1965), Transportation (in 1966), Energy (in 1977), and Education (in 1979; it had been a part of Health, Education and Welfare).

The largest new programs were created in the 1960s as part of President Lyndon Johnson's Great Society initiative. Medicare and Medicaid, which provide health care services to the elderly and the poor, were created in 1965 and expanded throughout the next fifteen years. Along with Social Security, they now are the largest entitlement programs.[13]

Federal spending generally fluctuated at just over 20 percent of GDP throughout the 1980s and early 1990s. However, in the last few years spending has sharply increased again as the war on terrorism collided with a domestic sending spree.

Over time, the composition of federal spending has evolved as well. Between 1962 and 2000, defense spending plummeted from 9.3 percent of GDP to 3.0 percent. Nearly all of funding shifted from defense spending went into mandatory spending (mostly entitlement programs), which jumped from 6.1 percent of GDP to 12.1 percent during that period.

The importance of this evolution cannot be understated. For most of the nation's history, the federal government's chief budgetary function was funding defense. The two-thirds decline in defense spending since 1962 has substantially altered the make-up and structure of the U.S. national defense.

At the same time, the expanding entitlement state has completely filled the spending void. Entitlements such as Social Security, Medicare, and Medicaid are projected to continue growing rapidly in coming decades—until they *alone* top 20 percent of GDP. If global events ever warranted a return to the defense spending levels of the 1960s, it would be nearly impossible to find room in the budget without raising taxes to catastrophic levels.

Budget Burdens

Defense. Those who are inclined to spend less on defense may argue that the nation's fiscal woes are not the result of the growth of domestic program spending, but that defense spending is the problem because it is crowding out other spending. History shows that this is not the case. While the overall level of federal government spending, relative to the size of the economy, has remained reasonably constant over the last 32 years, the same cannot be said regarding the major components of federal outlays. The defense budget has trended down, while entitlements in particular have trended up.

Other Budget Spending. Since 1962, defense outlays have grown from $52.6 billion to $404.9 billion. Major entitlement expenditures (Social Security, Medicare, and Medicaid), on the other hand, have exploded from $14.1 billion to $905.5 billion during the same period. Even outlays for all other federal programs (excluding defense and the three major entitlements) have grown faster than defense during this 42-year period. What is crystal clear, however, is that the spending on the three major entitlement programs has been growing at a rate that dwarfs all the other major categories of federal spending.[14] (See Appendix 10.) This is a huge concern for the defense budget, as well as the future implications for the economy, because this entitlement growth is unsustainable.

Share of Federal Outlays. As would be expected, the relatively rapid rise in entitlement spending during the last 42 years resulted in higher shares of overall federal outlays going to those programs. Meanwhile, restraints on defense expenditures resulted in a reduction in its share of the federal budget. In fiscal year 1962, defense outlays accounted for 46.2 percent of all federal outlays. By fiscal year 2003, the defense share of the budget had fallen to 18 percent. Meanwhile, outlays for the major entitlements grew from 12.9 percent of all federal outlays in 1962 to 40 percent in 2003. Outlays for other spending and interest on the national debt remained relatively constant from

1962 to 2003 in terms of their respective shares of overall federal spending.[15] (See Appendix 11.)

The Burden on the Economy. Not surprisingly, the same trends hold true for the burden these spending categories place on the economy. In 1962, defense absorbed roughly 9.2 percent of GDP. However, by 2003, defense outlays consumed only 3.7 percent of GDP.[16] The reverse trend occurs for the major entitlements. In 1962, major entitlement programs consumed 2.5 percent of GDP. By 2003, 8.3 percent of GDP went to these programs.[17] Spending on programs other than major entitlements and defense fluctuated during the same during this period, although spending growth in this category of the budget has outstripped economic performance in recent years.[18] Interest payments went up as a share of GDP in 1980s and 1990s, but have fallen back in recent years.[19] (See Appendix 12.)

Security Spending. Following the terrorist attacks of September 11, 2001, the federal government began tracking spending for homeland security outside the defense budget. In 2003, this spending (including a supplemental appropriation) totaled $34 billion.[20] This spending is distributed among a wide variety of federal departments and agencies, including the new Department of Homeland Security. Offsetting receipts, however, covered about $3.4 billion of this spending. The net outlay for homeland security outside the defense budget, therefore, constituted 0.28 percent of GDP in fiscal year 2003. Given the short record of tracking this spending, the question is whether this new category will expand to the degree that it outstrips overall federal spending or national economic performance.

Current Federal Spending Trends

After 28 consecutive years of budget deficits, the 1998 fiscal year ended with a $69 billion budget surplus. These budget deficits, which had reached 6 percent of GDP in 1983, were eliminated by a combination of three factors: First, real defense spending plummeted by 30 percent in the 1990s as a result of winning the Cold War. Second, tax revenues reached their highest level since World War II as a result of the economic boom. Third, legislative gridlock between Democratic President Bill Clinton and the Republican Congress doomed most new spending initiatives and allowed spending growth to slow to a crawl.

The arrival of budget surpluses, however, saw federal spending accelerating once again. These spending increases went mostly unnoticed because tax revenues continued pouring in at a pace rarely seen in American history, culminating in a $236 billion budget surplus in 2000.

With the economic boom predicted to continue indefinitely, a January 2001 Congressional Budget Office report forecast a cumulative budget surplus of $5.6 trillion over the next decade. In response, Congress adopted President George W. Bush's tax cut proposal, which was estimated to reduce revenues by up to $1.3 trillion over the decade, and in tandem accelerated the federal spending spree. Lawmakers were not yet aware that the technology bubble had burst, the economy was falling into recession, and tax revenues would soon begin plummeting. Against this budget backdrop came the September 11 attacks. A reeling economy was suddenly faced with a massive defense and homeland security mobilization.

Between 2001 and 2004, wars with Afghanistan and Iraq were funded by a 48 percent increase in defense spending. Homeland security spending, which had not even existed as a category before September 11, leapt from $16 billion to $33 billion.[21] The low defense spending that helped bring balanced budgets in the late 1990s was over.

Lawmakers typically blame war and homeland security costs for the barrage of new spending since 2001. That explanation is incomplete. In the two years following the terrorist attacks, federal spending jumped by $296 billion. Of this, $100 billion (34 percent) went for defense and $32 billion (11 percent) went for other 9/11–related costs such as homeland security, international assistance, rebuilding New York City, and compensating terrorism victims. This leaves $164 billion in new spending—which represents 55 percent of the total increase—unrelated to defense and the terrorist attacks.[22]

Furthermore, lawmakers usually cut non-security spending in time of war. Budgets are about setting priorities, and sometimes non-defense programs must take a back seat to the nation's security needs. During World War II, President Roosevelt reduced non–war-related spending by an average of 11 percent each year. President Truman signed budgets during the Korean War that reduced non-defense spending by 6 percent annually. This trend was reversed during the Vietnam War, as President Johnson signed budgets expanding the non-defense spending by 14 percent per year. Tax increases and economic stagnation followed.

Although not quite reaching the levels it did under Johnson, federal spending during the war on terrorism has more closely reflected the Vietnam-era spending binges than the spending restraint of World War II and the Korean War. Spending not related to defense and 9/11 increased by an average of 5 percent per year from 2001 through 2003. That two-year, 11 percent increase in non-security spending represents the fastest growth in a decade.[23] At a time when defense and homeland security priorities require especially tight non-security budgets, lawmakers have not made necessary trade-offs, and in fact, have *accelerated* non-security spending growth.

Where did all this money go? Apart from defense and homeland security, the 2001 through 2004 period saw:

- A 2002 farm bill that is estimated to cost $180 billion over ten years—an 80 percent increase over the baseline;
- A 2003 Medicare drug bill that is estimated to cost $534 billion in the first ten years, and as much as $2 trillion in the following decade, according to the Congressional Budget Office;
- The 2001 No Child Left Behind Act, which authorized billions in new education spending, and is largely responsible for the 77 percent education spending increase;
- Several extensions of unemployment benefits, combined with the automatic new costs that occur when recessions expand unemployment rolls, resulting in a 60 percent increase in unemployment spending;
- An amount of $20 billion in federal assistance to states; and
- Expansions of the refundable Earned Income Tax Credit and Child Tax Credit, resulting in $10 billion in new spending.[24]

From 2001 to 2004, a span of only three years, the following program categories received major spending increases: international affairs (108 percent), general government (78 percent), education (77 percent), unemployment benefits (60 percent), community and regional development (59 percent), and health research and regulation (54 percent).

Even on the lowest-priority programs, restraint remains absent. During that same three-year period, massive funding increases were granted to low-priority programs such as the National Technical Information Service (900 percent), Commerce Department management (311 percent), and the Natural Resources Conservation Service (205 percent).[25] The number of annual "pork" projects (grants for often unnecessary projects back in the lawmakers' districts) surpassed 10,000 for the first time ever, and this $23 billion cost included grants to the Please Touch Museum in Philadelphia ($725,000) and the Rock & Roll Hall of Fame in Cleveland ($200,000).[26] Each dollar given to these projects represents one less dollar for security, tax relief, or deficit reduction.

Waste has proliferated as well. The federal government was unable to account for $25 billion that was spent in 2003. Auditors estimated that employees embezzled 3 percent of the entire Department of Agriculture budget by placing personal purchases on their government credit cards. Over $20 billion in annual program overpayments plagues Washington's social programs.[27]

Overall, from 2001 through 2004, federal spending leaped 24 percent, from $1.86 trillion to $2.32 trillion. Discretionary spending increased 39 percent and mandatory spending surpassed 11 percent of GDP for the first time ever. Dozens of small, lower-priority programs received historic spending increases, and no programs of significance were eliminated or even substantially reduced. On a per household basis, federal spending exceeded $20,000 per household for the first time since World War II (adjusted for inflation).[28] In only four years, the $236 billion budget surplus was replaced with a budget deficit topping $400 billion.

Why Spending Accelerated

Most Americans say they prefer smaller government, yet majorities consistently support government expansion. The reason for this apparent contradiction is rooted in common sense. To wit: A bill in Congress would add $1 each to 100 million peoples' taxes and distribute that entire bounty to the pork industry. The 100 million people may oppose the tax, yet the small $1 cost is not worth the effort of discovering the legislation, fighting it, and voting against elected officials who favor the legislation. Because the pork industry has a $100 million stake in the legislation, they will produce more lobbying, campaign contributions, and electoral pressures on elected officials than the 100 million citizens combined. The legislation will likely pass.

Now, apply this logic to several hundred programs that benefit specific groups of people, each of which will fight to its subsidy. An iron triangle develops between the beneficiaries, the agency administering the program, and the congressional committee overseeing the program, all of which have an interest in preserving it.

A budget process that encourages federal spending has aided such special interest politics. Because there are no limits on federal spending, lawmakers can fund all spending demands and simply pass the cost on to taxpayers.

Although public choice theory explains the general growth of government, the acceleration of non-war spending during a time of higher priorities requires additional explanation. Three chief factors induced this recent spending spree.

No Discipline. The Republican majority in Congress, still haunted by the 1995–1996 government shutdown, began to consider spending cuts the new "third rail" of politics. The ambitious 104th Congress had sought such cuts to balance the budget, but oddly began by targeting the most popular programs, including many in which the savings would be miniscule. Its popularity plummeted when President Clinton capitalized on its tactical errors by forcing a government shutdown. Rather than regrouping and changing tactics, shell-shocked GOP legislators dropped spending restraint altogether. In the White House, as well as among congressional Republicans, "Remember the 104th" became checkmate against anyone foolish enough to suggest spending cuts.

No Limits. The balanced budgets of the late 1990s removed the most popular argument for spending restraint. Before then, lawmakers could use the deficit as a reason to keep spending for popular programs in check. Yet when a tax revenue boom first balanced the budget in 1998, the floodgates opened. Gloomy deficit reduction was replaced with a sunny "balanced budget liberalism," which funded colossal education, health, and social spending increases with soaring tax revenues from an economy that—it seemed—would boom forever. Economic reality quickly returned tax revenues to their historical levels, but it was too late: Both parties now measured their compassion by how much they spend on these popular programs. No one wanted the thankless job of setting limits and saying no.

No Majority. The nation's 50/50 partisan split accelerated pandering and special interest politics. Republicans and Democrats entered their campaign seasons believing that congressional control would be won or lost on the last few thousand votes. When both sides move so close to victory, bold political risks become too dangerous. Federal spending has been used to play to any remaining special interest that can provide support in elections. In 2002, Senate leaders identified farmers as the swing voters who would decide control of the Senate. The ensuing bipartisan bidding war resulted in the most expensive farm bill in American history. By 2004, all the momentum favored expanding government. It is critical that in the short term this momentum be upset in order to fund key priorities like defense and homeland security—and in the long term to protect economic security from huge tax increases necessary to address the entitlement explosion.

Future Spending Trends

Where do we go from here? Budgets are about setting priorities, and the central priorities of the federal budget are to defend the American people from external threats and to protect individuals' paychecks. This is what Eisenhower knew would help win the Cold War. It is what Glenn Hubbard believed would help win the war on terrorism. They were both right. We should learn the lessons of the Eisenhower presidency and stick to the economic strategies mapped out by the Bush Administration after 9/11. This requires appropriate funding for defense and homeland security while keeping taxes low. In doing so, policymakers must deal with two truths:

First, defense and homeland security spending are critical elements of our nation's future. The world has changed and so must America's security budget. Although defense and homeland security costs dropped to 3 percent of GDP in the 1990s, they have since rebounded to 4.4 percent of GDP—representing a $160 billion increase. Given the long-term dangers posed by transnational terrorist groups—as well as the proliferation of weapons of mass destruction and other dangers that might arise from aggressor, enabler, or slacker states—American security spending must likely remain at this higher level indefinitely.

Second, entitlements represent the largest challenge to the nation's ability to fund defense and still keep taxes low. Entitlement spending topped 11 percent of GDP for the first time ever in 2003, and yet even this high level is considered the calm before the budgetary storm. The Baby Boomers will begin retiring at the end of this decade and an unprecedented Social Security and Medicare liability will be handed over to younger generations. The ratio of workers to retirees will complete its drop from 16:1 in the 1930s to 2:1 in 2030. In other words, a two-income couple will be supporting themselves, their children, and the full retirement and health care expenses of their very own retiree.

The Congressional Budget Office has calculated the costs of this coming entitlement explosion. It has projected that federal spending will increase by 5 percent of GDP by 2030 (the current equivalent of $5,200 per household annually), and 13 percent of GDP by 2050 (the current equivalent of

$13,500 per household annually).[29] This will require either massive tax increases, the elimination of most other government programs (including defense and homeland security), or a combination of the two.

Spending Recommendations for the Long War

Reform Entitlements. Taxpayers cannot afford the massive intergenerational transfer of wealth that Social Security and Medicare will soon require. European economies are already being crushed under the weight of these expensive social insurance programs, and the United States must reform now to avoid a similar fate. This means transitioning Social Security from the current "pay-as-you-go" system (in which today's taxpayers fund today's retirees) into one in which taxpayers are allowed to save and invest their own payroll taxes. Taxpayers would actually own their personal retirement accounts as assets that they could control—and even pass down to their children. Similarly, Congress should look at reforming Medicare into a market-based system that provides seniors with choices and incentives to shop around for the best deals. Additionally, lawmakers must revisit the 2003 Medicare drug law that threatens to add trillions of dollars to the tax burden.

Eliminate Low-Priority Programs. A major theme of this chapter is that budgets are about setting priorities. Washington should fully fund its highest priorities (defense and homeland security) and eliminate unaffordable nonpriorities. Lawmakers should create a government waste commission that would submit legislation terminating all wasteful, ineffective, and outdated programs. Lawmakers should also eliminate corporate welfare, privatize functions that can be better run by the private sector, and devolve more functions to state and local governments that can best customize programs to match local needs.

Repair the Budget Process. Lawmakers still cling to the antiquated budget process created back in 1974. During the past thirty years, successive Congresses have punched this process full of holes and federal spending has correspondingly tripled. The current budget process provides no workable tools to limit spending, no restrictions on passing massive costs onto future generations, and no incentive to bring all parties to the table early in the budget to set a framework. America's budget priorities have changed, and so must its budget process.

Reform the Tax Code. The tax rate reductions championed by Glenn Hubbard and implemented by President Bush have rejuvenated today's economy.

Yet it sometimes seems as if tax policy is like running on a treadmill because the good tax legislation of some years is offset by bad developments in other years. Tax rates are increased in some years, the tax bias against saving and investment goes up in other years—and complexity gets worse every year.

As a result, today's tax system remains an obstacle to economic growth. Consider a few facts: Approximately 140 million taxpayers will send tax returns to Uncle Sam this year, a painful exercise involving 8 billion pages of paper that will help transfer more than $2 trillion from the productive sector of the economy to the government. For America's most productive residents, the tax system takes more than one-third of the additional wealth they generate for the nation. Those who save and invest in America's future are penalized with extra layers of taxation. Indeed, it is possible for a single dollar of income to be hit by the capital gains tax, the corporate income tax, the personal income tax, *and* the death tax.

With more than 1,000 forms, notices, and publications, the Internal Revenue Code imposes an enormous compliance burden on taxpayers. Businesses get hit the worst. Two-thirds of compliance costs are borne by companies—expenses that are ultimately paid by workers, shareholders, and consumers. Yet this is just the tip of the iceberg. Businesses also are hit by a 35 percent federal tax rate (in addition to the states' 5 percent); this represents the second-highest corporate tax burden in the industrialized world.

Academic experts estimate that the current tax system imposes mammoth costs on the U.S. economy. Economic output may be about 15 percent lower than it could be as a result of bad tax law, and annual growth rates could be much more impressive if the tax system did not punish productive behavior. There are many reasons why bad tax law reduces economic performance. High tax rates discourage work and entrepreneurship. Discriminatory taxes against capital undermine saving and investment. Special loopholes and penalties undermine efficient allocation of resources by giving people an incentive to make decisions for tax reasons rather than economic reasons. Complexity imposes deadweight costs and diverts intelligent and capable people to careers that add nothing to America's economic output.

Good Tax Policy Equals Good Long-War Strategy

To ensure that the economy grows faster and produces more wealth, jobs, and security, the tax system should be fixed. This requires both tax reduction and tax reform. It is important to understand, however, that not all tax cuts are created equal. Some tax cuts, specifically "supply-side" reductions in tax rates on work, saving, investment, and entrepreneurship, can yield large benefits to the economy. Properly designed, they even can simplify today's byzantine tax system. Yet it is also possible to cut taxes in ways that lead to a more complicated tax system, while simultaneously doing nothing to improve the economy's performance.

To judge the desirability of tax policy changes, there must be a yardstick—a benchmark, so to speak—of an ideal tax system. This theoretical ideal would have a low tax rate and it would tax income only *one* time. Such a system would not impose a second layer of tax on income earned in other nations, and taxpayers would find it easy to understand. The "flat tax" is the best example of such a system. It would minimize the tax penalties imposed on productive behavior and it would get politicians out of the business of trying to micromanage the economy through the tax code.

Yet even if politicians are reluctant to junk the tax code and implement a flat tax—because it would take away too much power from Washington—there are many incremental changes that can create a better tax system. However, to reap these benefits, lawmakers must understand how taxes affect the economy. They also need to realize that economic growth occurs when people work more, save more, and invest more—the behaviors that increase national income and boost the nation's wealth. When contemplating tax policy changes, policymakers should focus on the following questions:

- Will the provision lower the tax rate on productive behavior? To encourage growth, a tax cut should reduce the tax rates on work, saving, investment, risk-taking, and entrepreneurship. These are the activities that increase national income. As a general rule, credits, deductions, preferences, and exemptions do not help the economy grow faster.

- Will the provision make America more competitive in the global economy? It is increasingly easy for jobs and capital to migrate from high-tax jurisdictions to low-tax jurisdictions. The process, known as tax competition, enhances the rewards for nations that implement pro-growth tax policy.

- Will the provision encourage job creation? Companies do not hire workers because they feel sorry for them or because they have a social conscience. They hire workers in the expectation of making a profit. High tax rates increase the cost of labor and discourage the capital formation that is necessary to boost worker productivity.

- Will the provision reduce the tax bias against saving and investment? Because of the capital gains tax, the corporate income tax, the personal income tax, and the death tax, the Internal Revenue Code imposes as many as *four* layers of tax on income that is saved and invested. Reducing or eliminating any of these extra layers of tax will boost capital formation by creating a level playing field between current consumption and future consumption.

Fixing the Tax Mess

There are a number of tax policy changes that meet the above criteria. Reducing the top tax rate imposed on personal income would be a positive step, particularly because today's 35 percent rate is still significantly higher than it was when Ronald Reagan left office. A similar reduction in the corporate tax rate also would be beneficial, especially since U.S. companies face a disadvantage in a competitive global economy due to this aspect of our tax law. Having a tax rate higher than either France or Sweden is a black mark against America.

Policymakers also should concentrate on reducing the tax bias against saving and investing. For example, eliminating the capital gains tax and the second layer of tax on dividends would ensure that there is no double tax on corporate profit. Making individual retirement accounts unlimited and universal would protect all saving from double taxation.

To promote simplicity and fairness—as well as to reduce compliance costs and help finance the pro-growth tax changes—lawmakers should eliminate as many special loopholes and exemptions as possible. The tax code is littered with special preferences that benefit lawyers, lobbyists, and accountants. Politicians are the biggest winners from tax code complexity, which is why tax reform also would be an ideal way of reducing corruption in Washington.

Because of globalization, the benefits of good tax policy have never been greater. Yet this also means that the costs of bad tax policy have never been higher. Many nations have enjoyed dramatic growth as a result of pro-growth tax policy changes. Ireland, for instance, has transformed itself from the "Sick Man of Europe" into the "Celtic Tiger" thanks to lower tax rates (including a corporate tax rate of 12.5 percent, down from 50 percent less than twenty years ago). Former Soviet bloc jurisdictions, including Russia, are experiencing impressive results thanks to low-rate flat tax regimes. Hong Kong has been the world's fastest-growing economy since World War II, thanks in part to its flat tax.

The United States has been a modest winner in this international competition. America's aggregate tax burden may be high, but it is considerably lower than many other industrialized nations. The Reagan tax cuts certainly gave the United States a major boost in the 1980s, but there was backsliding in the 1990s: Policy mistakes in that decade have been only partially reversed by recent tax rate reductions. Ample room remains for tax reduction and tax reforms to improve America's competitive position. The better a competitor the United States is economically, the better able it will be to provide for its own security.

Spirit by Eisenhower, Economics by Hubbard

A strong economy is fundamental to winning the long war. Period. Solid economic policies not only stand side-by-side with good security practices, but they are natural partners in the war on terrorism. America *can* do both. If, when al-Qaeda is long gone, the United States does not stand as a stronger and more prosperous country than it did on September 10, 2001, it has no one to blame but itself. However, getting there will take more effort. Tax and spending reforms are the keys to the future prosperity that will provide a cornerstone to winning the war on terrorism.

Chapter 6

Trade in a Challenging World

William Appleman Williams was one of the Cold War's most notable historians. A Naval Academy graduate, World War II Naval officer, and civil rights activist, Williams was both prolific and controversial. He was a champion of the leftist-revisionist histories that began to come out of the academy in the wake of the Korean War. Williams's *Tragedy of American Diplomacy*, published in 1959, argued that the problem with the United States is that Americans thought they had all the answers and they didn't. America, Williams argued was engaged in "Open Door Imperialism," a ceaseless quest for economic dominance and the establishment of an informal empire designed to sustain U.S. economic prosperity and prevent revolutionary agitation against the American global system overseas.[1]

The Cold War, Williams argued, was just the United States looking out for itself. The Truman Doctrine and Marshall Plan were, he believed, an example of "two sides of the same coin of America's traditional program of opendoor expansion."[2] Although Williams had little use for Truman, he thought even less of Eisenhower, whom he considered the coldest of the Cold War warriors. As far as Williams was concerned, after Ike things did not get any better. Vietnam, for Williams, was the apogee of American hubris. He became a vocal critic, not just of U.S. history, but of contemporary foreign policy as well. "I prefer to die as a free man struggling to create a human community than as a pawn of empire," he wrote in 1976 in the wake of the tragedy of Vietnam.[3] Williams built a career out of speaking truth to power—or so he thought.

Trade during the Cold War. U.S. agricultural products loading for shipment overseas. (COURTESY OF THE U.S. DEPARTMENT OF AGRICULTURE)

At the University of Wisconsin–Madison, Williams became known as the father of the "Wisconsin School," a generation of leftist diplomatic historians that found economic determinism at the root of virtually every episode of American foreign policy. Sadly, the Wisconsin school generated more heat than light. The evils of dollar diplomacy made for good reading. Yet, as powerful and evocative as Williams's writings were seen to be in the 1960s and early 1970s, it is questionable how well they have stood the test of time and distance from the raw emotion of the Vietnam era. The Marxist view of the past that underpins Williams's analysis—the critique of capitalism based on the presumed exploitation of the masses—all seems a bit old-fashioned and silly in the wake of the collapse of the Soviet empire. In many ways Williams has become, like McCarthyism, another of the Cold War's ghosts from Wisconsin.

Sometimes it is more important to pay attention to history than to historians. Williams, like Charles Beard and other progressive historians, stretched the evidence to fit the thesis. Often, both the theses and the historians were simply wrong. Much of the United States' economic role in global affairs was simply Americans doing business in the world without any secret plan or ulterior motive. Likewise, although every major foreign policy decision may have had global economic consequences, that did not mean that checkbook strategy was behind every U.S. action.

Williams's history of the Cold War was more a reflection of the ideological debates that accompanied the long struggle between democracy and communism than an accurate and insightful analysis of the lessons that can be learned from that troubled time. Still, his writings remain a powerful and important reminder that U.S. history, particularly since the turn of the twentieth century has been the history of the United States in the world. It is virtually impossible to talk or think about the global economy without thinking about the American economy.

There were voices during the Cold War that called for retrenchment and disengagement from the global economy and global affairs. That was never a realistic choice. Neither is retreating from the global economy much of an option today. It is true that the trade and commerce that carry goods, services, ideas, and people to and from our shores can also carry terrorists and their weapons—but we cannot live in a world without global trade and commerce. America is inextricably linked to the global economy, because 96 percent of the world's consumers live outside the United States and America is the world's largest exporter. We have to trade. One of the principal tasks of long war strategy is to preserve both free trade and security—in equal measure.

Trading Places

William Appleman Williams got it exactly wrong. Trade was not the enemy of freedom during the Cold War; it was the West's savior and it remains the lifeblood of freedom today. In the modern world, free trade stands as the driving force in global economic growth. Countries that have pursued liberalization have witnessed an increase in GDP. As countries open their markets, per capita GDP increases. This is a simple fact. The International Monetary Fund (IMF) survey of the literature on trade and growth found that "many cross-country econometric studies have concluded that trade openness is a significant explanatory variable for the level or the growth rate of real GDP per capita."[4] In plain language, what the IMF found was that countries that opened their markets and became global traders made more money.

No country demonstrates the importance of free trade to economic growth more than the United States. One of the more remarkable achievements of the United States in its long confrontation with the Soviet Union was that it sustained a military standoff while becoming a more open society, not just as a civil society, but also as a global trading partner. "The growth in

President Dwight D. Eisenhower addresses the 15th Session of the General Assembly of the United Nations, September 22, 1960. (COURTESY OF THE UNITED NATIONS)

trade over the past 50 years," concludes a U.S. Commerce Department report, "fueled by falling trade barriers, has contributed directly to the most rapid sustained economic growth in U.S. history."[5] Throughout the darkest days of the Cold War, America kept its doors open, and as a result, it finished the long war stronger than it started.

Free trade has made the United States more competitive and innovative. Innovation constantly provides new technologies that allow Americans to produce more. The resulting economic growth generates jobs, higher standards of living, and a greater appreciation of the benefits of living in a peaceful society.[6]

Free and fair trade also spurs efficiency. The drive to produce "better, faster, cheaper" improves the competitiveness of manufacturing enterprises and service industries.[7] In turn, competition brings lower prices. The big winner is the American consumer. According to a University of Michigan study, the North American Free Trade Agreement (NAFTA) and the World Trade Organization's (WTO) Uruguay Round of trade negotiations have increased the savings and gains of the average American family by $1,300 to $2,000. The income gains and tariff cuts from NAFTA alone were worth up to $930 each year for the average American family of four.[8] Additionally, the

WTO found that "in the United States, 12 million people owe their jobs to exports; 1.3 million of those jobs were created between 1994 and 1998. And those jobs tend to be better-paid with better security."[9]

The benefits of free trade are not confined by borders. The achievements of trade in North America offers the best example. The gains from NAFTA and the WTO Uruguay Round can be seen across the board, ranging from manufacturing to the local farmer. U.S. manufacturing output rose 44 percent (in real terms) in the 1990s and real hourly compensation increased by 14.4 percent in the ten years following the signing of the NAFTA agreement.[10] American farmers have seen a huge increase in exports. Mexico has become one of the fastest growing markets for U.S. beef. U.S. pork exports to Mexico and Canada have increased by more than 230 percent since the implementation of NAFTA.[11] In 2003, total U.S. exports to Canada exceeded $169 billion and total exports to Mexico exceeded $97 billion. Likewise, Canada's export industry benefits greatly. According to Canadian Prime Minister Paul Martin, "Canada exports more to Home Depot [a U.S.-based company], than we do to France."[12] NAFTA has benefited Mexico as well. Gary Hufbauer of the Institute for International Economics notes, "Between 1993 and 1999, Mexican exports grew from $48 billion to $120 billion. If Mexican exports had grown only as fast as real Mexican GDP (plus U.S. inflation), the 1999 figure would have been $63 billion. The extra $57 billion of exports boosted Mexican GDP potential by $12 to $28 billion (3 to 6 percent)."[13]

Nor is the capacity of trade to stimulate economic growth limited to North America. Any country willing to tear down barriers and open its market can experience the benefits of these policies. (See Appendix 13.) Hong Kong embraced free trade and is now one of the premier centers of finance and commerce in the world.[14] Hong Kong has a per capita GDP that is nearly $25,000. Likewise, Singapore is very open—with a weighted average tariff rate of 0 percent.[15] Singapore's per capita GDP is over $27,000. In contrast, countries that have isolated themselves from the global economy have suffered as a result. Burma, which has restrictive trade policies, has a per capita GDP of only $152.[16]

Not only is free trade the right approach to promoting economic growth, it also serves to address, rather than exacerbate, many of the ills commonly (though often wrongly) associated with globalization. Free trade, for example, improves environmental standards. Mike Moore, former Director-General of the WTO, points out that, "All serious research shows that poverty is the greatest threat to the environment. People don't live in polluted squalor by choice, nor do they trek miles to strip trees for charcoal by choice. There is a direct connection with rising living standards and better environmental outcomes."[17] Countries enjoy a superior environmental quality when they can afford to establish and sustain environmental standards. Trade creates wealth. In turn, when incomes rise, more money becomes available to spend on the environment. (See Appendix 14.) In short, countries that have a higher degree of trade openness have a higher level of environmental sustainability.[18]

Trade also improves labor standards. Poverty, not trade, creates sweatshops, slumlords, and exploitative child labor. A Brookings Institution study found that in countries with a per capita income of $500 or less, 30 percent to 60 percent of children between the ages of 10 and 14 work, whereas in countries with a per capita income within the $500 to $1,000 range, only 10 percent of children in that age bracket work.[19] The increased per capita GDP that an open market brings can only help—not hurt—a country's labor standards.

Finally, free trade is the handmaiden of security. There is a reason why thriving democracies never go to war with each other. The U.S. National Security Strategy points out:

> A strong world economy enhances our national security by advancing prosperity and freedom in the rest of the world. Economic growth supported by free trade and free markets creates new jobs and higher incomes. It allows people to lift their lives out of poverty, spurs economic and legal reform, and the fight against corruption, and it reinforces the habits of liberty. We will promote economic growth and economic freedom beyond America's shores.[20]

In short, there are few better weapons in a long war than free trade. Trade makes a nation's economy stronger and it improves global conditions generally. The tide raises all boats.

Free Trade's Champion

No one is more passionate about the value of free trade than Robert Zoellick, the United States Trade Representative under the Bush Administration. If William Appleman Williams stood at one pole representing the way Americans thought about the impact of the U.S. economy on the world, Zoellick would be standing at the other. "Free trade is about freedom," Zoellick would often say. "Openness is America's trump card."

Even before 9/11, Zoellick passionately believed that free trade was as crucial to dealing with the ills of the post-Cold War world as it was in saving the West in the long struggle against communism. "Over the last decade," Zoellick is fond of reminding audiences, "trade helped to raise 140 million people out of poverty, spreading prosperity and peace to parts of the world that have seen too little of both."[21] The end of the Cold War, in fact, brought new opportunities to extend the advantages of free and open trade to virtually every nation in the world. Zoellick's mission was to ensure that no one—anti–free-traders, protectionists, or terrorists—closed the open door.

Zoellick's career as a high priest for free trade bridged the sunset of the Cold War and the rise of the so-called New World Order. The young man from Naperville, Illinois, armed with law and public policy graduate degrees from Harvard, joined the U.S. Treasury Department in 1985. Later, Zoellick served as State Department undersecretary beneath James Baker. In 1991 and 1992, he served as the President's personal representative at the G-7 economic summits.

On February 7, 2001, Zoellick assumed his duties as the nation's trade representative. The following year, Congress granted the President Trade Promotion Authority (TPA), often called "fast track authority." TPA involves special procedures for the negotiating and implementing of trade agreements. Although the Constitution gives Congress authority to set the terms of international commerce, fast track is a means for Congress to delegate responsibility to the President for speeding trade negotiations. Under fast track, once the President negotiates a deal and turns it over to the Hill to become law, Congress limits itself to twenty hours of debate and an up or down vote on the final bill (with no amendments allowed). Created in 1974, Congress allowed presidential negotiating authority to lapse in 1994. The United States had been falling behind ever since. Of the 150 free trade agreements in the world in 1994, the United States was party to only three.

It is not a coincidence that at the dawn of the war on terrorism, the Bush Administration turned its attention to rekindling momentum for the expansion of free trade. Long wars demand strong economies and free trade is the ultimate engine of economic growth.

Since Zoellick took over, the President has signed agreements with Chile and Singapore and has completed negotiations for agreements with Central

Robert Zoellick advocating to extend the President's authority to negotiate free trade agreements. (PHOTO FROM THE HERITAGE FOUNDATION COLLECTION)

America, Australia, Bahrain, and Morocco.[22] In 2004, the trade representative negotiated the Free Trade Agreement of the Americas, as well as conducting bilateral free trade agreement negotiations with Panama, Thailand, and the Andean countries. "By pursuing multiple free trade initiatives," Zoellick argues, "the United States is creating a 'competition for liberalization' that provides leverage for openness in all negotiations, establishes models of success that can be used on many fronts, and develops a fresh political dynamic that puts free trade on the offensive."[23] That is, simply put, the right trade strategy for a long war.

Advancing Free Trade

The United States is not alone in this endeavor. By the end of 2003 there were already 250 bilateral and multilateral agreements in place around the world. Over half of them have been put in place since 1995 and about fifty more are believed to be on the way.[24] With luck, that will be only the beginning. The WTO's Doha Round of trade negotiations (launched in Qatar in November 2001) began by calling, in particular, for ensuring the inclusion of the developing world. "International trade can play a major role in the promotion of economic development and the alleviation of poverty," the Doha Declaration concluded. "We recognize the need for all peoples to benefit from the increased opportunities and welfare gains that the multilateral trading system generates. The majority of WTO Members are developing countries. We seek to place their needs and interests at the heart of the Work Programme adopted in this Declaration."[25] The challenge now is to put these words into action.

Despite the emphasis Doha places on expanding the free trade agenda, negotiations have been slow. That is not surprising. WTO decisions are made by a consensus vote of its 147 members. Because the WTO membership chooses to point fingers over who has the highest barriers instead of simply advancing trade, the organization has become less of an engine for change and more of a speed bump to progress.

Past WTO agreements have greatly benefited global growth. Future agreements will contribute to that growth and will strengthen the ties that bind the global economy. Security regimes must take this global economic system into account. Re-energizing the WTO, as well as pushing forward with other bilateral and multilateral trade deals, has to remain a high priority.

Here are some additional steps that the United States should be taking right now. We can start by keeping America free of protectionism. To that end, the government should:

- Advance as many free trade agreements as possible. Thus far, the Bush Administration has advanced free trade agreements with Chile and Singapore and has completed negotiations with Central

America, Australia, and Morocco. It should continue to negotiate free trade agreements with other countries around the world.

- Eliminate agricultural subsidies, antidumping measures, and other protectionist policies. Subsidies and special protections benefit small economic interests or sectors at the expense of millions of consumers and producers. They translate into higher prices—the impact of which is felt primarily by poor Americans.
- At the same time, the United States should push other developed and developing nations to adopt these policies as well, creating a level playing field for global competition.

Terrorism and Trade

Clearly, free trade is here to stay. Likewise, security is not an option. Although free trade provides the strength to fight the long war, like every other instrument of conflict, it must be protected.

Transnational terrorism, if left unchecked, could represent a significant threat to the lifeblood of the global economy. For instance, in 2002, a labor dispute closed all ports on the West Coast for eleven days—ports that handled 60 percent of U.S. maritime imports and exports. Losses from the lockout stretched into "the billions of dollars."[26] The effects of this dispute reached beyond U.S. soil across the ocean to foreign producers trying to export their goods.

A terrorist attack might be capable of inflicting far more economic damage. The direct impact on the domestic economy would no doubt be substantial. The Port of Long Beach accounts for 30,000 jobs[27] and the Port of Miami-Dade generates more than 90,000 jobs and has an economic impact of $12 billion annually.[28] The consequences of shutting them down would be immediate and significant. Additionally, there could be huge ramifications on trade. U.S. producers and foreigner importers would likely face gridlock or a complete shutout for weeks—or even longer.

Thus, the United States faces a dual challenge. Asa Hutchinson, the Department of Homeland Security's Undersecretary for Border and Transportation Security, said it best: "[Our] borders and ports are not just 'openings' to be secured. They are economic doors that must remain open."[29] We must always keep both goals in mind.

In the wake of 9/11, trade quickly became a battleground for dueling experts. While economists argued for open borders, security experts campaigned

Trade and Transport: Lifeblood of the twenty-first century economy. (PHOTO FROM PHOTOS.COM)

for more regulations. Framing a debate between security and trade offers a false choice, much in the same way that arguing for security *or* civil liberties simply sets forth the wrong set of options. The answer is simple. It is security *and* trade. That is why the post-9/11 efforts to adopt layered security, public–private partnerships, and risk-management methods have established exactly the right kind of framework for providing good security for a global economy. This approach makes security simply another cost in the process of doing business, just like safety, labor, and environmental standards are factors that must also be account-ed for in global commerce. They represent the right approach for the long war, reasonable measures that provide real security with the public and private sector each fulfilling its responsibilities for the protection of global trade.

Advancing both security and trade, however, can be easier said than done. Although rich nations, such as the United States and its trading partners in Asia and Europe, can well afford the security initiatives introduced since 9/11 to protect global trade, other nations cannot. Rising tides cannot lift boats that have no bottoms.

Security and Emerging Economies

The U.S. National Security Strategy correctly calls for encouraging econom-ic development through free markets, free trade, and enhancing the capacity of developing nations to compete in the global economy. Concurrently, how-ever, the United States is rightly promoting international security regimes designed to prevent terrorists from attacking or exploiting the world's global trade networks. Meeting these requirements is difficult for developing coun-tries that lack mature infrastructure, robust human capital programs, and adequate financing. Today, many of these countries are not major trading partners with the United States. Unless they determine how best to meet emerging international measures to combat terrorism, they never will be.

Good security costs money. The International Shipping and Port Security (ISPS) Codes offer a case in point. Established by the International Maritime Organization in the wake of 9/11, ISPS mandates new, unprecedented meas-ures for securing commercial shipping. The "I code" requires that commercial ships carry an automatic identification system so that their location can be plotted moment by moment in the event of an onboard emergency.[30] Each must also appoint a security officer who must oversee the ship's security plan. Additionally, ships must provide a synopsis record of all movements, ports of call, cargoes, and ownership details.[31] Costs for non-compliance are likely to be very high. If a ship does not meet the new requirements, it is very possible that it will be turned away and not be allowed to dock at a U.S. port.[32]

Likewise, the ISPS code sets security requirements for ports, which must establish port security committees, conduct vulnerability assessments, and implement security plans. National authorities must certify that ports are

ISPS compliant. Ships that dock at non-compliant ports may also be denied entry to U.S. waters.

The cost of compliance appears to be substantial as well. More than 46,000 ships and almost 4,000 ports are involved in international trade and will be required to comply with ISPS. A 2003 Organisation for Economic Co-operation and Development report estimates the initial ISPS Code compliance burden on ship operators to be at least $1.3 billion and $730 million per year thereafter.[33] The costs of having to meet ISPS requirements are very difficult to estimate because of the variability of needs and costs (e.g., labor and materials) at the ports.[34]

There are a number of reasons why it will be hard for emerging economies to get there from here—and it's more than the problem of just lacking cold, hard cash to buy fences and guard dogs. Fundamentally, good security is about good governance. That means an established rule of law and law enforcement and trade officials that follow the law. It also requires an end to widespread corruption. It demands transparency in government action. It includes having personnel adequately equipped and trained to do their jobs. For some, it demands cultural change. It requires a mindset that envisions the role of customs, trade, and law enforcement to be the facilitation and protection of trade—not just generating revenue for the government by collecting tariffs, taking bribes, and pilfering goods. Finally, it demands governance that facilitates economic growth, which in turns creates the wealth that allows the public and private sectors to pay for the security their people deserve. Developing nations that lack the capacity for good governance will always lack the capability to provide good security.

Traditional foreign assistance programs have simply failed to address the issues of good governance or the need to help poor nations develop. The United States disbursed nearly $259 billion (in constant 1995 dollars) in development assistance between 1980 and 2001.[35] Yet the citizens of most recipient countries are no better off today (in terms of per capita GDP) than they were decades ago. Some, in fact, are poorer. Between 1980 and 2001, of the 77 countries that received economic assistance that accounted for at least 1 percent of their 2001 GDP (in constant 1995 dollars) and for which per capita GDP data are available:

- Thirty-three experienced a decline in real per capita GDP;
- Fifteen experienced negligible real growth—less than 1 percent compound annual growth—in per capita GDP; and

- Only 29 experienced real compound annual growth in per capita GDP exceeding 1 percent. Of these 29, only eight countries saw growth over 3 percent.[36]

U.S. aid programs are just not getting the job done. That is why President Bush proposed a new form of assistance in the Millennium Challenge Account (MCA)—a performance-based foreign aid program. The MCA is an innovative attempt to address the historic failure of foreign aid and to make it more effective. Under the MCA, nations would be eligible to receive assistance only if they adopt policies consistent with good governance and economic freedom—policies proven to lead to greater prosperity.

Will the MCA work? Probably, *if* it is done correctly. To manage the MCA, the government established the Millennium Challenge Corporation (MCC). The trick will be for the MCC to focus on each candidate country's progress toward more open markets. The Heritage Foundation's *Index of Economic Freedom* shows exactly how to do this.

Using the *Index* as a guide, the MCC could identify which candidate countries have been working hardest toward MCA goals. The *Index* measures economic freedom by examining ten factors: trade policy, fiscal burden of government, government intervention in the economy, monetary policy, capital flows and foreign investment, banking and finance, wages and prices, property rights, regulation, and informal market activity. As the *Index of Economic Freedom* has demonstrated for the past ten years, countries that open their markets have higher per capita GDP.

The MCC recently designated 63 countries as potential recipients of MCA grants. Appendix 15 shows the performance of the 49 of these 63 countries that are ranked in the *Index*. Using *Index* data, the table divides the 49 countries into quartiles based on the improvement in their levels of economic freedom during the past four years. Within each quartile, countries are listed according to degree of improvement, in descending order. Countries in the first quartile are progressing fastest toward economic freedom and would therefore benefit most from the MCA. Conversely, countries in the fourth quartile have shown the least improvement and, measured against the President's goal, are the least deserving of MCA grants.

The countries in the top quartile have slightly more than six times as much GDP growth over the past 10 years as those in the bottom quartile. Consistent with the President's mission, the top quartile countries are likely to move beyond their current dependence on aid. For instance, Cape Verde's level of economic freedom has steadily increased since 2000, directly contributing to Cape Verde's achieving a higher rate of economic growth than most other countries in the table. The Cape Verde government plans to continue this progress by privatizing the remaining state-owned companies, reducing the corporate income tax rate, and implementing other measures. On the other hand, Bolivia has failed to move steadily toward economic prosperity. As Appendix 16 shows, Bolivia's poor record in economic freedom is associated with plummeting economic growth.

The MCA represents a fundamental shift in development assistance because it would provide assistance only to countries with a proven record of adopting policies that are complementary and conducive to economic growth. Compared to traditional foreign aid, the MCA would be a far more effective means of providing assistance and of leading poor nations to adopt policies that would encourage economic growth and development—with or without foreign assistance. The MCA should be the centerpiece of U.S. foreign assistance efforts. It is the only initiative that, over the long term, offers the promise of adequately addressing the challenges of promoting economic growth and establishing international security regimes that incorporate the world's emerging economies.

In the short term, there is also more that can be done within existing assistance programs. Programs to provide technical help to countries for developing trade already exist. In fact, the United States is the largest single-country donor for Trade Capacity Building Assistance (TCB).[37] In 2003, the United States gave $752 million for TCB.[38] Currently, this assistance falls under two categories: addressing supply-side obstacles and assistance related to participation in the WTO Technical Assistance Plan and regional trade agreements.[39] These funds should be used to help developing countries comply with international security regimes by promoting good governance practices related to trade security. Just as we have given technical assistance to help countries join the WTO, the United States should assist countries in understanding and developing strategies to meet the requirements of global security regimes.[40] Helping these countries help themselves, in the end, helps all of us. Each country that joins the global security regime helps shrink the sanctuaries and opportunities for terrorists plying the global networks of trade and travel.

Protectionism and Homeland Security

Perhaps the greatest threat to free trade during the long war, however, will not come from the terrorists or our incapacity to assist the developing world, but in our ability to hurt ourselves. Kennan's caution in the Long Telegram bears repeating here. "The greatest danger that can befall us in coping with this problem," he wrote, "is that we shall allow ourselves to become like those with whom we are coping." The terrorists would like to wall themselves off and create a world in which they reign without influence or contact from the rest of the universe, insulated from the corrupting influence of freedom and democracy. America cannot fight this kind of fascism if, in the name of fighting fascism, it imitates its methods. Thus, we must be watchful for those who would close the lifeline of free trade that fuels the American economy in the name of protecting that same economy.

A Cautionary Tale

Like the ghosts from Wisconsin, the specter of protectionism—arguments that America would be better off eschewing free trade in favor of restrictive rules and tariffs that limit U.S. interaction with the global economy—visit us again and again. At the height of the Cold War, for example, congressional legislators smashed Sony TVs on the steps of the Capitol building and railed against Japanese and German cars under the impression that restricting trade with America's staunchest allies would somehow make us richer and safer. Today's version of mindless protectionism is found in complaints about outsourcing—the irrational fear that contracting with overseas companies for services will somehow destroy the American economy or open up new avenues for terrorists to threaten the United States.

It was bound to happen. Opponents of outsourcing have dragged the issue of homeland security into their protectionist arguments. Immediately after the Department of Homeland Security awarded a contract to Accenture LLP (the U.S. subsidiary of the Bermuda-chartered company, Accenture) to implement DHS's new U.S. Visitor and Immigrant Status Indicator Technology (US-VISIT), CNN's *Exporting America* ran a segment[41] about outsourcing America's security. In recent months, *Exporting America* has tried to tap into the public's fear of job losses by highlighting anecdotal stories while ignoring official statistics that show that fears about job loss are wildly overblown. Apparently, *Exporting America* has now incorporated homeland security concerns into its argument, claiming that outsourcing homeland security contracts poses a threat to America. The facts simply do not bear out these concerns.

Applying protectionist policies to homeland security would only work to compromise America's security. DHS's goal when awarding contracts should be to obtain the best security for the dollars invested. To ensure that America gets both good value and good security, Congress and the Bush Administration should:

- Remove all language from the Homeland Security Act and appropriations bills that restricts DHS's ability to award contracts to whomever is best equipped for the job;
- Insist that DHS establish and require companies to follow strict security practices in order to receive contracts;
- Direct DHS to establish a program comparable to the National Industrial Security Program (NISP), through which inspectors would inspect contractor facilities to verify that all security requirements are met; and
- Refrain from implementing protectionist policies that would limit DHS access to superior service and technology (and that might invite protectionist reprisals against the United States).

An Overstated Argument

Some critics do not even understand their own arguments. The Accenture controversy, for instance, has nothing to do with outsourcing—which occurs when a U.S. company subcontracts some element of its operations to a foreign entity. Instead, it is a fight about whether a company with a foreign "parent" should bid for U.S. government contracts, especially if the parent company rechartered in a jurisdiction with better tax laws. However, even by this criterion, opponents of the Accenture contract are inaccurate because Accenture was never a U.S. company. Rather, it is a related set of partnerships in various nations that chose Bermuda as a home base for purposes of incorporation.

In any event, complaints about outsourcing the US-VISIT contract are completely misdirected. They demonstrate how eager some are to link homeland security to the debate against outsourcing. Under the DHS contract, Accenture LLP will implement US-VISIT—a program that uses biometric identifiers, such as fingerprints and photographs, to make security determinations about individuals entering or exiting the United States. Accenture, the parent company, is a global management consulting and technology services company that is chartered in Bermuda. However, Accenture LLP—based in the U.S.—will do all of the contract work, and the dollars and tax revenue generated by the project will remain in the United States. Moreover, Accenture LLP met all of DHS's legal requirements for the US-VISIT bid and was awarded the contract based on its ability to do the job.

The Benefits of Outsourcing

Even though the Accenture debate is not really about outsourcing, it is important to realize that the ability to contract outside national borders benefits the American economy and national security. Outsourcing opponents routinely focus on only one side of the issue, while ignoring the gains in lower prices, higher efficiency, and insourced jobs.

More Americans are employed today than ever before—a record high of 139 million workers, as reported by the Bureau of Labor Statistics. The unemployment rate has been dropping for one year and is steady at a low 5.6 percent—all the more impressive because the American workforce has grown by 2.84 million people since late 2001.[42] This robust performance—particularly when compared to the economic stagnation and high unemployment rate in Europe—can be attributed to U.S. reliance on the free market to allocate resources.

This market flexibility and dynamism does mean that some jobs are lost, but those job losses tend to be small compared to the number of jobs that are created. The only official study on the impact of off-shoring jobs (released by the Department of Labor on June 10, 2004) found that only 4,633 job losses were associated with overseas relocations in the first quarter of 2004.[43] That represents only 2 percent of total layoffs in America.

Aside from debunking inflated fears about the export of American jobs, it is necessary to recognize the many benefits of outsourcing. Outsourcing is a two-way street. There are currently 6.4 million jobs in the U.S. in which the employer is a foreign company. These "insourced" jobs are growing at a faster rate than jobs in general are being lost. According to the Organization for International Investment, "Over the last 15 years, manufacturing 'insourced' jobs grew by 82%—at an annual rate of 5.5%; and manufacturing 'outsourced' jobs grew by 23 percent—at an annual rate of 1.5%."[44]

Furthermore, outsourcing is a means of increasing output while reducing input costs. This leads to lower consumer prices, higher living standards, and more jobs in a growing economy. Outsourcing also lets competition run its course and encourages companies to become more efficient. In the end, having a pool of highly competitive and efficient companies bidding for homeland security contracts will only further the quality of America's security.

Policies that punish businesses that outsource jobs are protectionist and isolationist—and such policies have a long history of failure. They also erode U.S. competitiveness. Policies that encourage free trade, free labor, and free capital are not only necessary for economic growth, but are crucial to America's national security because they ensure that the U.S. will have access to the best technologies and systems for homeland security.

Corporate Expatriation: Blame the Tax Code, Not the Companies

Much of the protectionist sentiment in the Accenture debate is not really about outsourcing, but is targeted at companies that choose to incorporate outside the United States. Many companies—including Tyco, Ingersoll–Rand, Cooper Industries, McDermott International, Nabors Industries, the Noble Corporation, and Foster–Wheeler—have dissolved their U.S. charters and reincorporated in low-tax jurisdictions that have territorial tax regimes. (This business practice is also known as inversion or expatriation.) Other companies, such as Accenture, chose low-tax jurisdictions when they first incorporated. On a similar note, a vice president of Intel remarked that, if Intel could start over, it would organize as a foreign company.[45]

The United States' high corporate tax rate and "worldwide taxation" policy simply make it difficult for corporations chartered in the United States to compete overseas. The federal government imposes a 35 percent tax on corporate income[46] and states take another 5 percent (on average). This cumulative 40 percent tax rate is significantly higher than the 29.96 percent average corporate tax burden in Organisation for Economic Co-operation and Development countries.[47] Indeed, the tax burden on U.S.-based corporations is currently the second highest in the industrialized world.[48] Additionally, U.S.-chartered firms must pay tax to the Internal Revenue Service on income earned in other countries, in addition to the local corporate tax. This "worldwide taxation" policy puts American-based companies at a disadvantage because most U.S. trading partners rely on "territorial taxation"—the commonsense notion that governments tax only income earned inside their borders.

The combination of these misguided policies is undermining U.S. competitiveness—as, for instance, when a U.S. company competes against a Dutch company in Ireland. Because Holland has a territorial tax system, the Dutch company pays only the 12.5 percent Irish corporate income tax on its Irish income.[49] The American company, though, must pay the 12.5 percent Irish tax and the 35 percent U.S. corporate income tax.

Companies like Accenture still have U.S. operations, and their U.S. subsidiaries pay tax to the IRS on all U.S. income. This certainly will be the case with Accenture's Illinois-based U.S. subsidiary. However, because the parent company is based in a jurisdiction with better tax laws, it avoids paying the punitive U.S. corporate tax rate on non-U.S. income. This is simply a smart business decision, which protects the interests of both workers and shareholders. In no way does this practice of having parent companies based in low-tax jurisdictions threaten America's homeland security.

Getting Homeland Security and Trade Right

Applying protectionist policies for the sake of homeland security would stifle innovation and increase costs—working against the goal of getting the best security (and the best value) for the dollars invested. Where the contract is fulfilled—whether in Boston, Britain, or Bermuda—does not necessarily add or detract from the end goal of obtaining safe and secure services. More important are the safeguards in the contract. The federal government should ensure that its contracts outline stringent security and data protection requirements. It is imperative that the government award contracts to companies that both meet those security standards *and* possess the expertise to complete the projects. In general, it should insist that contract work is conducted in countries that have a cooperative relationship with the United States across a broad spectrum of security initiatives, including:

- Harmonization of security requirements and acquisition processes;
- Security of supply;
- Export procedures;
- Security of information;
- Ownership and corporate governance;

- Research and development;
- Flow of technical information; and
- Security of trade.[50]

Additionally, both the federal government and the private sector have the responsibility to perform "due diligence," ensuring that services are being provided under conditions consistent with the rule of law and good management and security practices. These criteria, rather than geographic location, are the best guarantor of getting good value and good security. Improving homeland security is a vital national priority. Better security should not be sacrificed in the name of an emotional debate about outsourcing.

The homeland security "argument" against outsourcing and corporate inversion is a red herring. Instead of implementing protectionist measures that would harm the economy and impair national security, we should be exploiting the benefits of free trade to strengthen the nation.

Rising With the Tide

It is asking a lot to follow Kennan's advice and have the "courage and confidence" to steer the steady course. Nowhere is the challenge greater than in guiding the U.S. role in the world economy. A prescription of sticking to a steady diet of free trade may sound like an all-too-simplistic answer to a complex challenge, but it is most assuredly not. Speaking of war, Clausewitz wrote that in any conflict, "Even the simple is difficult." His maxim applies to global economic policy just as well. While free trade is the right answer, it is a tough task to remain true to its principles. There is, however, no better option. Free trade is a vital component of winning the long war.

The next steps will be difficult. The United States must rebuild the momentum for free trade agreements. America must promote the practices that will lead the developing world to grow their own economies and join as solid partners in the task of creating the global security regimes needed to fight terrorists. Finally, we must fight off the impulses of protectionism that appear to axiomatically accompany any downturn in the business cycle.

Chapter 7

The War of Ideas

On February 24, 2004, Colin Powell, the U.S. Secretary of State and former Chairman of the Joint Chiefs of Staff, traveled to Princeton, New Jersey. The occasion celebrated the 100th birthday of George Kennan. In a long, effusive speech Powell praised Kennan for many things, but most of all for his understanding of "human nature" and how the human heart shaped power politics, wars, and the fate of nations. Kennan's brilliance, Powell argued, was his ability to "get under the human skin of international politics, allowing us to see deeper into its very essence. Because George Kennan could see more deeply, he could foresee more accurately."[1] The capacity to grasp the human nature of conflict was, as Powell reminded us, the real genius of fighting the long war.

Powell reserved the remainder of his remarks to address the war on terrorism and, here too, he found Kennan uncannily relevant. "Few people ever find the right balance between the need to adopt a coldly objective attitude toward the world's danger, and the equally important need to allow oneself to embrace and to be guided by ideals. George Kennan found that balance, and so must we," the Secretary told the scions of Princeton. "We must acknowledge the power of ideas, and champion the nobility of democratic ideals, in our own times."[2] War is won in the minds of men.

Of the 8,000 words in Kennan's Long Telegram, most are reserved for a discussion of the sources of Soviet conduct. Kennan wanted Washington to understand the ideas that animated the Communists. Determining how to best to defeat an enemy always begins with understanding who they are and

President Dwight D. Eisenhower speaks to the world from the Voice of America microphones. (COURTESY OF THE VOICE OF AMERICA)

why they fight. It is a time-honored component of strategy that one most know his enemies in order to understand the enemies' strengths and weaknesses—and determine how to best defeat them.

There is, however, a second reason for understanding the enemy. All wars are wars of ideas. Both Kennan and Powell would readily have agreed with another conclusion in Clausewitz's *On War*—that defeat is in the mind of the enemy commander. Such reminders mattered less in the short war, when the enemy commander would know his defeat well when his armies were scattered, his generals in chains, and his land occupied. Defeat in the long war, however—in which a climactic battle might never be fought, and where indeed armies might never fight—could mean something very different.

Winning the long war is all about winning the struggle of ideas, destroying the legitimacy of a competing ideology, and robbing the enemy of the support of the people. Such an effort implies some essential tasks: 1) understanding the enemy; 2) de-legitimizing its view of the world; 3) offering a credible alternative; and 4) demonstrating the will to prevail in the long conflict. A strategy of security, economic growth, and the preservation of civil society satisfies the last two of these tasks, but the strategy for a long war also has to address the first two: Long war strategy has to understand the enemy and do battle with its ideas. In large part, this was the important message Kennan hoped to convey in the Long Telegram. It was a message that Powell heard loud and clear more than fifty years later when he helped craft strategy for the global war on terrorism.

The Enemy of Mankind

Terrorists are the enemy of all humanity. One of the difficulties of this long war is that we may not always know who they are. Aum Shinrikyo will always serve as a cautious *aide memoire* that in this conflict new foes may rise up against us, perhaps without warning or reason. However, in the current campaign against transnational terrorism there is one present and implacable enemy that cannot be ignored—an evil that must be understood and discredited.

At the root of the current wave of violence against the United States and its allies is a blasphemous interpretation of religion, which sanctions the killing of Americans—and citizens of all nations and religions, even moderate and Orthodox Muslims who do not agree with the radicalization of their religion. Religious extremists (and the allies they have found among secular, radical Arab-nationalist movements) not only justify the murder and maiming of civilians, they glorify suicide bombings and other terror tactics.[3] There appears to be no limit to their appetite for violence and the murder of innocents. They have tried to obtain and use weapons of mass destruction and they will likely continue to do so until they succeed or they are stopped.

The Nature of Evil

The terrorist interpretation of Islam is both universal and totalitarian. It brooks no argument and tolerates no differences—neither within the Realm of Islam (known as *Dar al-Islam*) nor in the rest of the world (known as the Realm of War, or *Dar ul-Harb*). Just as Nazism, Japanese militarism, and Soviet communism were inimical to the values of Western democracy in general—and to American values in particular—so, too, are the values of the totalitarian Islamists who inspired al-Qaeda, the Taliban, Hezbollah, Hamas, and other organizations of mass murder.

These voices are not practicing Islam—they are perverting it. As Angelo Codevilla wrote, "Murderous heresies arise as revolutionary movements. They take one, or more, of the faith's central tenets and twist it into a warrant for overthrowing the norms and practices first of the ordinary faithful, then of mankind. This kind of heresy sets itself apart by entitling the heretics to do whatever they want. The heretics…slip the bounds of orthodoxy and endow themselves with boundless, revolutionary discretion."[4] Radical Islam is not terrorism in the name of religion; it is terrorism hiding behind a mask of religion.

The main perpetrators of anti-American and anti-Western jihad today are the radical Wahhabi/Salafi sects and their twentieth century mutations: The Muslim Brotherhood (which was founded in 1929 by an Egyptian, Hassan al Banna) and Jamaat-i Islami (started by Maulana Sayyid Abul-Ala Mawdudi in Pakistan in 1941). These are also extremist elements of Shia Islam, supported by the radical factions of the Iranian government.[5]

Why They Fight

Why these groups have embraced terrorism as their weapon of choice has been the subject of endless academic debates. In Europe, as in the American left, policy analyses of the root causes of terrorism range from neo-Marxist (exploitation) to economic determinism, and from "victimology" and anti-imperialism to "Orientalism," a pejorative thrown out by the late Edward Said to denote what he considered the inadequate, misguided, and value-laden Western scholarship of the Middle East.[6] Thus, the notion of a "war" on terrorism is derided, and policy prescriptions for responses to terrorist attacks range from rejecting violence to more economic development and health care to promoting the European Union constitution and addressing the Arab–Israeli conflict.[7]

The origins of terrorism, however, spring from the realm of ideas, not the material world. Poverty, frustration, and humiliation are not the driving forces behind militant extremists: Ideology is. This is nothing new. The origins of long wars are often found in evil ideas. Karl Marx's *Communist Manifesto*, Adolf Hitler's *Mein Kampf*, and V.I. Lenin's *What Is to Be Done?* were all about ideas. The spread of those ideas fueled the movements they spawned and brought hundreds of millions of people under their sway, leading their millions of victims to misery.

Bin Laden's brand of terrorism has deep ideological roots, particularly in Wahhabism, the most fundamentalist interpretation of Sunni Islam. These roots date back to the very beginning of Islamic history and the Khariji sect

The battle for hearts and minds during the Cold War: a rope jumping session at the Thanh Haf Orphanage near Nah Trang, South Vietnam, April 1968. (COURTESY OF THE U.S. AIR FORCE)

in the eighth century A.D.[8] The Khariji sect was responsible for killing of Ali bin Abu Talib, the fourth Caliph and the Prophet Muhammad's cousin, adopted son, and son-in-law—generating a split in the faith, which later became the Sunni/Shia schism.[9] Khariji Islam, and the teachings of a fourteenth century Muslim scholar, Ibn Taymiyya (who justified the killing of Muslim rulers considered insufficiently pious), were both theologically extreme. The two have reincarnated into the Saudi state's religious ideology, Wahhabism, which was developed by Abdul Wahhab in the Arabian Peninsula in the eighteenth century. Today, Ibn Taymiyya is particularly popular with al-Qaeda leadership.

The Ibn Saud tribe has created a political–religious alliance with Abdul Wahhab and his tribe and has appropriated his teachings. Wahhabism became the ideological justification for launching a self-proclaimed jihad and subjugating other Muslims of the Arabian Peninsula during the eighteenth century. This culminated in a war against the Ottoman Sultan, the Caliph himself,

Osama Bin Laden propaganda poster found in Eastern Afghanistan, January 14, 2002. (COURTESY OF THE U.S. DEPARTMENT OF DEFENSE)

under British imperial tutelage from the late nineteenth to early twentieth centuries. Moreover, Wahhabi jihad, which justifies the murder of other Muslims and the plunder of their caravans and cities, provided perfect legitimacy for the Ibn Saud extended family business of tribal raiding. The combination of extreme Wahhabist ideology and the violence and determination of Ibn Saud overwhelmed the non-Wahhabi Muslim elements of the Arabian Peninsula. The region was almost cleansed of non-Wahhabi Muslims during the Wahhabi conquests in the nineteenth and early twentieth centuries. The Wahhabi doctrine also supplanted the traditional respect for "People of the Book" (Jews and Christians), declaring jihad against them and expelling them from the Arabian Peninsula as well.[10]

By the 1830s, Wahhabism had spread to the Indian subcontinent. In the early twentieth century, with British support, it overthrew Ottoman domination of the Middle East. The Saudi kingdom shifted its foreign patronage from the British Empire to the U.S. in the 1930s and 1940s. In the 1970s and 1980s, boosted by oil wealth and a tactical alliance with Washington, Wahhabism launched a global challenge to mainstream Islam and to the Soviet domination of Afghanistan, attempting to spearhead jihad against the Soviets in that country, which in fact was fought by traditional Sunni Afghans. With complacent and non-comprehending U.S. administrations, Wahhabism went on to spawn global terrorist movements backed by oil power and oil money.[11]

The xenophobic, extremist ideology of the Kharijis and Wahhabis developed new manifestations in the modern era with the Muslim Brotherhood (1929) and the Jama'at ul-Islam movement (1941) in today's Pakistan, inspired by Maulana Mawdudi. The combination of radical Wahhabism, the Muslim Brotherhood, and the followers of Maulana Mawdudi gave birth to al-Qaeda, as well as to other Islamic terrorist organizations. All of these groups—the Khariji in early Islam, the Wahhabis beginning in the eighteenth century, the Muslim Brotherhood, and the followers of Maulana Mawdudi—have two totalitarian characteristics in common. First, they draw a strict line between themselves and all other Muslims, who are then labeled as unbelievers and designated targets to be converted or killed. The second distinction is between the Islamic and non-Islamic worlds—the Land of Islam (*Dar al-Islam*) and the Land of War (*Dar ul-Harb*), which ultimately needs to be converted and subjugated.

Fanatics such as Ayman al-Zawahiri (leader of the Egyptian Islamic Jihad organization) and 9/11 hijacker Mohammed Atef were both loyal Osama bin

Laden deputies. Zawahiri's Egyptian Islamic Jihad assassinated President Anwar el-Sadat in 1981 for concluding a peace with Israel and being "un-Islamic." The Egyptian Islamic Jihad and al-Qaeda formally merged in 1998 to create the World Islamic Front for Jihad Against Jews and Crusaders.[12] A crusader, of course, is an Islamist code word for Christians and for any Western presence in the Middle East—in particular, the U.S. military and energy industry support operations in Saudi Arabia.

Wahhabi-influenced and -funded groups include Hamas; the Egyptian Islamic Jihad (Gama'at al-Islamiyya); the Pakistan-based terrorist organizations that are now recruiting for resumption of jihad in Afghanistan, massacring Shias in Pakistan, and attacking Kashmir; the Chechen Wahhabi faction led by Shamil Basaev; the Islamic Front of Uzbekistan, which was connected to bin Laden and fought with al-Qaeda in Afghanistan; Jama'at Islamiya of Indonesia, led by Muhammad Bakr El Bashir; and many others.[13]

Under the Banner of Jihad

The incitement of Muslims to hatred and violence, the plotting, and the killing are all being done under the banner of jihad—Holy War. The word jihad has two main connotations: that of personal self-improvement (the greater jihad) and of armed warfare against unbelievers (the lesser jihad).[14] Traditional Muslims do not recognize military jihad to be legitimate unless it is called by a *khilafa* (caliphate) and fought between regular armies according to specific rules, including exemption of noncombatants from attack. Some argue that as the Caliphate no longer exists, therefore there can be no jihad. Others advocate defensive jihad waged by Muslim states against armed aggressors who prevent Muslims from practicing their religion, but still condemn the killing of civilians.

To close the gap between existing Islamic law and their own desire to wage terror, the Wahhabis, followers of the Muslim Brotherhood, and the Pakistani Jammat i-Islami argued that, given the power and extent of the rule of the unbelievers, jihad can and should be waged by revolutionary means. These include militias and irregular forces utilizing terrorist tactics. This entire concept remains a fratricidal and dangerous heresy in traditional Sunni Islam. Nevertheless, it succeeded in generating an appreciative echo among Shia Muslims in Lebanon and Iran, where religion is suffused with a cult of death and sacrifice.[15]

Westerners often feed the perception of religious war by carelessly using the term jihad. Although they intend this to be a pejorative description of terrorists every time they use it, they are merely clothing their enemy with the robes of religious sanctity. The terrorists know this well.

Extremist clerics and terrorist leaders advocate the murder of innocent civilians and suicide bombings in the prosecution of jihad—notwithstanding the glaring contradiction between this practice and the traditional conception of jihad as waged by Muslim armies. Once again, the innovation came from the "modernist" views of the Wahhabis and Sayyid Qutb (who was executed for conspiracy to overthrow the Gamal Abd el-Nasser regime in 1966). It was Qutb who ruled, after Ibn Taymiyya, that not only infidels, but also "not sufficiently Islamic" Arab rulers, whom he labeled as equivalent to *kuffar* (unbelievers), should be killed. Thus, violence is sanctioned against those Muslims who do not accept Islamist ideology. This premise was used to justify the 1952 killing of King Abdallah of Jordan, grandfather of the late King Hussein (and great-grandfather of King Abdallah II, the current monarch), by the Muslim Brotherhood. Qutb and Maulana Mawdudi have influenced terrorists to declare that all Americans, British, Australians, Israelis, etc., are "combatants" and therefore legitimate enemies, or that all Americans pay taxes to support the armed forces and are therefore legitimate targets.

The essence of the conflict is this: "The Americans are fighting so they can live and enjoy the material things of life," said Mohammad Hussein Mostassed, a Taliban official, "but we are fighting so we can die in the cause of God."[16] This motif infuses the rhetoric of jihadis in Afghanistan, Madrid, Chechnya, Gaza, and Kashmir. It also inspires the slaughter of "black-skinned indigenous animists and Christians" by the government-backed, Arabic-speaking radical Islamist Janjiweed militia of the Sudan. The terrorists do not lack for targets.

Terrorist Strategy

The terrorists have their own version of Clausewitz. They too have strategies of ends, ways, and means. Their end is to attain total domination of the Islamic religion and over Islamic politics and states. The goal is the establishment of a Caliphate—a militarist, nuclear-armed, global Muslim state, strictly governed by the Sharia law. The purpose of this Muslim super-state is to engage in jihad with the rest of the world in order to convert it to Islam. The ultimate goal, then, is a global Islamic religious government. This is an alternative view to globalization based on free markets, tolerance, and diversity promoted by proponents of global institutions and norm-based international politics.

Bringing down moderate and pro-Western regimes in the Islamic world and replacing them with dictatorships is an interim objective of the jihadi movement. The terrorists have given themselves carte blanche to repress and kill those who challenge their political interpretations of the Qur'an and Hadith (oral commentaries of the Prophet). Islamic jurisprudence, and plural-ist, moderate, and secular Islamic ideas, leaders, and regimes are under threat.

The Word and the Sword

Terrorist strategy also is animated by ways and means. The physical instru-ments of terrorism are well-known, but the enemy has also turned words into weapons. Sheikh Yussuf Al-Qaradhawi, who resides in Qatar and runs a mas-sive outreach program on television and the Internet, heads the Muslim Brotherhood. In concert with many radical religious authorities, he has adju-dicated that Islamic law permits suicide bombings ("martyrdom operations").

In truth, many traditional Sunnis do not accept this point of view, since Islam abhors suicide under any conditions. Militant Sunnis still use this rea-soning to justify suicide bombings, and the intimidation and silence of those who disagree with them. Some of these militants include: Qaradhawi; Sheikh Mohammed al-Sayed Tantawi (the 43rd sheikh of Al Azhar Mosque in Egypt—the primary center of Sunni learning—who was appointed by Presi-dent Hosni Mubarak); and Sheikh Ahmad Kuftaro (the Grand Mufti of Syria).

The fact that their ideas are illegitimate, however, has not slowed the ter-rorist call to arms. A great number of radical preachers and terrorist ringlead-ers and their supporters have abused the freedoms found in the West to pro-mote radical causes. Western legal systems fail to see that for terrorists, first comes the jihad of the tongue, then that of the purse, and finally that of the sword, which is supreme. Thus, jihad represents a continuum of action, not a single criminal act—a concept beyond Western jurisprudence and Western jurists' understanding. The career of Abdurrahman Alamoudi, former Execu-tive Director of the American Muslim Council and a former U.S. Depart-ment of State "goodwill ambassador" to the Muslim countries offers a case in point. He has consistently and publicly called for support of the terrorist organizations Hamas and Hezbollah. Alamondi defended Hamas leader Musa Abu Marzuk, who was arrested by the FBI in 1995 and subsequently expelled from the United States. Alamoudi's organization also arranged for fundraising visits for radical Islamic organizations such as Egypt's Muslim Brotherhood.[17] Until 2004, little has been done to disrupt these networks of mosque-based "charities," which fund terrorist activities.[18]

There is a simple reason why the hijacking of Islam has brought terror to our doorstep. The voices of terrorism are being heard around the world. And people are listening. Anti-Americanism is predominant in the Muslim world. As a 2002 Gallup poll has shown, large majorities in the Islamic world (more than 80 percent), from Morocco to Indonesia, are strongly anti-American. They believe that the wars in Afghanistan and Iraq were unjustified and they maintain that Arabs did not carry out the 9/11 terrorist attacks.[19] The poll indicates that there is a large gap between perceptions of reality in the Islamic world and those of the West.

Battling Bad Ideas

The United States has no choice but to engage in a war of ideas. We have been attacked and are continually attacked every day. The war of ideas must be joined and fought. In the struggle of ideas, failure is not an option. Neutralizing the militant ideology fueling terrorism is a key factor if the world—and moderate Islam—are to succeed in the current conflict.

It is encouraging that the first statements of U.S. strategy that came out after the 9/11 attacks committed the nation to an ideological battle as well as a contest of military force and diplomacy. The 2002 *National Security Strategy* calls for:

- Using the full influence of the United States and working closely with allies and friends to make clear that all acts of terrorism are illegitimate so that terrorism will be viewed in the same light as slavery, piracy, or genocide—behavior that no respectable government can condone or support, and which all must oppose;
- Supporting moderate and modern governments, especially in the Muslim world, to ensure that the conditions and ideologies that promote terrorism do not find fertile ground in any nation;
- Diminishing the underlying conditions that spawn terrorism by enlisting the international community to focus its efforts and resources on areas most at risk; and

- Using effective public diplomacy to promote the free flow of information and ideas to kindle the hopes and aspirations of freedom of
  those in societies that are ruled by global terrorism's sponsors.[20]

The bad news is that U.S. public diplomacy has been ineffective and
unimaginative. The State Department hired a few Arabic speakers to handle
media, and produced expensive TV commercials for Muslim countries hail-
ing religious tolerance toward moderate Muslims and the United States.
Commendable as such efforts might be, they are carried out on too small a
scale to make a difference, and are too remote from real problems. Traditional public diplomacy, aimed at winning the media and elite opinion, needs to
be supplemented by more innovative approaches, ones that combine public
diplomacy as well as politically overt action (democracy promotion, education reform) and covert action—all aimed at discrediting terrorism.

In fighting the battle to loosen terrorism's grip on the world, the United
States need not reinvent the wheel. Credible spiritual and political alternatives
to Islamist ideology already exist within the traditional Islamic global community, or *umma*—including the Middle East, South and Southeast Asia, Central Asia, and in the Muslim immigrant communities around the world.

It is highly significant that radical Islamists have thus far failed to obtain
majority popular support even in the most traditional Muslim countries.
Only Saudi Arabia, Afghanistan (behind the iron veil of the Taliban), and
Sudan (under the rule of Islamists), can be described as exclusively Sharia
states. Except for Saudi Arabia, the rest of the Gulf states maintain Sharia for
personal and family law alongside Western commercial, civil, and criminal
law. Qatar, for example, although it nominally maintains the Wahhabi or
"reformed" Sharia as its official law, does not permit rulings of Sharia judges
to take precedence over those based on Western law. Oman, which maintains
a form of extremely conservative Sharia, also keeps Sharia separate from commercial, civil, and criminal law. This is, in fact, the model in place throughout the Islamic world, except in a number of provinces in Pakistan, Nigeria,
and Malaysia, which have come under Islamist control in recent years due to
the steady buildup of well-funded Wahhabi educational programs, institutions, and campaigns led by Wahhabi religious leaders with a definite mission
to spread Sharia. Everywhere else (except in secularized Turkey), Sharia and
Western legal models coexist.

The threat to states, as well as Muslim diaspora communities in countries throughout the world, is penetration of the institutions of worship and

education by Wahhabi-directed organizations, missionaries, and funding. *These ways and means are the taproot of terrorism.* The results are known: radical mosques serving as safe havens and religious sanctuaries for the planners of 9/11 and for the recruitment of future generations of terrorists. Clausewitz called this the enemy's "center of gravity," a concept he wrote about extensively in *On War*. The center of gravity represented the hub of the wheel, the key source of power that enabled the enemy to act. In conventional war, the center of gravity might be a certain military unit or leader; in shadow war it could be some other animating feature. For the terrorists, it is their ability to harness the institutions of Islam to plan, organize, prepare, and kill.

The Need for Religious Pluralism

The problem with the war of ideas is that even after 9/11, the terrorist center of gravity remains largely unthreatened. Today, the voices of traditional, moderate Islam and of liberal secularism inside the Islamic world are seldom heard. Extremists dominate the Islamic discourse. While it is laudable that the Saudi state claims to have taken some steps to curb terrorist funding in the aftermath of al-Qaeda terrorist attacks in the kingdom, and some religious authorities in Saudi Arabia were enticed by the state to distance themselves from bin Laden's suicide attacks, Saudi Arabia continues massive funding of the global Wahhabi network of mosques and madrassas (religious schools). This infrastructure has been providing an enabling environment for jihad for at least 25 years.

The much-advertised calls for moderation in Saudi Arabia must be taken in context. The House of Saud is well aware that the United States, and the West in general, may justly lay the blame for support of terrorism upon a number of prominent individuals and "charities" operating freely within the kingdom. For example, the wealthy Muwafaq Foundation, run by prominent Saudi businessman Yasin al-Qadi and the bin Mahfouz family, has been accused of channeling funds to terrorists. According to the *New York Times*, this charity, which works openly in Saudi Arabia and the Gulf states, has been placed on the U.S. Department of State's list of terrorism-sponsoring organizations.[21] Charitable entities such as the Muwafaq Foundation have funded extremism, including those who have long been linked with terrorist masterminds—and continue to do so even in the aftermath of the September 11 attacks.[22] Other example of international charities with alleged terrorist links are Moslem World League, the World Association of Muslim Youth, the International Islamic Relief Organization, and al-Haramain.[23]

The majority of Muslims around the world may not support terrorism against the United States. Their voices, however, are not heard. Neither is the voice of another important minority—that of progressive liberals, who recognize the need to integrate their countries into the global community, which shares democratic and human rights values and recognizes that a sophisticated market economy is the most viable pathway toward economic development and increased living standards.

Media, Education, and Political Mythology in the Islamic World

Lack of education for tolerance, pluralism, human rights, and gender equality may be the Achilles' heel of Greater Middle Eastern and South Asian societies. Even though radicals blast "apostates" and "non-believers" (including Christians, Hindus, Buddhists, and Jews) for everything they consider to be wrong in the world, most practicing Muslims do not read classical Arabic, and therefore cannot read the original Qur'an. In addition, tradition dictates that the faithful are dependent upon clerics and the media for interpretation of the scriptures.

It is the governments, especially their information/propaganda ministries, the mosques, and the media, which largely determine the attitude of the "street" by issuing guidance to the muftis, editors, and censors. Because many preachers, journalists, and editors in the Muslim world are either government employees or work within the narrow confines of state censorship, they cannot openly criticize their domestic regimes or challenge the dogmas of Islam. Still, many of them are aware of the economic backwardness, educational failures, and lack of human rights that characterize their respective societies.[24] They air their frustrations in the only fashion allowed: by attacking the United States, the West, and Israel—and their alleged conspiracies against the Muslim world. They support jihad against the West, fanning the flames of terrorist activities.

Most government-sponsored and opposition media in the Islamic world were vehemently anti-American before 9/11. However, the reaction of the media to the attacks brought their anti-U.S. and anti-Western bias into sharp focus. Many columnists proceeded to lay the blame on everyone but the real culprit. Samir Atallah, a columnist for the London-based *Al-Sharq Al-Awsat* wrote, "I have a sneaking suspicion that George W. Bush was involved in the operation...as well as Colin Powell.... Every George Bush in the family has his own world war."[25] The journalist went on to claim that President Bush had little popular support before 9/11, but received bipartisan backing thereafter.

The journalists take their cues from higher ups: In the aftermath of the May 1, 2004, attack on Western workers for the oil industry in the Red Sea port of Yanbu, Crown Prince Abdullah of Saudi Arabia claimed that he is 95 percent sure that Zionists were behind the attack.[26] After al-Qaeda claimed responsibility for the Yanbu operation and a similar attack in Dhahran almost one month later (in which 22 Westerners were murdered),[27] he refrained from repeating such claims.

As if these conspiracy theories were not enough, some Arab media also suggested that U.S. militias may have committed the 9/11 attack by hacking into air traffic control computers,[28] or that perhaps it was Japan—in revenge for the bombings of Hiroshima and Nagasaki,[29] or Russia, China, or anonymous opponents of globalization who did it.[30] Khalid Amayreh, a Palestinian Islamist journalist, published an article in the London-based *Palestine Times*, entitled "Why I Hate America." He writes, "I do hate it (the American government) so really, so deeply and yes, so rightly.... America is the all-powerful devil that spreads oppression and death.... America is the tyrant, a global dictatorship that robs hundreds of millions of Arabs and Muslims of their right to freely elect their government because corporate America dreads the outcome of democracy in the Muslim world.... It is almost impossible for me, as indeed is the case for most Palestinians, Arabs, or Muslims, not to hate America so much."[31]

The Hamas terrorist organization's weekly publication went so far as to praise the anthrax attack on America, and to advocate wreaking further damage by introducing anthrax bacteria into the U.S. water supply.[32] However, the problem of anti-American influence in the Muslim world—and even in the United States—does not start with the adults who read newspapers. Unfortunately, it is inculcated much earlier—at the elementary and secondary school level.[33]

Poverty remains extreme throughout the Islamic world. Religious schools, or madrassas, are often the only sources of free education for the poor. However, many of these schools often fail to teach marketable skills, such as math and computers, but are instead focused on arms training and religious hate indoctrination. Tens of thousands of mosques and madrassas throughout the Islamic world and the West have been overtaken by radical Islamists and turned into schools for terrorists, funded directly or indirectly by nationals and foundations from Saudi Arabia and the Gulf states. The massive involvement of Saudi charities in funding terrorist education (including in the United States) is well known and amply documented.[34]

The phenomenon is most pronounced in the Sunni world, but applies to the Shiites in Iran and Lebanon as well.[35] In Pakistan, the madrassas were turned into factories to prepare "holy warriors" to fight first against the Soviets in Afghanistan, and later against the Indians in Kashmir. Today, the jihad seminaries also target "battlefronts" in the United States, Central Asia, Turkey, Russia, and Israel by sending recruits to fight far and wide. In April 2001, the Pakistani government acknowledged that the schools had become a serious security threat, but no decisive action was taken to stop their practices. In December 2001, Pakistan's President Pervez Musharraf finally ordered the former interior minister to investigate the madrassas' connection with the Taliban—with no significant results.[36]

During the last two decades, between 15,000 to 25,000 madrassas in Pakistan alone have churned out 4 million alumni of these terrorism training grounds, and between 500,000 to one million students are currently in their classrooms, according to veteran journalist Arnaud de Borchgrave, who traveled in Pakistan to study the phenomenon.[37] Dar-al Ulum Haqqania (University for Education of Truth) in Akora Khatak counts nine out of ten of the Taliban leaders among its alumni.[38] According to Arasiab Khattak, chairman of the Human Rights Commission of Pakistan, "The madrassas indulge in brainwashing on a large scale, of the young children and those in their early teens."[39]

Nor is the penetration of educational institutions a problem only for the greater Middle East. In the fall of 2003, the United States expelled over a dozen Saudi clerics and propagandists, traveling on Saudi diplomatic passports, for engaging in Wahhabi Islamist "education" in a religious college in Northern Virginia (the Institute of Islamic and Arabic Studies). The institute trained scores of members of the U.S. armed forces to be chaplains.[40] Two similar institutes that train U.S. military and prison clergy are the American Muslim Armed Forces and Veteran Affairs Council (which Alamoudi founded) and the Islamic Society of North America (ISNA) and its Graduate School of Islamic Social Sciences. These institutions have ties to Saudi Wahhabi operatives, including Alamoudi, who served as ISNA's regional representative.[41] These activities are a terrorist time bomb waiting to explode. The education factor, much like the prolific anti-American media, will prove to be a challenge in the war of ideas, but this does not suggest that the fight is unwinnable.

Europe shares America's problem. Recently several British Islamic officials complained that the mosques in that country have lost control over teaching religion to youngsters. Leading British Muslims decried the proliferation of jihadi extra-curricular instruction, which is used, as in from Pakistan to Lebanon, to recruit terrorists. Muslim officials also admitted that "volunteers" enter Britain from the Middle East to engage in brainwashing the youth.[42] Muslim leaders in the United Kingdom lobbied the Cabinet to forbid the "weekend imams" to jet in from the Persian Gulf to deliver incendiary sermons and radical religious training. They also requested that only British Muslim clerics engage in education, while banning extremist religious instructors who promote terrorism.[43]

Winning Hearts and Minds

The key to overcoming the rhetoric and practice of terrorism justified as religion is to empower moderate Muslims and secularists who consider Islam a personal religion, and Islamists who strive for the creation of a Caliphate and world domination. Sheikh Muhammad Hisham Kabbani, Chairman of the Islamic Supreme Council of America and a profound authority in Islamic law, is promoting Islam that is tolerant, engaged in genuine dialogue with other faiths, and opposed to violence.[44]

Sheikh Abdul Hadi Palazzi, the Secretary General of the Italian Muslim Association, is one of the most coherent critics of the radicals. He provides learned criticism of the radical interpretations of Islam.[45] In addition to Sheikh Hadi Palazzi, there are many others calling for co-existence and mutual respects inside various Islamic communities and between religions, for observance of democratic norms, and for respect of human rights.

The Ibn Khaldoun Society, led by Dr. Fatima Mernissi of Morocco, is calling upon the West to cease supporting backward governments in the Arab world that violate the rights of women and minorities. While sometimes critical of Western policy towards the Middle East, Dr. Mernissi a unique perspective on the Islamic world as seen from inside, and has become an outspoken advocate of women's rights in the Muslim world.[46]

A Canadian of South Asian origin, Irshad Manji, author of *The Trouble with Islam*, has exposed the suffocating atmosphere in Islamic educational institutions and strongly advocates a significant change in the status of women in the Muslim world, including the use of micro-loans to allow women to start small businesses, thus taking a first step toward liberating themselves and their families from chattel status within their societies.[47] Others, such as Ibn

Warraq, call for reconciling Islam with the modern world, and have publicized stories of Muslims who chose to leave their religion—a "sin," which in some places even today can be punishable by death.[48]

Professor Muqtedar Khan termed the 9/11 attacks "a horrible scar on the history of our religion," while calling upon Muslims "to remember the verses in the Qur'an in which Allah says in unequivocal terms that to kill an innocent being is like killing humanity itself." Khan reminded his fellow Muslims that Israel treats its one million Arab citizens with greater respect and dignity than most Arab nations show to their own people, and he pointed out the double standard of the Islamic world, which remains silent when fellow Muslims are murdered or treated harshly by the regimes of Islamic countries: Iraqi Kurds, the Bengalis under Pakistani rule, or the Afghans under the Taliban.[49]

Abd al-Hamid al-Ansari, dean of the faculty of Islamic Law at the University of Qatar and a prominent Islamic scholar, has called for deep changes in school curricula, as well as educational and media reform, to oppose the current trend toward justifying and training for terrorism. Al-Ansari and others compare today's radicals with the ancient terrorist sect of Khariji, which is blamed for the death of the imam Ali, the son-in-law of the Prophet Muhammad and which pioneered the political killing of Muslims who were considered heretics. Professor al-Ansari has openly criticized the Al-Jazeera satellite TV channel for opening the airwaves to al-Qaeda supporters, Taliban fans, bin Laden loyalists, and other propagandists of violence. He believes that the terrorism in the prevailing culture is "rooted in the minds of those who suffered from a closed education that leaves no room for pluralism."[50]

The Islamic world, however, is still waiting for the emergence of a robust liberal intellectual movement and media, which would promote toleration and ask the difficult questions in a language that key Islamic target audiences, including traditional believing Muslims, can appreciate and understand. Just as Solidarity in Poland and Charter 77 in then-Czechoslovakia benefited from Western assistance and support, reformers in the Muslim world are awaiting a helping hand from the free world. Yet before we can help, we need to understand what we are doing and who we are talking to.

It is totally erroneous to view the Muslim world, and particularly the Middle East, as a single monolith of "Arabs" or "Muslims."[51] The majority of the world's Muslims reside in Indonesia, Pakistan, and Bangladesh—not in the Arab countries. Writers and broadcasters must differentiate target audiences by their levels of education and religious observance. The Middle East is home to many ethnic groups, languages, religions, and denominations—from Assyrians to Zoroastrians—who are oppressed.

According to a Freedom House report, seven out of ten of the least-free countries in the world are predominantly Islamic. These are: Afghanistan (under the Taliban), Iraq (under Saddam Hussein), Libya, Saudi Arabia, Sudan, Syria, and Turkmenistan. They achieved Freedom House's lowest rating of "unfree" in a 2001 global survey of political rights and civil liberties.[52] Thus, radical Islamism or Arab nationalist/socialist ideology (in the case of Libya and Syria) are a driving force behind oppression in this century.

The Islamic world is socially and economically diverse. In designing communications strategies and messages, this must be kept in mind, as well as the fact that many of these groups have different (often competing) interests. It is in America's interest to promote debate and plurality of opinions, and to appeal to those who are likely to receive and disseminate U.S. messages.

Among the primary audiences for U.S. public diplomacy and information should be:

Women. The role of women and discrimination against them in Islamic societies is a well-known phenomenon, one that has tremendous potential for furthering the debate about the nature of Muslim societies, the role of Sharia, the necessity of reform, and the constitutional rights and underpinnings of Islamic states. After all, women comprise half of these societies, but they generally suffer from inequality and oppression. Given the opportunity, they may emerge as the best allies of those who support freedom. As mothers, they influence the next generations of Muslims. For example, the majority of women passionately hated the Taliban regime in Afghanistan, and many express their disapproval of the religious dictatorship in Iran.

The Business and Entrepreneurial Class. The business community has little influence in many Muslim countries, especially in the most authoritarian ones, where power belongs to the royal families and military rulers. Chambers of Commerce, businesspeople, and entrepreneurs are mired in corruption, over-regulation, and extortion by officials. The Heritage Foundation's *Index of Economic Freedom* puts many Islamic countries in the category of "mostly unfree."[53] Elevating considerations of economic reform in the decision making process may encourage governments to curb radical activities.

Ethnic Minorities and Guest Workers. In many countries of the Middle East, ethnic minorities are denied linguistic, cultural, and religious rights. For example, the Berbers in Algeria, Tunisia, and Morocco have fought for their rights—to no avail—for decades. The Kurds have been brutally persecuted in

Iraq and Iran. Over 20 million Shi'a Turkic Iranians are indistinguishable from their brethren in Azerbaijan, but are denied linguistic and cultural autonomy, as are the Turkmen who live in Iran and Iraq.

Intelligentsia and the Artistic Community. The ability to dream, write, publish, and express oneself in art and film is cherished among intellectuals. U.S. and Western policies against censorship and in favor of freedom of expression may also strengthen dissent and provoke debate about modernization, including questioning and redefining the role of Islam in a modern state as a private religious practice, not a totalitarian and oppressive doctrine.

Youth. Because the economies of most Islamic countries (with the exception of Malaysia) are stagnant and their populations continue to grow rapidly, the quality of life in many of these lands deteriorates from year to year. Often, youth in these countries are the most frustrated with the status quo, specifically the corruption and lack of popular participation in government and politics. In some countries, such as Pakistan, Central Asia, and the Arabian peninsula, young people easily fall prey to totalitarian Islamic preachers. However, in Iran, the youth are the ones who strive for a chance to pursue a meaningful career and to access the knowledge and the opportunities offered by the globalizing world. These are tomorrow's leaders for change, whether through peaceful evolution or violent revolution. The terrorists understand the importance of gaining the allegiance of the youth, and actively recruit their cadres, including terrorists and suicide bombers, from among the madrassa students. Moderate Muslims and the West have to beat them at their own game.

The Next Steps

The 9/11 attacks on the United States were a clarion call to engage in battle for the hearts and minds of the peoples of the Middle East, Central Asia, the Indian subcontinent, and Southeast Asia; however, it is now three years after 9/11 and the West has yet heard the call. The war of ideas will require presidential leadership and a comprehensive strategy, including the development and mobilization of area and linguistic expertise and a long-term investment of wealth and stamina, comparable to that of the Cold War. This consideration extends well beyond any U.S. war against Afghanistan or Iraq. To be victorious, knowledge of history, religion, languages, economics, and politics must be combined with operational political skills aimed at changing the opinion of elites and the broader public in key areas from Marrakesh to Mindanao.

Thus far, attempts within the Department of State, the Pentagon, and the White House to launch successful public affairs operations aimed at foreign audiences have lacked leadership, area skills, or intellectual heft. Unsurprisingly, these campaigns have met with limited success at best. Institutional capabilities and budgets were slashed in the aftermath of the Cold War, public servants with expertise retired, and the federal government rarely rewarded language and area expertise. Above all, no one expected that the United States Information Agency, which had a Cold War mission, would be so necessary once again—and so soon.

The creation of effective mechanisms to fight this war, the recruitment of personnel, and the formulation of key messages combined with their successful delivery to target audiences around the world are some of the greatest foreign policy challenges facing the U.S.

The United States should not go it alone. Some states will be more willing to work with America than others. This is an area in which coalition-building with the European Union, Russia, Turkey, and even with China and Japan, is feasible. Although the elements of civil society in some Muslim regions may for now be anti-American, it is important to develop indigenous institutions that can work with American bodies.

The war of ideas will aim to undermine and destroy the credibility of those who use and support the use of terrorism against the United States and its allies. The battle for hearts and minds is not a short-term campaign, but a protracted conflict that will take years, decades, and possibly generations. It should be guided by an integrated strategy of public diplomacy and politically overt and covert action, something that the United States has not attempted for half a century, ever since the early stages of the Cold War. This will be a campaign in the information and media battlefields, fought not against a state or a coalition of states, but against an array of radical organizations and the governments and sub-rosa institutions and networks supporting them.

The nature of the enemy, the spectrum of threats, and the environment in which the conflict is waged require that the war of ideas be conducted overtly when possible, and covertly when necessary. Al-Qaeda and other terrorist organizations operate by stealth. So do the funders who subsidize radical Islamic brainwashing in the guise of religious "education." The boards of madrassas do not post their curricula and audits on the Internet. Foreigners are not allowed to participate in religious seminars in Pakistan and the Gulf, where agent penetration is required. Regimes in Iran, Libya, and Syria do not welcome the U.S. Foreign Service officers with public diplomacy expertise who explain American values to their domestic audiences. Thus, the CIA's political action capabilities need to be rebuilt, or another agency capable of handling the job needs to be created.

During the Cold War, the United States cooperated with its allies in developing and waging the war of ideas against communism. Similarly, today's United States should reach out to the countries of Europe and beyond, including moderate segments in the greater Middle East (e.g., Turkey and Morocco) to cooperate in formulating and disseminating the ideas of moderate Islam and other non-threatening forms of personal faith, including secularism.

Although the U.S. Constitution prohibits the "establishment" of religion domestically, this does not apply abroad. Nor is this clause relevant to the implementation of U.S. foreign and security policy. Some believe that the United States should not pick and choose religious faiths. However, a distorted and hijacked "faith" that has turned into a threatening political ideology and a component of warfare needs to be dealt with—preferably *before* it acquires weapons of mass destruction. U.S.-funded programs should prioritize moderate Sufi and Ismaili Islam in their assistance programs; moderate schools of both Sunni and Shia; the Bahai faith; and universal and tolerant forms of Christianity, both indigenous to the region and those willing to expand there. The United States should support secularization of curricula in the Muslim world, the introduction of programs that teach tolerance and diversity, and the introduction of American studies and Holocaust studies into middle school, high school, and college curricula. America and its allies should actively promote the universal values of tolerance, human rights, gender and religious equality, and ideas of economic and personal freedom, secularism, and faiths indigenous to these troubled regions.

The main weapon of the United States in the battle of ideas should be truth— truth about America, the societies of the greater Middle East and South Asia, including their social problems, their rulers, and the terrorist leaders who prey on them. The truth should be disseminated through open channels where possible, and covertly where necessary, but the promotion of individual freedom and respect for other peoples' lives, faiths, and property must remain at the heart of the suggested strategy. The United States has to set the record straight about American achievements, values, and policies— including its protection of Muslims in Kuwait, Bosnia, Kosovo, and Afghanistan.[54]

We must formulate strategies to engage radicals and extremists who support terrorism, discredit their basic premises, and dismantle their organizational infrastructure. In the aftermath of the Cold War, the United States Information Agency, which was created to counter Communist propaganda, was collapsed into the U.S. Department of State. Many public diplomacy functions were dispersed throughout the regional units or integrated in the Public Diplomacy Bureau at the State Department. Many important initiatives, such as storefront libraries and book translation programs were cancelled or de-funded. International broadcasting suffered drastic cuts.

In a post-9/11 world, the State Department Arabic media initiatives, which brought from retirement a few Arabic-speaking former U.S. Ambassadors, and launched stolid, text-heavy Web sites, will simply not be enough.[55] The Middle Eastern Broadcast Network has turned out to be exceptionally slow to launch. Whereas the Voice of America got on the air in February 1942, three months after the attack on Pearl Harbor, the new Arabic radio network was not broadcasting even six months after the 9/11 attacks. The Arabic TV channel Al-Hurra was launched in 2004—three years after 9/11. Additionally, questions have been raised by international broadcasting professionals about the efficiency of editorial control over radio talent locally hired in the Muslim world.[56]

Leadership in the effort to win hearts and minds will require humility and realism, as well as the talents and skills of dedicated linguists, writers, editors, and public affairs and area experts. Changing hostile perceptions will not be easy.

The Administration must re-evaluate, revive, and upgrade its public diplomacy "tool box," as well as invent new and specific tools for fighting aggressive, anti-Western sentiment among fundamentalists. The overarching principle and the key to disarming an ideological enemy is changing the perception of the elite—through publications of new ideas in their languages, broadcasting, personal contacts and exchanges, and other means.

The dissemination of information within oppressed societies, countries, and targeted communities will be vital to ensure understanding both of where extreme Islam went wrong (in its advocacy of violence and terrorism) and what the West truly stands for. In order to do this, it will be necessary to expand funding for, and further develop, the Al-Hurra TV channel and possibly to launch privately owned channels aimed at Islamic audiences. Programming for Radio Sawa (Arabic) and Radio Farda (Farsi) as surrogate AM/FM broadcasting, similar to the short wave Radio Free Europe and Radio Liberty of the Cold War era should be improved and expanded. However, innovative approaches to cooperation with privately owned Muslim TV channels and radio stations and indigenous print media need to be developed beyond today's renting of airwaves.

The U.S. government and private foundations should expand the publication of books, journals, and newspapers that promote views opposing radical Islam and provide the truth about America—in languages of the greater Middle East and South and Southeast Asia. In the realm of education, diplomatic action should be initiated against the state-supported incitement to violence prevalent in mosques, education systems, and Islamist media under the banner of jihad. The State Department has to play a pro-active role in stopping hatred, which breeds terrorist violence. Demands should be made for Islamic states to reform educational systems and develop new curricula for both religious schools and colleges, as well as for public schools. Another beneficial change would be to expand inter- and intra-confessional religious dialogue, identifying and cooperating with moderate clerics. The United States and other states which would confront the spread of religious intolerance and incitement to violence should identify and recruit talent for the new war of ideas by utilizing the talents of people from the Islamic world residing in their countries.

The Banner of Freedom

In July 2004, Colin Powell celebrated another hero of the Cold War, George Marshall. Marshall, like Powell, had traded in an Army uniform and desk in the Pentagon for a desk at State Department headquarters in Foggy Bottom. Marshall's greatest achievement as Secretary—the Economic Recovery Plan for Europe (popularly known as the Marshall Plan)—proved to be one of the most decisive instruments of the Cold War. The Marshall Plan was an embodiment of the instruments Kennan had called for in the Long Telegram. It was more important than the economic aid it provided. In fact, Marshall Plan funds were only a fraction of the monies used to rebuild Europe. It was the "idea" of the Marshall Plan that proved most decisive—the idea of American commitment to an investment in democracy that wedded Europe and the United States together for the remainder of the Cold War. The Marshall plan proved, perhaps more than another American initiative, that ideas really mattered.

The plan was, as Powell noted in his speech at the opening of an exhibit crediting Marshall's achievement, a remarkable feat. There were lessons that could be learned. "The first," Powell contended, "is that the character of the solution to any problem has to fit the problem. If you've got a big problem, you need a big solution. If you've got a novel problem, you need a creative solution. George Marshall recognized that the Western democracies were in uncharted waters after World War II, with both dangers and opportunities ahead. He had a vision that was built to scale for the challenges of that moment in history. He wasn't afraid to think boldly. He was afraid of what would happen if we didn't think boldly."[57] Powell's advice could serve as well to describe the challenge facing America in the war of ideas. We know it is a struggle we must engage in. We know we don't have the instruments or the programs to do it right. We know we must act boldly—or the banner of freedom will never supplant the face of terrorism.

A New (Shorter) Long Telegram —Strategy for a New Century

Our effort to understand the challenge of crafting strategy for a long war took its inspiration from George Kennan's Long Telegram of 1946. As a final measure of analysis we have chosen to put it to the test of brevity. Thus, we provide here a summary of the ideas we have presented in *Winning the Long War*. We hope it serves as another reminder of the power of Kennan's brilliant strategic analysis presented over a half-century ago and its enduring relevance to the world we face today.

In view of recent events the following might be of interest.

Knowing the enemy and knowing yourself is the acme of strategy. Strategy is the secret to winning the long war. George F. Kennan understood that well as he scribbled the Long Telegram in his apartments at the Moscow Embassy. And so he wrote. He explained who the enemy was, who we are, and how we would win the long war.

We have tried to do the same.

Describing the enemy is perhaps a more formidable task than the one faced by Kennan. It is not that our enemy is inscrutable. In fact, the opposite is true. They are all too predictable. We know them. We know them well. They are old terrors with new names. They are those who will accept no dominion over men and women other than their own. Their message is the same old lie: Somehow the slaughter of innocents will redress social, political, cultural, or economic ills. They use the same old tools. They clothe lies in a veneer of religion, creed, or ideology. They pervert the instruments of the everyday world and turn them against us. Yet describing them is difficult because they wear no uniforms; they use the benefits of an open society to hide their faces; and they can rise up against us with little or no warning.

The world has always had to bear the burden of evil, yet this evil—the threat of transnational terrorism—merits special attention. Today our planet is united by networks that freely carry goods, services, peoples, and ideas. It is the source of our prosperity and the hope for ramping up the economies of the developing world. It must be preserved, even though it also provides the means for terrorists to turn themselves into world-class dangers. As long as we live in a globalized world, we will live with the potential for global terror.

We must also remember that we no longer live in a time in which only great powers can bring great powers to their knees. There are weapons that virtually any enemy can get hold of and, under the right circumstances, threaten tens of thousands of lives and cause hundreds of billions of dollars in damages.

Finally, we must take terrorists seriously because they are an enemy that will never leave us alone. They can't. They are our enemy not because we have attacked them, but because we exist—and our continued existence is the obstacle to their empires.

For these reasons, this is an enemy that cannot be ignored. We will always have to be vigilant; the sad truth is that such enemies are endemic to the modern world.

However, we also know that our enemy is not invincible. In fact, as long as we do not lose courage and confidence in ourselves, terrorists cannot win. They have limited resources. They cannot threaten us everywhere, all the time. They have few friends. The United States is

Two banks of lights pierce the New York City skyline in tribute to the fallen, March 14, 2002. (PHOTO BY KENN MANN COURTESY OF THE U.S. AIR FORCE)

far from alone in the war against terrorism. Other countries may disapprove of our methods and our foreign policy, but with few exceptions, nations recognize that transnational terrorism is a threat to them as well. Some may lack the capacity or will to engage the enemy with as much vigor as the United States, but the era when terrorists could freely transit the world without fear of interference or establish sanctuaries without threat of attack is over.

Because they are scattered among the nations of the earth, because they may be difficult to find, because others may come to take their place, this will likely be a long war. And winning the long war requires a long-war strategy—one that provides for security, economic growth, the protection of civil society, and the struggle of ideas.

Our advocacy for a long-war strategy is animated by the same reasoning by which Kennan argued we must approach the Cold War. This is a war that cannot be won on the battlefield. It can only be won by prevailing. Victory is occasioned by just being there. Long-war strategies are designed to sustain a nation for the long fight. Indeed, the goal is to grow and prosper, even as the enemy drifts into memory.

Long-war strategies begin with a good offense. The goal of the offense is to destroy that which makes the enemy formidable— its capacity to reach out across distances and mobilize people and resources. In short, victory means taking the "transnational" out of transnational terrorism. That will require destroying sanctuaries, incapacitating leaders, and crippling networks. We have argued that there are three critical enablers for long-war offense: good strategic intelligence, a solid base of military might, and the means for harnessing all the instruments of national power in the campaign to root out the terrorists' centers of gravity.

Strategies for the long war also require defense. In a world linked by global lifelines, some enemy will inevitably find a gap to slip through. There is no silver-bullet solution to stopping every terrorist threat. Simply throwing money at the problem is not the answer either. It did not work during the Cold War and it will not work here. A layered defense in which governments, the private sector, and citizens each fulfill their responsibilities is the only prudent course. There is still much work to be done in establishing these appropriate roles and linking them together into a true national homeland security system. That must be our primary effort.

Preserving both liberty and order is equally important to winning the long war. A strong civil society is all that sustains the will of a democratic people in a protracted conflict. We must fight hard and be free. Debates that frame our choices between civil liberties or security are offering us the wrong options. In a long war you need both. We must provide better tools for finding and stopping the terrorists among us; ones that do not endanger the foundations of a healthy civil society. We believe the Patriot Act is an example of the kind of instrument that successfully accomplishes this goal. The scrutiny given to this law, however, needs to be extended to *all* our domestic counterterrorism instruments. They must be efficient, effective, and appropriately applied.

Economic growth is equally vital for success. In this we face perhaps our greatest challenge. Sustaining long-term growth will depend on restraining both non-security–related mandatory *and* discretionary spending and using tax reform to unleash the full potential of the American economy. At the same time, we must aggressively pursue a free-trade agenda, ending our own protectionist practices and pushing others to follow suit. These are perhaps the toughest of tasks, but if we fail to undertake them, America may not have the stamina to sustain itself for the long fight.

Finally, we must be prepared to engage on the battlefield of ideas. Terrorists win when they can walk into any community (in nations rich and poor) and, unchallenged, seek out the downtrodden and disaffected, the poor and the poor in spirit. We have to break the nexus between the preachers of hate and their potential victims. In part, this must be done by drying up funding and prosecuting agitators. In other cases, the answer will be education reform and public diplomacy. Either way, the objective will be the same—to discredit the ideologies that feed terrorism. At the same time, the United States must continually make the case that democracy and free markets offer a credible alternative to extremism and repression. Finally, the United States must make clear that it will never retrench or retreat. The idea offensive must destroy any glimmer of hope among the terrorists that we will ever let them prevail in their fascist schemes.

Foremost, however, we must heed Kennan's most critical warning: "The greatest danger that can befall us...is that we shall allow ourselves to become like those with whom we are coping." We must retain the courage and confidence to remain true to what has made this nation great, to the values that make the idea of America worth defending. The banner that we must carry into every battle in the long war must read: "Freedom."

Appendix 1

The Long Telegram

861.00/2 - 2246: Telegram[1]

The Charge in the Soviet Union (Kennan) to the Secretary of State

SECRET

Moscow, February 22, 1946—9 p.m. [Received February 22—3: 52 p.m.]

511. Answer to Dept's 284, Feb 3 [13] involves questions so intricate, so delicate, so strange to our form of thought, and so important to analysis of our international environment that I cannot compress answers into single brief message without yielding to what I feel would be dangerous degree of over-simplification. I hope, therefore, Dept will bear with me if I submit in answer to this question five parts, subjects of which will be roughly as follows:

(1) Basic features of post-war Soviet outlook.

(2) Background of this outlook.

(3) Its projection in practical policy on official level.

(4) Its projection on unofficial level.

(5) Practical deductions from standpoint of US policy.

I apologize in advance for this burdening of telegraphic channel; but questions involved are of such urgent importance, particularly in view of recent events, that our answers to them, if they deserve attention at all, seem to me to deserve it at once. There follows

Part 1: Basic Features of Post War Soviet Outlook, as Put Forward by Official Propaganda Machine Are as Follows:

(a) USSR still lives in antagonistic "capitalist encirclement" with which in the long run there can be no permanent peaceful coexistence. As stated by Stalin in 1927 to a delegation of American workers:

"In course of further development of international revolution there will emerge two centers of world significance: a socialist center, drawing to itself the countries which tend toward socialism, and a capitalist center, drawing to itself the countries that incline toward capitalism. Battle between these two centers for command of world economy will decide fate of capitalism and of communism in entire world."

(b) Capitalist world is beset with internal conflicts, inherent in nature of capitalist society. These conflicts are insoluble by means of peaceful compromise. Greatest of them is that between England and US.

(c) Internal conflicts of capitalism inevitably generate wars. Wars thus generated may be of two kinds: intra-capitalist wars between two capitalist states, and wars of intervention against socialist world. Smart capitalists, vainly seeking escape from inner conflicts of capitalism, incline toward latter.

(d) Intervention against USSR, while it would be disastrous to those who undertook it, would cause renewed delay in progress of Soviet socialism and must therefore be forestalled at all costs.

(e) Conflicts between capitalist states, though likewise fraught with danger for USSR, nevertheless hold out great possibilities for advancement of socialist cause, particularly if USSR remains militarily powerful, ideologically monolithic and faithful to its present brilliant leadership.

(f) It must be borne in mind that capitalist world is not all bad. In addition to hopelessly reactionary and bourgeois elements, it includes (1) certain wholly enlightened and positive elements united in acceptable communistic parties and (2) certain other elements (now described for tactical reasons as progressive or democratic) whose reactions, aspirations and activities happen to be "objectively" favorable to interests of USSR These last must be encouraged and utilized for Soviet purposes.

(g) Among negative elements of bourgeois-capitalist society, most dangerous of all are those whom Lenin called false friends of the people, namely moderate-socialist or social-democratic leaders (in other words, non-Communist left-wing). These are more dangerous than out-and-out reactionaries, for latter at least march under their true colors, whereas moderate left-wing leaders confuse people by employing devices of socialism to seine interests of reactionary capital.

So much for premises. To what deductions do they lead from standpoint of Soviet policy? To following:

(a) Everything must be done to advance relative strength of USSR as factor in international society. Conversely, no opportunity most be missed to reduce strength and influence, collectively as well as individually, of capitalist powers.

(b) Soviet efforts, and those of Russia's friends abroad, must be directed toward deepening and exploiting of differences and conflicts between capitalist powers. If these eventually deepen into an "imperialist" war, this war must be turned into revolutionary upheavals within the various capitalist countries.

(c) "Democratic-progressive" elements abroad are to be utilized to maximum to bring pressure to bear on capitalist governments along lines agreeable to Soviet interests.

(d) Relentless battle must be waged against socialist and social-democratic leaders abroad.

Part 2: Background of Outlook

Before examining ramifications of this party line in practice there are certain aspects of it to which I wish to draw attention.

First, it does not represent natural outlook of Russian people. Latter are, by and large, friendly to outside world, eager for experience of it, eager to measure against it talents they are conscious of possessing, eager above all to live in peace and enjoy fruits of their own labor. Party line only represents thesis which official propaganda machine puts forward with great skill and persistence to a public often remarkably resistant in the stronghold of its innermost thoughts. But party line is binding for outlook and conduct of people who make up apparatus of power—party, secret police and Government—and it is exclusively with these that we have to deal.

Second, please note that premises on which this party line is based are for most part simply not true. Experience has shown that peaceful and mutually profitable coexistence of capitalist and socialist states is entirely possible. Basic internal conflicts in advanced countries are no longer primarily those arising out of capitalist ownership of means of production, but are ones arising from advanced urbanism and industrialism as such, which Russia has thus far been spared not by socialism but only by her own backwardness. Internal rivalries of capitalism do not always generate wars; and not all wars are attributable to this cause. To speak of possibility of intervention against USSR today, after elimination of Germany and Japan and after example of recent war, is sheerest nonsense. If not provoked by forces of intolerance and subversion "capitalist" world of today is quite capable of living at peace with itself and with Russia. Finally, no sane person has reason to doubt sincerity of moderate socialist leaders in Western countries. Nor is it fair to deny success of their efforts to improve conditions for working population whenever, as in Scandinavia, they have been given chance to show what they could do.

Falseness of those premises, every one of which predates recent war, was amply demonstrated by that conflict itself Anglo-American differences did not turn out to be major differences of Western World. Capitalist countries, other than those of Axis, showed no disposition to solve their differences by joining in crusade against USSR. Instead of imperialist war turning into civil wars and revolution, USSR found itself obliged to fight side by side with capitalist powers for an avowed community of aim.

Nevertheless, all these theses, however baseless and disproven, are being boldly put forward again today. What does this indicate? It indicates that Soviet party line is not based on any objective analysis of situation beyond Russia's borders; that it has, indeed, little to do with conditions outside of Russia; that it arises mainly from basic inner-Russian necessities which existed before recent war and exist today.

At bottom of Kremlin's neurotic view of world affairs is traditional and instinctive Russian sense of insecurity. Originally, this was insecurity of a peaceful agricultural people trying to live on vast exposed plain in neighborhood of fierce nomadic peoples. To this was added, as Russia came into contact with economically advanced West, fear of more competent, more powerful, more highly organized societies in that area. But this latter type of insecurity was one which afflicted rather Russian rulers than Russian people; for Russian rulers have invariably sensed that their rule was relatively archaic in form fragile and artificial in its psychological foundation, unable to stand comparison or contact with political systems of Western countries. For this reason they have always feared foreign penetration, feared direct contact between Western world and their own, feared what would happen if Russians learned truth about world without or if foreigners learned truth about world within. And they have learned to seek security only in patient but deadly struggle for total destruction of rival power, never in compacts and compromises with it.

It was no coincidence that Marxism, which had smoldered ineffectively for half a century in Western Europe, caught hold and blazed for first time in Russia. Only in this land which had never known a friendly neighbor or indeed any tolerant equilibrium of separate powers, either internal or international, could a doctrine thrive which viewed economic conflicts of society as insoluble by peaceful means. After establishment of Bolshevist regime, Marxist dogma, rendered even more truculent and intolerant by Lenin's interpretation, became a perfect vehicle for sense of insecurity with which Bolsheviks, even more than previous Russian rulers, were afflicted. In this dogma, with its basic altruism of purpose, they found justification for their instinctive fear of outside world, for the dictatorship without which they did not know how to rule, for cruelties they did not dare not to inflict, for sacrifice they felt bound to demand. In the name of Marxism they sacrificed every single ethical value in their methods and tactics. Today they cannot dispense with it. It is fig leaf of their moral and intellectual respectability. Without it they would stand before history, at best, as only the last of that long succession of cruel and wasteful Russian rulers who have relentlessly forced country on to ever new heights of military power in order to guarantee external security of their internally weak regimes. This is why Soviet purposes most always be solemnly clothed in trappings of Marxism, and why no one should underrate importance of dogma in Soviet affairs. Thus Soviet leaders are driven [by?] necessities of their own past and present position to put forward which [apparent omission] outside world as evil, hostile and menacing, but as bearing within itself germs of creeping disease and destined to be wracked with growing internal convulsions until it is given final *Coup de grace* by rising power of socialism and yields to new and better world. This thesis provides justification for that increase of military and police power of Russian state, for that isolation of Russian population from outside world, and for that fluid and constant pressure to extend limits of Russian police power which are together the natural and instinctive urges of Russian rulers. Basically this is only the steady advance of uneasy Russian nationalism, a centuries old movement in which conceptions of offense and defense are inextricably confused. But in new guise of international Marxism, with its honeyed promises to a desperate and war torn outside world, it is more dangerous and insidious than ever before.

It should not be thought from above that Soviet party line is necessarily disingenuous and insincere on part of all those who put it forward. Many of them are too ignorant of outside world and mentally too dependent to question [apparent omission] self-hypnotism, and who have no difficulty making themselves believe what they find it comforting and convenient to believe. Finally we have the unsolved mystery as to who, if anyone, in this great land actually receives accurate and unbiased information about outside world. In atmosphere of oriental secretiveness and conspiracy which pervades this Government, possibilities for distorting or poisoning sources and currents of information are infinite. The very disrespect of Russians for objective truth—indeed, their disbelief in its existence—leads them to view all stated facts as instruments for furtherance of one ulterior purpose or another. There is good reason to suspect that this Government is actually a conspiracy within a conspiracy; and I for one am reluctant to believe that Stalin himself receives anything like an objective picture of outside world. Here there is ample scope for the type of subtle intrigue at which Russians are past masters. Inability of foreign governments to place their case squarely before Russian policy makers—extent to which they are delivered up in their relations with Russia to good graces of obscure and unknown advisors whom they never see and cannot influence—this to my mind is most disquieting feature of diplomacy in Moscow, and one which Western statesmen would do well to keep in mind if they would understand nature of difficulties encountered here.

Part 3: Projection of Soviet Outlook in Practical Policy on Official Level

We have now seen nature and background of Soviet program. What may we expect by way of its practical implementation?

Soviet policy, as Department implies in its query under reference, is conducted on two planes: (1) official plane represented by actions undertaken officially in name of Soviet Government; and (2) subterranean plane of actions undertaken by agencies for which Soviet Government does not admit responsibility.

Policy promulgated on both planes will be calculated to serve basic policies (a) to (d) outlined in part 1. Actions taken on different planes will differ considerably, but will dovetail into each other in purpose, timing and effect.

On official plane we must look for following:

(a) Internal policy devoted to increasing in every way strength and prestige of Soviet state: intensive military-industrialization; maximum development of armed forces; great displays to impress outsiders; continued secretiveness about internal matters, designed to conceal weaknesses and to keep opponents in dark.

(b) Wherever it is considered timely and promising, efforts will be made to advance official limits of Soviet power. For the moment, these efforts are restricted to certain neighboring points conceived of here as being of immediate strategic necessity, such as Northern Iran, Turkey, possibly Bornholm However, other points may at any time come into question, if and as concealed Soviet political power is extended to new areas. Thus a "friendly Persian Government might be asked to grant Russia a port on Persian Gulf. Should Spain fall under Communist control, question of Soviet base at Gibraltar Strait might be activated. But such claims will appear on official level only when unofficial preparation is complete.

(c) Russians will participate officially in international organizations where they see opportunity of extending Soviet power or of inhibiting or diluting power of others. Moscow sees in UNO not the mechanism for a permanent and stable world society founded on mutual interest and aims of all nations, but an arena in which aims just mentioned can be favorably pursued. As long as UNO is considered here to serve this purpose, Soviets will remain with it. But if at any time they come to conclusion that it is serving to embarrass or frustrate their aims for power expansion and if they see better prospects for pursuit of these aims along other lines, they will not hesitate to abandon UNO. This would imply, however, that they felt themselves strong enough to split unity of other nations by their withdrawal to render UNO ineffective as a threat to their aims or security, replace it with an international weapon more effective from their viewpoint. Thus Soviet attitude toward UNO will depend largely on loyalty of other nations to it, and on degree of vigor, decisiveness and cohesion with which those nations defend in UNO the peaceful and hopeful concept of international life, which that organization represents to our way of thinking. I reiterate, Moscow has no abstract devotion to UNO ideals. Its attitude to that organization will remain essentially pragmatic and tactical.

(d) Toward colonial areas and backward or dependent peoples, Soviet policy, even on official plane, will be directed toward weakening of power and influence and contacts of advanced Western nations, on theory that in so far as this policy is successful, there will be created a vacuum which will favor Communist-Soviet penetration. Soviet pressure for participation in trusteeship arrangements thus represents, in my opinion, a desire to be in a position to complicate and inhibit exertion of Western influence at such points rather than to provide major channel for exerting of Soviet power. Latter motive is not lacking, but for this Soviets prefer to rely on other channels than official trusteeship arrangements. Thus we may expect to find Soviets asking for admission everywhere to trusteeship or similar arrangements and using levers thus acquired to weaken Western influence among such peoples.

(e) Russians will strive energetically to develop Soviet representation in, and official ties with, countries in which they sense Strong possibilities of opposition to Western centers of power. This applies to such widely separated points as Germany, Argentina, Middle Eastern countries, etc.

(f) In international economic matters, Soviet policy will really be dominated by pursuit of autarchy for Soviet Union and Soviet-dominated adjacent areas taken together. That, however, will be underlying policy. As far as official line is concerned, position is not yet clear. Soviet Government has shown strange reticence since termination hostilities on subject foreign trade. If large scale long term credits should be forthcoming, I believe Soviet Government may eventually again do lip service, as it did in 1930's to desirability of building up international economic exchanges in general. Otherwise I think it possible Soviet foreign trade may be restricted largely to Soviet's own security sphere, including occupied areas in Germany, and that a cold official shoulder may be turned to principle of general economic collaboration among nations.

(g) With respect to cultural collaboration, lip service will likewise be rendered to desirability of deepening cultural contacts between peoples, but this will not in practice be interpreted in any way which could weaken security position of Soviet peoples. Actual manifestations of Soviet policy in this respect will be restricted to arid channels of closely shepherded official visits and functions, with superabundance of vodka and speeches and dearth of permanent effects.

(h) Beyond this, Soviet official relations will take what might be called "correct" course with individual foreign governments, with great stress being laid on prestige of Soviet Union and its representatives and with punctilious attention to protocol as distinct from good manners.

Part 4: Following May Be Said as to What We May Expect by Way of Implementation of Basic Soviet Policies on Unofficial, or Subterranean Plane, i.e. on Plane for Which Soviet Government Accepts no Responsibility

Agencies utilized for promulgation of policies on this plane are following:

1. Inner central core of Communist Parties in other countries. While many of persons who compose this category may also appear and act in unrelated public capacities, they are in reality working closely together as an underground operating directorate of world communism, a concealed Comintern tightly coordinated and directed by Moscow. It is important to remember that this inner core is actually working on underground lines, despite legality of parties with which it is associated.

2. Rank and file of Communist Parties. Note distinction is drawn between those and persons defined in paragraph 1. This distinction has become much sharper in recent years. Whereas formerly foreign Communist Parties represented a curious (and from Moscow's standpoint often inconvenient) mixture of conspiracy and legitimate activity, now the conspiratorial element has been neatly concentrated in inner circle and ordered underground, while rank and file—no longer even taken into confidence about realities of movement—are thrust forward as bona fide internal partisans of certain political tendencies within their respective countries, genuinely innocent of conspiratorial connection with foreign states. Only in certain countries where communists are numerically strong do they now regularly appear and act as a body. As a rule they are used to penetrate, and to influence or dominate, as case may be, other organizations less

likely to be suspected of being tools of Soviet Government, with a view to accomplishing their purposes through [apparent omission] organizations, rather than by direct action as a separate political party.

3. A wide variety of national associations or bodies which can be dominated or influenced by such penetration. These include: labor unions, youth leagues, women's organizations, racial societies, religious societies, social organizations, cultural groups, liberal magazines, publishing houses, etc.

4. International organizations which can be similarly penetrated through influence over various national components. Labor, youth and women's organizations are prominent among them. Particular, almost vital importance is attached in this connection to international labor movement. In this, Moscow sees possibility of sidetracking western governments in world affairs and building up international lobby capable of compelling governments to take actions favorable to Soviet interests in various countries and of paralyzing actions disagreeable to USSR

5. Russian Orthodox Church, with its foreign branches, and through it the Eastern Orthodox Church in general.

6. Pan-Slav movement and other movements (Azerbaijan, Armenian, Turcoman, etc.) based on racial groups within Soviet Union.

7. Governments or governing groups willing to lend themselves to Soviet purposes in one degree or another, such as present Bulgarian and Yugoslav Governments, North Persian regime, Chinese Communists, etc. Not only propaganda machines but actual policies of these regimes can be placed extensively at disposal of USSR

It may be expected that component parts of this far-flung apparatus will be utilized in accordance with their individual suitability, as follows:

(a) To undermine general political and strategic potential of major western powers. Efforts will be made in such countries to disrupt national self confidence, to hamstring measures of national defense, to increase social and industrial unrest, to stimulate all forms of disunity. All persons with grievances, whether economic or racial, will be urged to spelt redress not in mediation and compromise, but in defiant violent struggle for destruction of other elements of society. Here poor will be set against rich, black against white, young against old, newcomers against established residents, etc.

(b) On unofficial plane particularly violent efforts will be made to weaken power and influence of Western Powers of [on] colonial backward, or dependent peoples. On this level, no holds will be barred. Mistakes and weaknesses of western colonial administration will be mercilessly exposed and exploited. Liberal opinion in Western countries will be mobilized to weaken colonial policies. Resentment among dependent peoples will be stimulated. And while latter are being encouraged to seek independence of Western Powers, Soviet dominated puppet political machines will be undergoing preparation to take over domestic power in respective colonial areas when independence is achieved.

(c) Where individual governments stand in path of Soviet purposes pressure will be brought for their removal from office. This can happen where governments directly oppose Soviet foreign policy aims (Turkey, Iran), where they seal their territories off against Communist penetration (Switzerland, Portugal), or where they compete too strongly, like Labor Government in England, for moral domination among elements which it is important for Communists to dominate. (Sometimes, two of these elements are present in a single case. Then Communist opposition becomes particularly shrill and savage.[)]

(d) In foreign countries Communists will, as a rule, work toward destruction of all forms of personal independence, economic, political or moral. Their system can handle only individuals who have been brought into complete dependence on higher power. Thus, persons who are financially independent—such as individual businessmen, estate owners, successful farmers, artisans and all those who exercise local leadership or have local prestige, such as popular local clergymen or political figures, are anathema. It is not by chance that even in USSR local officials are kept constantly on move from one job to another, to prevent their taking root.

(e) Everything possible will be done to set major Western Powers against each other. Anti-British talk will be plugged among Americans, anti-American talk among British. Continentals, including Germans, will be taught to abhor both Anglo-Saxon powers. Where suspicions exist, they will be fanned; where not, ignited. No effort will be spared to discredit and combat all efforts which threaten to lead to any sort of unity or cohesion among other [apparent omission] from which Russia might be excluded. Thus, all forms of international organization not amenable to Communist penetration and control, whether it be the Catholic [apparent omission] international economic concerns, or the international fraternity of royalty and aristocracy, must expect to find themselves under fire from many, and often [apparent omission].

(f) In general, all Soviet efforts on unofficial international plane will be negative and destructive in character, designed to tear down sources of strength beyond reach of Soviet control. This is only in line with basic Soviet instinct that there can be no compromise with rival power and that constructive work can start only when Communist power is doming But behind all this will be applied insistent, unceasing pressure for penetration and command of key positions in administration and especially in police apparatus of foreign countries. The Soviet regime is a police regime par excellence, reared in the dim half world of Tsarist police intrigue, accustomed to think primarily in terms of police power. This should never be lost sight of in ganging Soviet motives.

Part 5: [Practical Deductions From Standpoint of US Policy]

In summary, we have here a political force committed fanatically to the belief that with US there can be no permanent *modus vivendi* that it is desirable and necessary that the internal harmony of our society be disrupted, our traditional way of life be destroyed, the international authority of our state be broken, if Soviet power is to be secure. This political force has complete power of disposition over energies of one of world's greatest peoples and resources of world's richest national territory, and is borne along by deep and powerful currents of Russian nationalism. In addition, it has an elaborate and far flung apparatus for exertion of its influence in other countries, an apparatus of amazing flexibility and versatility, managed by people whose experience and skill in underground methods are presumably without parallel in history. Finally, it is seemingly inaccessible to considerations of reality in its basic reactions. For it, the vast fund of objective fact about human society is not, as with us, the measure against which outlook is constantly being tested and re-formed, but a grab bag from which individual items are selected arbitrarily and tendenciously to bolster an outlook already preconceived. This is admittedly not a pleasant picture. Problem of how to cope with this force in [is] undoubtedly greatest task our diplomacy has ever faced and probably greatest it will ever have to face. It should be point of departure from which our political general staff work at present juncture should proceed. It should be approached with same thoroughness and care as solution of major strategic problem in war, and if necessary, with no smaller outlay in planning effort. I cannot attempt to suggest all answers here. But I would like to record my conviction that problem is within our power to solve—and that without recourse to any general military conflict.. And in support of this conviction there are certain observations of a more encouraging nature I should like to make:

(1) Soviet power, unlike that of Hitlerite Germany, is neither schematic nor adventunstic. It does not work by fixed plans. It does not take unnecessary risks. Impervious to logic of reason,

and it is highly sensitive to logic of force. For this reason it can easily withdraw—and usually does when strong resistance is encountered at any point. Thus, if the adversary has sufficient force and makes clear his readiness to use it, he rarely has to do so. If situations are properly handled there need be no prestige-engaging showdowns.

(2) Gauged against Western World as a whole, Soviets are still by far the weaker force. Thus, their success will really depend on degree of cohesion, firmness and vigor which Western World can muster. And this is factor which it is within our power to influence.

(3) Success of Soviet system, as form of internal power, is not yet finally proven. It has yet to be demonstrated that it can survive supreme test of successive transfer of power from one individual or group to another. Lenin's death was first such transfer, and its effects wracked Soviet state for 15 years. After Stalin's death or retirement will be second. But even this will not be final test. Soviet internal system will now be subjected, by virtue of recent territorial expansions, to series of additional strains which once proved severe tax on Tsardom. We here are convinced that never since termination of civil war have mass of Russian people been emotionally farther removed from doctrines of Communist Party than they are today. In Russia, party has now become a great and—for the moment—highly successful apparatus of dictatorial administration, but it has ceased to be a source of emotional inspiration. Thus, internal soundness and permanence of movement need not yet be regarded as assured.

(4) All Soviet propaganda beyond Soviet security sphere is basically negative and destructive. It should therefore be relatively easy to combat it by any intelligent and really constructive program.

For those reasons I think we may approach calmly and with good heart problem of how to deal with Russia. As to how this approach should be made, I only wish to advance, by way of conclusion, following comments:

(1) Our first step must be to apprehend, and recognize for what it is, the nature of the movement with which we are dealing. We must study it with same courage, detachment, objectivity, and same determination not to be emotionally provoked or unseated by it, with which doctor studies unruly and unreasonable individual.

(2) We must see that our public is educated to realities of Russian situation. I cannot over-emphasize importance of this. Press cannot do this alone. It must be done mainly by Government, which is necessarily more experienced and better informed on practical problems involved. In this we need not be deterred by [ugliness?] of picture. I am convinced that there would be far less hysterical anti-Sovietism in our country today if realities of this situation were better understood by our people. There is nothing as dangerous or as terrifying as the unknown. It may also be argued that to reveal more information on our difficulties with Russia would reflect unfavorably on Russian-American relations. I feel that if there is any real risk here involved, it is one which we should have courage to face, and sooner the better. But I cannot see what we would be risking. Our stake in this country, even coming on heels of tremendous demonstrations of our friendship for Russian people, is remarkably small. We have here no investments to guard, no actual trade to lose, virtually no citizens to protect, few cultural contacts to preserve. Our only stake lies in what we hope rather than what we have; and I am convinced we have better chance of realizing those hopes if our public is enlightened and if our dealings with Russians are placed entirely on realistic and matter-of-fact basis.

(3) Much depends on health and vigor of our own society. World communism is like malignant parasite which feeds only on diseased tissue. This is point at which domestic and foreign policies meets Every courageous and incisive measure to solve internal problems of our own society, to improve self-confidence, discipline, morale and community spirit of our own people, is a diplomatic victory over Moscow worth a thousand diplomatic notes and joint communiqués. If we cannot abandon fatalism

and indifference in face of deficiencies of our own society, Moscow will profit—Moscow cannot help profiting by them in its foreign policies.

(4) We must formulate and put forward for other nations a much more positive and constructive picture of sort of world we would like to see than we have put forward in past. It is not enough to urge people to develop political processes similar to our own. Many foreign peoples, in Europe at least, are tired and frightened by experiences of past, and are less interested in abstract freedom than in security. They are seeking guidance rather than responsibilities. We should be better able than Russians to give them this. And unless we do, Russians certainly will.

(5) Finally we must have courage and self-confidence to cling to our own methods and conceptions of human society. After Al, the greatest danger that can befall us in coping with this problem of Soviet communism, is that we shall allow ourselves to become like those with whom we are coping.

KENNAN

800.00B International Red Day/2 - 2546: Airgram

Appendix 2

Unprecedented Commitment —NSC 68 and the Cold War

In the fall of 1949, after the communist takeover of China and the Soviet atomic bomb test, President Harry Truman ordered an analysis of Soviet and American capabilities.[1] In April 1950, the National Security Council produced a policy paper known as "NSC 68." Among its most important recommendations, it called for an unprecedented peacetime military buildup. Three months after the report was written, North Korea attacked South Korea and the military buildup began.

Excerpts from NSC 68
United States Objectives and Programs for National Security
A Report to the President Pursuant to the President's Directive of January 31, 1950

A more rapid build-up of political, economic, and military strength and thereby of confidence in the free world than is now contemplated is the only course which is consistent with progress toward achieving our fundamental purpose. The frustration of the Kremlin design requires the free world to develop a successfully functioning political and economic system and a vigorous political offensive against the Soviet Union. These, in turn, require an adequate military shield under which they can develop. It is necessary to have the military power to deter, if possible, Soviet expansion, and to defeat, if necessary, aggressive Soviet or Soviet-directed actions of a limited or total character. The potential strength of the free world is great; its ability to develop these military capabilities and its will to resist Soviet expansion will be determined by the wisdom and will with which it undertakes to meet its political and economic problems.

1. Military aspects....The two fundamental requirements which must be met by forces in being or readily available are support of foreign policy and protection against disaster....In the broadest terms, the ability to perform these tasks requires a build-up of military strength by the United States and its allies to a point at which the combined strength will be superior for at least these tasks, both initially and throughout a war, to the forces that can be brought to bear by the Soviet Union and its satellites.

2. Political and economic aspects. The immediate objectives— to the achievement of which such a build-up of strength is a necessary though not a sufficient condition—are a renewed initiative in the cold war and a situation to which the Kremlin would find it expedient to accommodate itself, first by relaxing tensions and pressures and then by gradual withdrawal.

A program for rapidly building up strength and improving political and economic conditions will place heavy demands on our courage and intelligence; it will be costly; it will be dangerous. But half-measures will be more costly and more dangerous, for they will be inadequate to prevent and may actually invite war. Budgetary considerations will need to be subordinated to the stark fact that our very independence as a nation may be at stake.

Appendix 3

National Strategies and the Extent They Address GAO's Desirable Characteristics

National Strategy (short titles)	Purpose, Scope, and Methodology	Problem Definition and Risk Assessment	Goals, Subordinate Objectives, Activities, and Performance Measures	Resources, Investments, and Risk Management	Organizational Roles, Responsibilities, and Coordination	Integration and Implementation
National Security	Does Not Address	Does Not Address	Partially Addresses	Does Not Address	Does Not Address	Does Not Address
Homeland Security	Addresses	Addresses	Partially Addresses	Partially Addresses	Addresses	Partially Addresses
Combatting Terrorism	Partially Addresses	Addresses	Partially Addresses	Does Not Address	Partially Addresses	Partially Addresses
Weapons of Mass Destruction	Does Not Address	Does Not Address	Partially Addresses	Does Not Address	Partially Addresses	Partially Addresses
Physical Infrastructure	Addresses	Addresses	Partially Addresses	Partially Addresses	Partially Addresses	Partially Addresses
Secure Cyberspace	Partially Addresses	Addresses	Partially Addresses	Partially Addresses	Partially Addresses	Partially Addresses
Money Laundering	Partially Addresses	Partially Addresses	Partially Addresses	Partially Addresses	Partially Addresses	Partially Addresses

SOURCE: United States General Accounting Office, "Combatting Terrorism: Evaluation of Selected Characteristics in National Strategies Related to Terrorism," statement of Randall A. Yim to the Subcommittee on National Security, Emerging Threats, and International Relations, Committee on Government Reform, U.S. House of Representatives, February 3, 2004, at *www.gao.gov/new.items/d04408t.pdf* (September 20, 2004).

Appendix 4

Preemption and Strategy
Excerpt from the 2002 National Security Strategy

While the right of preemption is well-established in international law, the United States has never included a statement in its national security strategy that explicitly addressed the issue prior to the 9/11 attacks. The 2002 National Security Strategy released in the wake of 9/11 contained explicit language on the subject.[1]

> For centuries, international law recognized that nations need not suffer an attack before they can lawfully take action to defend themselves against forces that present an imminent danger. Legal scholars and international jurists often conditioned the legitimacy of preemption upon the existence of an imminent threat—most often a visible mobilization of armies, navies, and air forces preparing for attack.

> We must adapt the concept of imminent threat to the capabilities and objectives of today's adversaries. Rogue states and terrorists do not seek to attack us using conventional means. They know such attacks would fail. Instead, they rely on acts of terrorism and, potentially, the use of weapons of mass destruction—weapons that can be easily concealed, covertly delivered, and used without warning.

The targets of these attacks are our military forces— and our civilian population, in direct violation of one of the principal norms of the law of warfare. As was demonstrated by the losses on September 11, 2001, a specific objective of terrorists is to cause mass civilian casualties. These casualties would be exponentially more severe if terrorists acquired and used weapons of mass destruction.

The United States has long maintained the option of preemptive actions to counter a sufficient threat to our national security. The greater the threat, the greater is the risk of inaction— and the more compelling the case for taking anticipatory action to defend ourselves, even if uncertainty remains as to the time and place of the enemy's attack. To forestall or prevent such hostile acts by our adversaries, the United States will, if necessary, act preemptively.

The United States will not use force in all cases to preempt emerging threats, nor should nations use preemption as a pretext for aggression. Yet in an age where the enemies of civilization openly and actively seek the world's most destructive technologies, the United States cannot remain idle while dangers gather. We will always proceed deliberately, weighing the consequences of our actions. To support preemptive options, we will:

- build better, more integrated intelligence capabilities to provide timely, accurate information on threats, wherever they may emerge;

- coordinate closely with allies to form a common assessment of the most dangerous threats; and

- continue to transform our military forces to ensure our ability to conduct rapid and precise operations to achieve decisive results.

The purpose of our actions will always be to eliminate a specific threat to the United States or our allies and friends. The reasons for our actions will be clear, the force measured, and the cause just.

Appendix 5

The Intelligence Community

According to President Ronald Reagan's Executive Order 12333, "The United States intelligence effort shall provide the President and the National Security Council with the necessary information on which to base decisions concerning the conduct and development of foreign, defense and economic policy, and the protection of United States national interests from foreign security threats. All departments and agencies shall cooperate fully to fulfill this goal." The departments and agencies cooperating to fulfill the goals of EO 12333 constitute the U.S. Intelligence Community (IC). They include:

- **Army, Navy, Air Force, and Marine Corps Intelligence Organizations**—individually collect and process intelligence relevant to their particular Service needs;
- **Central Intelligence Agency (CIA)**—provides accurate, comprehensive, and timely foreign intelligence about national security topics to national policy and decision makers;
- **Coast Guard Intelligence**—deals with information related to U.S. maritime borders and homeland security;
- **Defense Intelligence Agency (DIA)**—provides timely and objective military intelligence to warfighters, policymakers, and force planners;
- **Department of Energy**—performs analyses of foreign nuclear weapons, nuclear non-proliferation, and energy security-related

intelligence issues in support of U.S. national security policies, programs, and objectives;

- **Department of Homeland Security (DHS)**—prevents terrorist attacks within the United States, reduces America's vulnerability to terrorism, and minimizes the damage and recovers from attacks that do occur;
- **Department of State**—deals with information affecting U.S. foreign policy;
- **Department of the Treasury**—collects and processes information that may affect U.S. fiscal and monetary policy;
- **Federal Bureau of Investigation**—deals with counterespionage and data about international criminal cases;
- **National Geospatial-Intelligence Agency (NGA)**—provides timely, relevant, and accurate geospatial intelligence in support of national security;
- **National Reconnaissance Office (NRO)**—coordinates collection and analysis of information from airplane and satellite reconnaissance by the military services and the CIA; and
- **National Security Agency (NSA)**—collects and processes foreign signals intelligence information for our nation's leaders and warfighters and protects critical U.S. information security systems from compromise.

All the responsibilities of the CIA, DIA, NSA, NRO, and NGA are concerned with intelligence. Therefore each of these organizations in its entirety is considered to be a member of the Intelligence Community.

The other organizations are concerned primarily with missions and businesses other than intelligence, but do have intelligence responsibilities. In these cases, only the part of the organization charged with intelligence responsibility is considered to be a part of the Intelligence Community. In the case of the U.S. Navy, for instance, only its Office of Naval Intelligence is an IC member. The rest of the Navy supports the DoD in missions other than intelligence.

Appendix 6

The Army–McCarthy Hearings

The thirty-six days of the Senate Permanent Subcommittee on Investigations hearings, popularly known as the Army–McCarthy hearings, resulted from charges leveled by Senator Joseph R. McCarthy (R–WI) claiming that the Army was interfering with a consultant on his staff, G. David Schine, who had been drafted. The Army, McCarthy contended, was holding Schine "hostage" to deter McCarthy's committee from exposing communists within the military ranks. Eisenhower revealed his view of the hearings during a meeting with the White House staff.[1]

Notes By L. Arthur Minnich, Assistant White House Staff Secretary Concerning the McCarthy hearings May 17, 1954

5/17/54
McCARTHY HEARINGS
– x Privacy of Personal Advice

At the Legislative Conference of May 17, 1954, the President brought up the matter of the McCarthy hearings. He recalled his efforts to "stay out of this damn business on the Hill", but the demands for testimony from and about his immediate assistants had caused him to write a letter defining what he believed could or could not be subject to testimony. He said he was attaching to the letter a long historical recital by the Attorney General so that the President's views would be better understood. After noting the great pressures he had experienced for getting into the fray, he emphasized that his letter did not touch upon the matter of subpoenas but concentrated on the proposition that personal advice constitutes confidential and privileged material which cannot properly be brought into testimony. He hoped that no one would view the statement as an act by the Administration to stir up needlessly a struggle between the Executive and Legislative branches. Of course, there were always present some elements of struggle between the two, but the President thought it a virtue that such rivalry existed so long as respect and mutual confidence were maintained.

In the brief discussion that followed, several of the leaders pointed to the desirability of not bringing into question the power of Congress to subpoena members of the Executive Branch. The President saw a distinction between replying to a subpoena and giving sworn testimony. As for members of his staff, the President stated that they have no political existence apart from himself and no legislative responsibility such as that assigned in some cases by Congress directly to Department heads.

The matter was raised again later in the meeting when it was suggested that controversy over the President's letter could be held to a minimum by keeping the emphasis on the peculiar position occupied by Presidential assistants. The President thoroughly agreed and compared this position to that of staff officers in any military organization, and whose duties consisted of advising and counseling, not deciding affairs. He went on to restate how he had gone to the utmost lengths to be cooperative and to avoid creating crises in Executive–Legislative relations—and all this "despite terrific needling".

The discussion concluded with constructive suggestions from the leadership on the possibility of Congressional action to lay down some ground rules on the activities of investigative committees, and with a comment from the President on how he believed only the Senate could accomplish the necessary action. He added that he had long thought the particular Committee had gotten way out of line but that he couldn't presume to tell the Senate about its own business.

Minnich

Appendix 7

Proclamation Suspending the Writ of Habeas Corpus

Abraham Lincoln
September 24, 1862

Proclamation Suspending the Writ of Habeas Corpus[1]

BY THE PRESIDENT OF THE UNITED STATES OF AMERICA:

A PROCLAMATION

Whereas, it has become necessary to call into service not only volunteers but also portions of the militia of the States by draft in order to suppress the insurrection existing in the United States, and disloyal persons are not adequately restrained by the ordinary processes of law from hindering this measure and from giving aid and comfort in various ways to the insurrection;

Now, therefore, be it ordered, first, that during the existing insurrection and as a necessary measure for suppressing the same, all Rebels and Insurgents, their aiders and abettors within the United States, and all persons discouraging volunteer enlistments, resisting militia drafts, or guilty of any disloyal practice, affording aid and comfort to Rebels against the authority of United States, shall be subject to martial law and liable to trial and punishment by Courts Martial or Military Commission:

Second. That the Writ of Habeas Corpus is suspended in respect to all persons arrested, or who are now, or hereafter during the rebellion shall be, imprisoned in any fort, camp, arsenal, military prison, or other place of confinement by any military authority of [sic] by the sentence of any Court Martial or Military Commission.

In witness whereof, I have hereunto set my hand, and caused the seal of the United States to be affixed.

Done at the City of Washington this twenty fourth day of September, in the year of our Lord one thousand eight hundred and sixty-two, and of the Independence of the United States the 87th.

ABRAHAM LINCOLN

By the President:

WILLIAM H. SEWARD, Secretary of State

Appendix 8

Report of the Church Committee

In the 1970s, the Senate Select Committee to Study Governmental Operations With Respect to Intelligence Activities (popularly known as the "Church Committee," after Committee Chairman Frank Church) published a series of reports detailing U.S. intelligence operations during the Cold War. This excerpt from the report details domestic surveillance that was run by the FBI from 1956 until 1971.[1]

COINTELPRO:

The FBI'S Covert Action Programs Against American Citizens[2]

I. Introduction and Summary

COINTELPRO [Counterintelligence Programs] is the FBI acronym for a series of covert action programs directed against domestic groups. In these programs, the Bureau went beyond the collection of intelligence to secret action defined to "disrupt" and "neutralize" target groups and individuals. The techniques were adopted wholesale from wartime counterintelligence, and ranged from the trivial (mailing reprints of Reader's Digest articles to college administrators) to the degrading (sending anonymous poison-pen letters intended to break up marriages) and the dangerous (encouraging gang warfare and falsely labeling members of a violent group as police informers).

This report is based on a staff study of more than 20,000 pages of Bureau documents, depositions of many of the Bureau agents involved in the programs, and interviews of several COINTELPRO targets. The examples selected for discussion necessarily represent a small percentage of the more than 2,000 approved COINTELPRO actions. Nevertheless, the cases demonstrate the consequences of a Government agency's decision to take the law into its own hands for the "greater good" of the country.

COINTELPRO began in 1956, in part because of frustration with Supreme Court rulings limiting the Government's power to proceed overtly against dissident groups; it ended in 1971 with the threat of public exposure. In the intervening 15 years, the Bureau conducted a sophisticated vigilante operation aimed squarely at preventing the exercise of First Amendment rights of speech and association, on the theory that preventing the growth of dangerous groups and the propagation of dangerous ideas would protect the national security and deter violence.

Many of the techniques used would be intolerable in a democratic society even if all of the targets had been involved in violent activity, but COINTELPRO went far beyond that. The unexpressed major premise of the programs was that a law enforcement agency has the duty to do whatever is necessary to combat perceived threats to the existing social and political order.

A. *"Counterintelligence Program": A Misnomer for Domestic Covert Action*

COINTELPRO is an acronym for "counterintelligence program."

Counterintelligence is defined as those actions by an intelligence agency intended to protect its own security and to undermine hostile intelligence operations. Under COINTEL-PRO certain techniques the Bureau had used against hostile foreign agents were adopted for use against perceived domestic threats to the established political and social order. The formal programs which incorporated these techniques were, therefore, also called "counterintelligence."

"Covert action" is, however, a more accurate term for the Bureau's programs directed against American citizens. "Covert action" is the label applied to clandestine activities intended to influence political choices and social values.

B. Who Were the Targets?

1. The Five Targeted Groups

The Bureau's covert action programs were aimed at five perceived threats to domestic tranquility: the "Communist Party, USA (CPUSA)" program (1956–1971); the "Socialist Workers Party (SWP)" program (1961–1969); the "White Hate Group" program (1964–1971); the "Black Nationalist-Hate Group" program (1967–1971); and the "New Left" program (1968–1971).

2. Labels Without Meaning

The Bureau's titles for its programs should not be accepted uncritically. They imply a precision of definition and of targeting which did not exist.

Even the names of the later programs had no clear definition. The Black Nationalist program, according to its supervisor, included "a great number of organizations that you might not today characterize as black nationalist but which were in fact primarily black." Indeed, the nonviolent Southern Christian Leadership Conference was labeled as a Black Nationalist "Hate Group." Nor could anyone at the Bureau even define "New Left," except as "more or less an attitude."

Furthermore, the actual targets were chosen from a far broader group than the names of the programs would imply. The CPUSA program targeted not only Party members but also sponsors of the National Committee to Abolish the House Un-American Activities Committee and civil rights leaders allegedly under Communist influence or simply not "anti-Communist." The Socialist Workers Party program included non-SWP sponsors of antiwar demonstrations which were cosponsored by the SWP or the Young Socialist Alliance, its youth group. The Black Nationalist program targeted a range of organizations from the Panthers to Student Nonviolent Coordinating Committee to the peaceful Southern Christian Leadership Conference, and included most black student groups. New Left targets ranged from the Students for a Democratic Society to the Interuniversity Committee for Debate on Foreign Policy, from all of Antioch College ("vanguard of the New Left") to the New Mexico Free University and other "alternate" schools, and from underground newspapers to students protesting university censorship of a student publication by carrying signs with four-letter words on them.

C. What Were the Purposes of COINTELPRO?

The breadth of targeting and lack of substantive content in the descriptive titles of the programs reflect the range of motivations for COINTELPRO activity: protecting national security, preventing violence, and maintaining the existing social and political order by "disrupting" and "neutralizing" groups and individuals perceived as threats.

1. Protecting National Security

The first COINTELPRO, against the CPUSA, was instituted to counter what the Bureau believed to be a threat to the national security. As the chief of the COINTELPRO unit explained it:

We were trying first to develop intelligence so we would know what they were doing [and] second, to contain the threat ... To stop the spread of communism, to stop the effectiveness of the Communist Party as a vehicle of Soviet intelligence, propaganda and agitation.

Had the Bureau stopped there, perhaps the term "counterintelligence" would have been an accurate label for the program. The expansion of the CPUSA program to non-Communists, however, and the addition of subsequent programs, make it clear that other purposes were also at work.

2. Preventing Violence

One of these purposes was the prevention of violence. Every Bureau witness deposed stated that the purpose of the particular program or programs with which he was associated was to deter violent acts by the target groups, although the witnesses differed in their assessment of how successful the programs were in achieving that goal. The preventive function was not, however, intended to be a product of specific proposals directed at specific criminal acts. Rather, the programs were aimed at groups which the Bureau believed to be violent or to have the potential for violence.

The programs were to prevent violence by deterring membership in the target groups, even if neither the particular member nor the group was violent at the time. As the supervisor of the Black Nationalist COINTELPRO put it, "Obviously you are going to prevent violence or a greater amount of violence if you have smaller groups." The COINTELPRO unit chief agreed: "We also made an effort to deter or counteract the propaganda ... and to deter recruitment where we could. This was done with the view that if we could curb the organization, we could curb the action or the violence within the organization." In short, the programs were to prevent violence indirectly, rather than directly, by preventing possibly violent citizens from joining or continuing to associate with possibly violent groups.

The prevention of violence is clearly not, in itself, an improper purpose; preventing violence is the ultimate goal of most law enforcement. Prosecution and sentencing are intended to deter future criminal behavior, not only of the subject but also of others who might break the law. In that sense, law enforcement legitimately attempts the indirect prevention of possible violence and, if the methods used are proper, raises no constitutional issues. When the government goes beyond traditional law enforcement methods, however, and attacks group membership and advocacy, it treads on ground forbidden to it by the Constitution. In *Brandenberg v. Ohio* the Supreme Court held that the government is not permitted to "forbid or proscribe advocacy of the use of force or law violation except where such advocacy is directed toward inciting or producing imminent lawless action and is likely to incite or produce such action." In the absence of such clear and present danger, the government cannot act against speech nor, presumably, against association.

3. Maintaining the Existing Social and Political Order

Protecting national security and preventing violence are the purposes advanced by the Bureau for COINTELPRO. There is another purpose for COINTELPRO which is not explicit but which offers the only explanation for those actions which had no conceivable rational relationship to either national security or violent activity. The unexpressed major premise of much of COINTELPRO is that the Bureau has a role in maintaining the existing social order, and that its efforts should be aimed toward combating those who threaten that order.

The "New Left" COINTELPRO presents the most striking example of this attitude. As discussed earlier, the Bureau did not define the term "New Left," and the range of targets went far beyond alleged "subversives" or "extremists." Thus, for example, two student participants in a "free speech" demonstration were targeted because they defended the use of the classic four-letter word. Significantly, they were made COINTELPRO subjects even though the demonstration "does not appear to be inspired by the New Left" because it "shows obvious disregard for decency and established morality." In another case, reprints of a newspaper article entitled "Rabbi in Vietnam Says With-drawal Not the Answer" were mailed to members of the Viet-nam Day Committee "to convince [them] of the correctness of the U.S. foreign policy in Vietnam." Still another document weighs against the "liberal press and the bleeding hearts and the forces on the left" which were "taking advantage of the situa-tion in Chicago surrounding the Democratic National Con-vention to attack the police and organized law enforcement agencies." Upholding decency and established morality, defending the correctness of U.S. foreign policy, and attacking those who thought the Chicago police used undue force have no apparent connection with the expressed goals of protecting national security and preventing violence. These documents, among others examined, compel the conclusion that Federal law enforcement officers looked upon themselves as guardians of the status quo. The attitude should not be a surprise; the dif-ficulty lies in the choice of weapons.

D. What Techniques Were Used?

1. The Techniques of Wartime

Under the COINTELPRO programs, the arsenal of techniques used against foreign espionage agents was transferred to domes-tic enemies. As William C. Sullivan, former Assistant to the Director, put it,

This is a rough, tough, dirty business, and dangerous. It was dangerous at times. No holds were barred ....We have used [these techniques] against Soviet agents. They have used [them] against us.... [The same methods were] brought home against any organization against which we were targeted. We did not differentiate. This is a rough, tough business.

Mr. Sullivan's description—rough, tough, and dirty—is accu-rate. In the course of COINTELPRO's fifteen-year history, a number of individual actions may have violated specific crimi-nal statutes; a number of individual actions involved risk of serious bodily injury or death to the targets (at least four assaults were reported as "results"; and a number of actions, while not illegal or dangerous, can only be described as "abhorrent in a free Society." On the other hand, many of the actions were more silly than repellent.

The Bureau approved 2,370 separate counterintelligence actions. Their techniques ranged from anonymously mailing reprints of newspaper and magazine articles (sometimes Bureau-authored or planted) to group members or supporters to convince them of the error of their ways, to mailing anonymous letters to a member's spouse accusing the target of infidelity; from using informants to raise controversial issues at meetings in order to cause dissent, to the "snitch jacket" (falsely labeling a group member as an informant) and encouraging street warfare between violent groups; from contacting members of a "legitimate group to expose the alleged subversive background of a fellow member to contacting an employer to get a target fired; from attempting to arrange for reporters to interview targets with planted questions, to trying to stop targets from speaking at all; from notifying state and local authorities of a target's criminal law violations, to using the IRS to audit a professor, not just to collect any taxes owing, but to distract him from his political activities.

Appendix 9

The Patriot Act

The Patriot Act served to improve U.S. counterterrorism in four critical areas. First, it promoted the sharing of information between intelligence and law enforcement investigations—tearing down the "wall" that hampered investigations prior to 9/11. Second, the act authorized additional law enforcement tools for pursuing terrorists—tools that were already available for investigating other serious crimes, such as drug smuggling. Third, it facilitated surveillance of terrorists using new technologies like cell phones and the Internet. Fourth, the act provided for judicial and congressional oversight of the new authorities granted in the legislation. The excerpt from the act given here describes provisions in the law for sharing information.

Excerpt from the USA Patriot Act[1]

SEC. 203. AUTHORITY TO SHARE CRIMINAL INVESTIGATIVE INFORMATION

(a) AUTHORITY TO SHARE GRAND JURY INFORMATION

(1) IN GENERAL—Rule 6(e)(3)(C) of the Federal Rules of Criminal Procedure is amended to read as follows:

(C)(i) Disclosure otherwise prohibited by this rule of matters occurring before the grand jury may also be made—

(I) when so directed by a court preliminarily to or in connection with a judicial proceeding;

(II) when permitted by a court at the request of the defendant, upon a showing that grounds may exist for a motion to dismiss the indictment because of matters occurring before the grand jury;

(III) when the disclosure is made by an attorney for the government to another Federal grand jury;

(IV) when permitted by a court at the request of an attorney for the government, upon a showing that such matters may disclose a violation of state criminal law, to an appropriate official of a state or subdivision of a state for the purpose of enforcing such law; or

(V) when the matters involve foreign intelligence or counter-intelligence (as defined in section 3 of the National Security Act of 1947 [50 U.S.C. 401a]), or foreign intelligence information (as defined in clause (iv) of this subparagraph), to any Federal law enforcement, intelligence, protective, immigration, national defense, or national security official in order to assist the official receiving that information in the performance of his official duties.

(ii) If the court orders disclosure of matters occurring before the grand jury, the disclosure shall be made in such manner, at such time, and under such conditions as the court may direct.

(iii) Any Federal official to whom information is disclosed pursuant to clause (i)(V) of this subparagraph may use that information only as necessary in the conduct of that person's official duties subject to any limitations on the unauthorized disclosure of such information. Within a reasonable time after such disclosure, an attorney for the government shall file under seal a notice with the court stating the fact that such information was disclosed and the departments, agencies, or entities to which the disclosure was made.

(iv) In clause (i)(V) of this subparagraph, the term 'foreign intelligence information' means—

(I) information, whether or not concerning a United States person, that relates to the ability of the United States to protect against—

(aa) actual or potential attack or other grave hostile acts of a foreign power or an agent of a foreign power;

(bb) sabotage or international terrorism by a foreign power or an agent of a foreign power; or

(cc) clandestine intelligence activities by an intelligence service or network of a foreign power or by an agent of foreign power; or

(II) information, whether or not concerning a United States person, with respect to a foreign power or foreign territory that relates to—

(aa) the national defense or the security of the United States; or

(bb) the conduct of the foreign affairs of the United States.

Appendix 10

Outlays for Major Components of the Federal Budget, 1962–2003

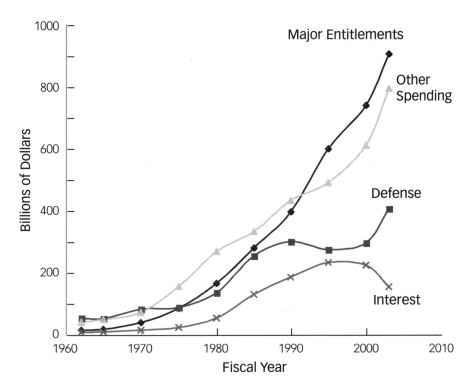

SOURCE: Calculations courtesy of Baker Spring, based on numbers found in U.S. Department of Defense, "Quadrenial Defense Review Report," September 30, 2001, at *www.loyola.edu/dept/politics/intel/qdr2001.pdf* (September 27, 2004).

Appendix 11

Major Component Shares of the Federal Budget, 1962–2003

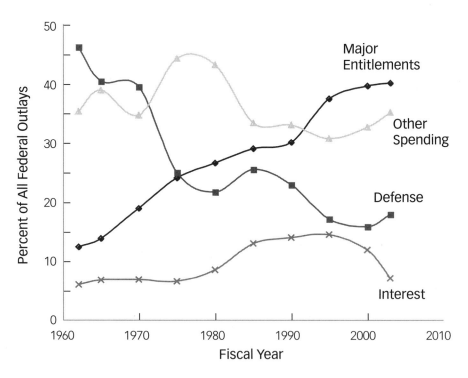

SOURCE: Calculations courtesy of Baker Spring, based on numbers found in U.S. Department of Defense, "Quadrenial Defense Review Report," September 30, 2001, at *www.loyola.edu/dept/politics/intel/qdr2001.pdf* (September 27, 2004).

Appendix 12

GDP Shares of Major Components of the Federal Budget, 1962–2003

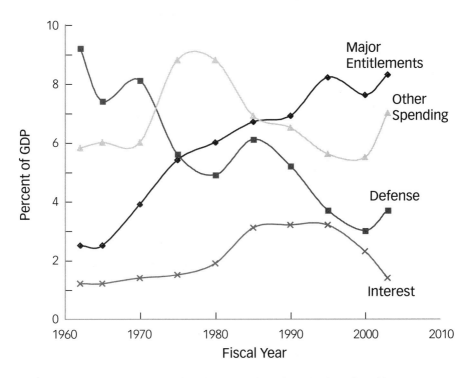

SOURCE: Calculations courtesy of Baker Spring, based on numbers found in U.S. Department of Defense, "Quadrenial Defense Review Report," September 30, 2001, at *www.loyola.edu/dept/politics/intel/qdr2001.pdf* (September 27, 2004).

Appendix 13

Trade Openness Index and Per Capita Income

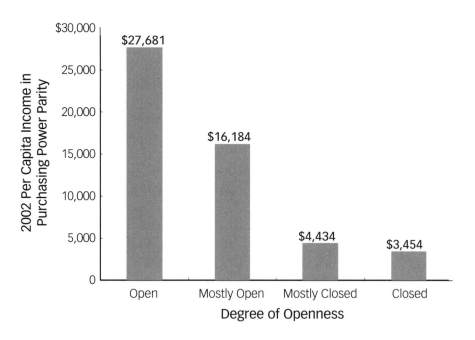

NOTE: Trade Openness Index equals the average score of the trade policy, capital flows and foreign investment, property rights, and regulation from the 2004 Index of Economic Freedom

SOURCES: The World Bank, *World Development Indicators Online*, at *www.worldbank. org/data* (September 27, 2004), and Marc A. Miles, Edwin J. Feulner, and Mary Anastasia O'Grady, *2004 Index of Economic Freedom* (Washington, D.C.: The Heritage Foundation and Dow Jones & Company, Inc., 2004).

Appendix 14

Environmental Sustainability and Trade Openness

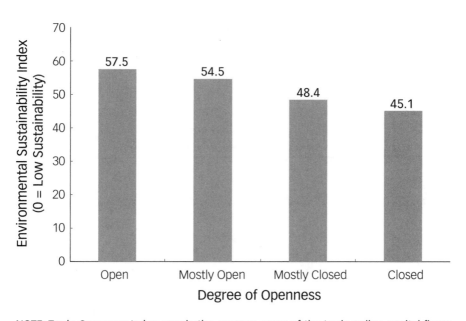

NOTE: Trade Openness Index equals the average score of the trade policy, capital flows and foreign investment, property rights, and regulation from the 2004 Index of Economic Freedom

SOURCES: The World Economic Forum, CIESIN, and Yale Center for Environmental Law and Policy, *Environmental Sustainability Index*, February 2002 at *www.ciesin.columbia.edu/ indicators/ESI/* (September 27, 2004); Marc A. Miles, Edwin J. Feulner, and Mary Anastasia O'Grady, *2004 Index of Economic Freedom* (Washington, D.C.: The Heritage Foundation and Dow Jones & Company, Inc., 2004).

Appendix 15

Economic Freedom and Economic Growth

Countries Eligible for Millennium Challenge Account Grants

Ranked by Improvement in Economic Freedom		Compound Per Capita GDP Growth Rate, 1992–2002
MOST IMPROVED	**1st Quartile** – Bosnia and Herzegovina*, Mauritania, Azerbaijan, Rwanda, Cape Verde, Nicaragua, Albania, Mozambique, Niger, Georgia, Armenia, Vietnam	**3.7%**
	2nd Quartile – Haiti, Chad, Uganda, Kyrgyz Republic, India, Malawi, Ethiopia, Laos, Senegal, Bangladesh, Burkina Faso, Togo	**1.5%**
	3rd Quartile – Republic of Congo, Tanzania, Moldova, Nepal, Madagascar, Yemen, Guyana, Mongolia, Djibouti, Pakistan, Gambia, Guinea, Cameroon	**0.3%**
LEAST IMPROVED	**4th Quartile** – Tajikistan, Bolivia, Honduras, Lesotho, Sri Lanka, Indonesia, Ghana, Kenya, Mali, Benin, Zambia, Nigeria	**0.6%**

*GDP per capita for 1994–2002
NOTE: The 49 countries included in this list are the 49 covered in the *2004 Index of Economic Freedom* that were also designated by the Millennium Challenge Corporation as potential recipients of Millennium Challenge Account grants earlier this year.
SOURCE: Marc A. Miles, Edwin J. Feulner, and Mary Anastasia O'Grady, *2004 Index of Economic Freedom* (Washington, D.C.: The Heritage Foundation and Dow Jones & Company, Inc., 2004) at *www.heritage.org/index*.

Appendix 16

Bin Laden's Fatwa

The following statement from Osama bin Laden and his associates purports to be a religious ruling (fatwa) requiring the killing of Americans, both civilian and military.[1]

Jihad Against Jews and Crusaders
World Islamic Front Statement
February 23, 1998

Sheikh Osama bin Muhammad bin Laden
Ayman al-Zawahiri, amir of the Jihad Group in Egypt
Abu-Yasir Rifa'i Ahmad Taha, Egyptian Islamic Group
Sheikh Mir Hamzah, secretary of the
    Jamiat-ul-Ulema-e-Pakistan
Fazlur Rahman, amir of the Jihad Movement in Bangladesh

Praise be to Allah, who revealed the Book, controls the clouds, defeats factionalism, and says in His Book: "But when the forbidden months are past, then fight and slay the pagans wherever ye find them, seize them, beleaguer them, and lie in wait for them in every stratagem (of war)"; and peace be upon our Prophet, Muhammad Bin-'Abdallah, who said: I have been sent with the sword between my hands to ensure that no one but Allah is worshipped, Allah who put my livelihood under the shadow of my spear and who inflicts humiliation and scorn on those who disobey my orders.

The Arabian Peninsula has never—since Allah made it flat, created its desert, and encircled it with seas—been stormed by any forces like the crusader armies spreading in it like locusts, eating its riches and wiping out its plantations. All this is happening at a time in which nations are attacking Muslims like people fighting over a plate of food. In the light of the grave situation and the lack of support, we and you are obliged to discuss current events, and we should all agree on how to settle the matter.

No one argues today about three facts that are known to everyone; we will list them, in order to remind everyone:

First, for over seven years the United States has been occupying the lands of Islam in the holiest of places, the Arabian Peninsula, plundering its riches, dictating to its rulers, humiliating its people, terrorizing its neighbors, and turning its bases in the Peninsula into a spearhead through which to fight the neighboring Muslim peoples.

If some people have in the past argued about the fact of the occupation, all the people of the Peninsula have now acknowledged it. The best proof of this is the Americans' continuing aggression against the Iraqi people using the Peninsula as a staging post, even though all its rulers are against their territories being used to that end, but they are helpless.

Second, despite the great devastation inflicted on the Iraqi people by the crusader-Zionist alliance, and despite the huge number of those killed, which has exceeded 1 million ... despite all this, the Americans are once again trying to repeat the horrific massacres, as though they are not content with the protracted blockade imposed after the ferocious war or the fragmentation and devastation.

So here they come to annihilate what is left of this people and to humiliate their Muslim neighbors.

Third, if the Americans' aims behind these wars are religious and economic, the aim is also to serve the Jews' petty state and divert attention from its occupation of Jerusalem and murder of Muslims there. The best proof of this is their eagerness to destroy Iraq, the strongest neighboring Arab state, and their endeavor to fragment all the states of the region such as Iraq, Saudi Arabia, Egypt, and Sudan into paper statelets and through their disunion and weakness to guarantee Israel's survival and the continuation of the brutal crusade occupation of the Peninsula.

All these crimes and sins committed by the Americans are a clear declaration of war on Allah, his messenger, and Muslims. And ulema have throughout Islamic history unanimously agreed that the jihad is an individual duty if the enemy destroys the Muslim countries. This was revealed by Imam Bin-Qadamah in "Al- Mughni," Imam al-Kisa'i in "Al-Bada'i," al-Qurtubi in his interpretation, and the shaykh of al-Islam in his books, where he said: "As for the fighting to repulse [an enemy], it is aimed at defending sanctity and religion, and it is a duty as agreed [by the ulema]. Nothing is more sacred than belief except repulsing an enemy who is attacking religion and life."

On that basis, and in compliance with Allah's order, we issue the following fatwa to all Muslims:

The ruling to kill the Americans and their allies—civilians and military—is an individual duty for every Muslim who can do it in any country in which it is possible to do it, in order to liberate the al-Aqsa Mosque and the holy mosque [Mecca] from their grip, and in order for their armies to move out of all the lands of Islam, defeated and unable to threaten any Muslim. This is in accordance with the words of Almighty Allah, "and fight the pagans all together as they fight you all together," and "fight them until there is no more tumult or oppression, and there prevail justice and faith in Allah."

This is in addition to the words of Almighty Allah: "And why should ye not fight in the cause of Allah and of those who, being weak, are ill-treated (and oppressed)? [sic]—women and children, whose cry is: 'Our Lord, rescue us from this town, whose people are oppressors; and raise for us from thee one who will help!'"

We—with Allah's help—call on every Muslim who believes in Allah and wishes to be rewarded to comply with Allah's order to kill the Americans and plunder their money wherever and whenever they find it. We also call on Muslim ulema, leaders, youths, and soldiers to launch the raid on Satan's U.S. troops and the devil's supporters allying with them, and to displace those who are behind them so that they may learn a lesson.

Almighty Allah said: "O ye who believe, give your response to Allah and His Apostle, when He calleth you to that which will give you life. And know that Allah cometh between a man and his heart, and that it is He to whom ye shall all be gathered."

Almighty Allah also says: "O ye who believe, what is the matter with you, that when ye are asked to go forth in the cause of Allah, ye cling so heavily to the earth! Do ye prefer the life of this world to the hereafter? But little is the comfort of this life, as compared with the hereafter. Unless ye go forth, He will punish you with a grievous penalty, and put others in your place; but Him ye would not harm in the least. For Allah hath power over all things."

Almighty Allah also says: "So lose no heart, nor fall into despair. For ye must gain mastery if ye are true in faith."

Notes

Prologue
The Long Shadow of the Long Telegram

1. For an introduction to the debate about Kennan's place in Cold War historiography, see John Lamberton Harper, *American Visions of Europe: Franklin D. Roosevelt, George F. Kennan, and Dean G. Acheson* (Cambridge: Cambridge University Press, 1996), p. 183.
2. Described in Harper, *American Visions,* pp. 77–131.
3. John Morton Blum, ed., *From the Morgenthau Dairies,* Vol. 3 (Boston: Houghton Mifflin, 1967), p. 197.
4. Michael Beschloss, *The Conquerors: Roosevelt, Truman and the Destruction of Hitler's Germany, 1941–1945* (New York: Simon & Schuster, 2002), p. 262.
5. Robert E. Wood, "From the Marshall Plan to the Third World," in Melvyn P. Lefler and David S. Painter, eds., *Origins of the Cold War: An International History* (London: Routledge, 1994), pp. 201–214.
6. Ernest May, ed., *American Cold War Strategy: Interpreting NSC 68* (Boston : Bedford Books of St. Martin's Press, 1993), p. 14–15. For an interesting comparative analysis of NSC 68 and the Long Telegram, see also Efstathios T. Fakiolas, "Kennan's Long Telegram and NSC-68: A Comparative Analysis," *East European Quarterly,* Vol. 31, No. 4 (January 1998), at *www.mtholyoke.edu/acad/intrel/fakiolas.htm* (August 19, 2004). Fakiolas argues that Kennan's writing represents a more coherent strategic concept.
7. For an introduction to the reception of the Mr. X article, see John Lewis Gaddis, *Strategies of Containment: A Critical Appraisal of Postwar American National Security Policy* (Oxford: Oxford University Press, 1982), pp. 25–26.
8. Ernest May, *American Cold War Strategy,* p. 96.
9. For an overview of Eisenhower's decision and his assignment at NATO, see William B. Pickett, *Eisenhower Decides to Run: Presidential Politics & Cold War Strategy* (Chicago: Ivan R. Dee, Inc., 2000), pp. 92–129.
10. Christopher Bassford, *Clausewitz in English: The Reception of Clausewitz in Britain and America 1815–1945* (Oxford: Oxford University Press, 1994), pp. 160–161.
11. For a critical discussion of policy formulation during the Eisenhower Administration, see Stephen G. Rabe, "Eisenhower Revisionism: A Decade of Scholarship," *Diplomatic History,* Vol. 17 (Winter 1993), pp. 97–115. For more positive assessments, see Robert R. Bowie and Richard H. Immerman, *Waging Peace: How Eisenhower Shaped an Enduring Cold War Strategy* (New York: Oxford University Press,

1998), and Harold Stassen and Marshall Houts, *Eisenhower: Turning the World Toward Peace* (St. Paul: Merrill/ Magnus, 1991).

12. Aaron L. Friedberg, *In the Shadow of the Garrison State: America's Anti-Statism and Its Cold War Strategy* (Princeton, N.J.: Princeton University Press, 2000), p. 341.

13. Alice C. Coles, *et al.*, eds., *The Department of Defense: Documents on Establishment and Organization* (Washington, D.C.: Office of the Secretary of Defense, 1978), p. 177.

14. James R. Locher III, *Victory on the Potomac: The Goldwater–Nichols Act Unifies the Pentagon* (College Station: Texas A&M University Press, 2002), p. 29.

15. Jeffrey Record, "Bounding the Global War on Terrorism," U.S. Army War College, Strategic Studies Institute, December 2003, p. 4. See also Michael Vlahos, "Terror's Mask: Insurgency Within Islam," Johns Hopkins University, Applied Physics Laboratory, May 2002, p. 2.

16. Roland Jacquard, *In the Name of Bin Laden: Global Terrorism and the Bin Laden Brotherhood* (Durham, N.C.: Duke University Press, 2002), p. 260.

17. Ever since the mid-1990s, Osama bin Laden has repeatedly threatened violence against the United States to coerce withdrawal of U.S. troops from Saudi Arabia. However, in recent years his rhetoric has expanded to include a call for a campaign against U.S. interests in general. Magnus Ranstorp, "Interpreting the Broader Context and Meaning of Bin-Laden's Fatwa," *Studies in Conflict and Terrorism*, Vol. 21, No. 4 (October/December 1998), pp. 321–330. For an analysis of possible motivations that may have inspired the September 11 attacks, see Ahmed S. Hashim, "The World According to Usama Bin Laden," *Naval War College Review*, Vol. LIV, No. 4 (Autumn 2001), pp. 11–36.

18. The National Commission on Terrorist Attacks Upon the United States, "Outline of the 9/11 Plot: Staff Statement No. 16," p. 2, at *www.9-11commission.gov/hearings/hearing12/staff_statement_16.pdf.* The commission concluded that Khalid Sheikh Mohammad began discussions with Osama bin Laden in 1996.

19. "Part VI: Overseas Operations," in staff statement, "A Case Study on the Aum Shinrikyo," October 31, 1995, in hearings, *Global Proliferation of Weapons of Mass Destruction*, Permanent Subcommittee on Investigations, Committee on Governmental Affairs, U.S. Senate, 104th Cong., 1st and 2nd Sess., at *del.fas.org/irp/congress/1995_rpt/aum/* (September 2, 2004).

20. The scope of the cult's chemical weapons program is described in Robert Jay Lifton, *Destroying the World to Save It: Aum Shinrikyo, Apocalyptic Violence, and the New Global Terrorism* (New York: Henry Holt, 2000), *passim.*

Chapter 1
Taking the Offensive

1. Henry A. Kissinger, *Years of Renewal* (New York: Simon & Schuster, 1999), p. 232.

2. Robert Schulzinger, *Henry Kissinger: Doctor of Diplomacy* (New York: Columbia University Press, 1989), p. 238.

3. *Ibid.*, p. 128.

4. *Ibid.*, pp. 108–109.

5. For an explanation of competing international relations theories, see Michael W. Doyle and John Ikenberry, eds., *New Thinking in International Relations Theory* (Boulder, Colo.: Westview, 1997), and Ken Booth and Steve Smith, eds., *International Relations Theory Today* (Cambridge, Mass.: Polity Press, 1995). For the impact of international relations theory on winning the Cold War, see John Lewis Gaddis, "International Relations Theory and the End of the Cold War," *International Security*, Vol. 17 (Winter 1992/1993), pp. 5–58, and Robert O. Keohane, "Institutional Theory and the Realist Challenge After the Cold War," in David A. Baldwin, ed., *Neorealism and Neoliberalism: The Contemporary Debate* (New York: Columbia University Press, 1993).

6. John Lewis Gaddis, "Rescuing Choice from Circumstance: The Statecraft of Henry Kissinger," in Gordon A. Craig and Francis L. Loewenheim, eds., *The Diplomats, 1939–1979* (Princeton, N.J.: Princeton University Press, 1994), pp. 564–592.

7. For an overview, see Jussi M. Hanhimäki, "Dr. Kissinger or 'Mr. Henry'? Kissingerology, Thirty Years and Counting," *Diplomatic History*, Vol. 27, No. 5 (November 2003), pp. 637–676.

8. Striking preemptively at terrorist threats has been among the most controversial measures suggested for the global war on terrorism. See, for example, Michael E. O'Hanlon, Susan E. Rice, and James B. Steinberg, "The New National Security Strategy and Preemption," Brookings Institution *Policy Brief* No. 113, December 2002. The 2002 national security strategy reaffirmed the nation's right of preemption, which allows countries to defend themselves against an imminent threat before they are attacked. The strategy broadly interpreted the United States' right to forestall or prevent terrorist acts, particularly when the threat of weapons of mass destruction might be involved. Although the right of preemption is recognized in international law and has long been a tenet of U.S. security policy, the 2002 strategy was the first public strategy statement to outline explicitly how it might be exercised. The debate about preemption serves as an example of reductionist arguments that do little to clarify how the United States employs power in the world. The strategy, for example, only reaffirms existing policy. Additionally, the strategy does not call for "preventive" war (initiating conflict not based on a perceived imminent threat), but does allow for war occasioned by the fear of potential aggression in the future. The United States considered, and rightly rejected, the concept of preventive war during the Cold War. See Gian P. Gentile, "Planning for Preventive War, 1945–1950," *Joint Force Quarterly*, Spring 2000, pp. 68–74. Nor does the strategy imply that preemption is the only instrument that the nation would employ. Preemption is not the cornerstone of the 2002 strategy, but it is another—justifiable—tool in the toolbox.

9. Perhaps the best introduction to the subject is Paul Pillar, *Terrorism and U.S. Foreign Policy* (Washington, D.C.: Brookings Institution, 2001).

10. The overwhelming bulk of American military power is still moved around the world by ship. Most military supplies and hardware move through only 17 seaports worldwide. Only four of these ports are designated specifically for the shipment of arms, ammunition, and military units through facilities owned by the Department

of Defense. For an overview of the military's reliance on ports and associated security risks, see U.S. General Accounting Office, *Combating Terrorism: Preliminary Observations on Weaknesses in Force Protection for DOD Deployments Through Domestic Seaports*, GAO–02–955TNI (July 23, 2002), and William G. Schubert, statement before the Subcommittee on National Security, Veterans Affairs, and International Relations, Committee on Government Reform, U.S. House of Representatives, July 23, 2002, at *www.marad.dot.gov/Headlines/testimony/homesecurity.html*. See also U.S. General Accounting Office, *Combating Terrorism: Actions Needed to Improve Force Protection for DOD Deployments Through Domestic Seaports*, GAO–03–15, October 2002, pp. 5–10. In another example of the application of an anti-access strategy, in January 2003, U.S. officials claimed to have credible evidence of a plot to sabotage commercial airliners transporting U.S. troops to the Middle East. During major military mobilizations, most forces are deployed by contract carriers. Thom Shanker, "Officials Reveal Threat to Troops Deploying to Gulf," *The New York Times*, January 13, 2002, p. A1. Even if this report proves unfounded, it nevertheless illustrates ways in which an enemy could attempt to interfere with the deployment of U.S. forces. A series of recent Army war games postulated various options for employing attacks on the homeland as a component of an anti-access strategy. In one game, for example, the enemy forced the United States to withhold troop deployments until terrorist sabotage cells throughout the country had been neutralized. Richard Brennan, *Protecting the Homeland: Insights from Army Wargames* (Santa Monica, Calif.: Rand, 2002), pp. 21–22.

11. Ivan Arreguín-Toft, "How the Weak Win Wars: A Theory of Asymmetric Conflict," *International Security*, Vol. 26, No. 1 (Summer 2001), pp. 93–128.

12. Sam J. Tangedi, *All Possible Wars? Toward a Consensus View of the Future Security Environment, 2001–2025* (Washington, D.C.: National Defense University, 2000), p. 52.

13. Central Intelligence Agency, *Unclassified Report to Congress on the Acquisition of Technology Relating to Weapons of Mass Destruction and Advanced Conventional Munitions, 1 July Through 31 December 1999*, August, 2000, at *www.cia.gov/cia/publications/bian/bian_aug2000.htm#14*.

14. Brian Nichiporuk, *The Security Dynamics of Demographic Factors* (Santa Monica, Calif.: Rand, 2000), and Myron Weiner, "Security, Stability, and International Migration," *International Security*, Vol. 17, No. 3 (Winter 1992/1993), pp. 91–126.

15. U.S. Department of State, *Patterns of Global Terrorism 1991*, April 1991, at *www.fas.org/irp/threat/terror_91/*, Appendix C.

16. Gilles Kepel, *Jihad: The Trial of Political Islam* (Cambridge, Mass.: Harvard University Press, 2002), p. 124.

17. Peter L. Bergen, *Holy War Inc.: Inside the Secret World of Osama Bin Laden* (New York: Free Press, 2001), pp. 76–91.

18. John McCain, "Axis of Evil: Belarus, The Missing Link," keynote address at The New Atlantic Initiative Conference Summary, Washington, D.C., November 14, 2002, at *www.aei.org/cs/cso21114.htm* (September 13, 2004).

19. Douglas Farah, "Report Says Africans Harbored Al-Qaeda," *The Washington Post*, December 29, 2002, p. A1.

20. Bergen, *Holy War Inc.,* pp. 92–104.
21. Audrey Kurth Cronin, "Rethinking Sovereignty: American Strategy in the Age of Terrorism," *Survival,* Vol. 44 (Summer 2002), pp. 119–139. See also Robert E. Hunter, "Global Economics and Unsteady Regional Geopolitics," *The Global Century,* pp. 109–126.
22. James Bissett, "Canada's Asylum System: A Threat to American Security?" Center for Immigration Studies, May 2002, p. 1.
23. Ted Morgan, *Reds: McCarthyism in Twentieth-Century America* (New York: Random House, 2003), p. 44.
24. Ken Alibek and Stephen Handleman, *Biohazard: The Chilling True Story of the Largest Covert Biological Weapons Program in the World—Told from Inside by the Man Who Ran It* (New York: Delta, 2000).
25. The inability of the intelligence community to reach clear assessments on the nature of global terrorism and state sponsorship should have been a strong signal that the United States lacked the ability to analyze transnational threats adequately. In the 1980s, some argued that Soviet sponsorship was at the root of the threat, although this conclusion was hotly debated. The most controversial claims were made in Claire Sterling, *The Terror Network: The Secret War of International Terrorism* (New York: Holt, Reinhart, and Winston, 1981). See also Bob Woodward, *Veil: The Secret Wars of the CIA, 1981–1987* (New York: Simon & Schuster, 1990) p. 127. Woodward concludes that Sterling's research drew heavily on CIA disinformation efforts inflating the threat of Soviet state-sponsored terrorism. Nevertheless, in the early 1990s, Russian officials, including deputy minister Sergei Shakhari and information minister Mikhail Poltoranin, suggested that there was credible archival material substantiating the role of terrorism sponsorship by the Soviet Union and its client states. Many of the relevant archives continue to be closed to Western researchers. For example, see Mark Kramer, "Archival Research in Moscow: Progress and Pitfalls," *Cold War International History Project,* at *wwics.si.edu/index.cfm?fuseaction=library.document&topic_id=1409&id=516,* and Gary Bruce, "Update on the Stasi Archives," *Cold War International History Project,* at *wwics.si.edu/index.cfm?fuseaction=library.document&topic_id=1409&id=15618.*
26. See James Jay Carafano, Ph.D., "The Senate Intelligence Report: Fair and Balanced?" Heritage Foundation *Web Memo* No. 534, July 13, 2004, at *www.heritage.org/Research/HomelandDefense/wm534.cfm.*
27. For a list of recommendations, see James Jay Carafano, Ph.D., "An Agenda for Responsible Intelligence Reform," Heritage Foundation *Executive Memorandum* No. 931, May 13, 2004, at *www.heritage.org/Research/HomelandDefense/em931.cfm.*
28. In 1980, Army Chief of Staff General Edward C. Meyer used the term "hollow Army" in congressional testimony to describe the shortage of soldiers available to fill the service's field units. The term is now widely used to characterize shortages of personnel, training, and equipment that significantly impinge on military readiness. U.S. Department of Defense, *C JSC Guide to the Chairman's Readiness System,* September 1, 2000, p. 3. For an illustration of the "hollow force" and its impact on the Korean War, see William W. Epley, "America's First Cold War Army, 1945–1950," Association of the United States Army, Institute for Land Warfare Studies *Land*

Warfare Paper No. 32, August 1999, at *www.ausa.org/PDFdocs/lwp32.pdf.* A similar pattern of neglect occurred after the Vietnam War. See U.S. Department of the Army, *Historical Summary FY 1989*, updated May 19, 2003, p. 4, at *www.army. mil/cmh-pg/books/DAHSUM/1989/CH1.htm.*

29. The Reserve Component represents 47 percent of the nation's available military forces and consumes approximately 8.3 percent of the annual national defense budget. It consists of the Army and Air National Guard and the Army, Navy, Marine Corps, and Air Force Reserves, totaling over 1,200,000 men and women. (These figures do not include the 13,000 men and women in the Coast Guard Reserve.) The National Guard of each state or territory is commanded by its governor. Governors can assign state missions as allowed by state constitutions and statutes. Individuals or units are called into federal service under either Title 32 or Title 10 of the U.S. Code. Title 32 covers federally funded, non-federal duty status, which includes periodic training periods and participation in congressionally directed domestic programs (such as drug interdiction). Under Title 10, Guard forces perform federal duty under the command of the President. Reserves are federal troops whose sole mission is to augment and reinforce active duty forces. Most Reserve personnel spend only a limited amount of time performing military duties. The majority of units assemble for training one weekend per month and two weeks per year. Some Reserve members are called up to serve for several weeks or months. A few remain on active duty full time (often called "full time manning"), normally to provide support to Reserve forces. At the end of fiscal year 2001, the "active reserve" accounted for 866,000 personnel, or 72 percent of the Reserve Component. The rest do no periodic service or training and are often referred to as the "inactive reserve." Limited service makes the citizen-soldier—a tradition derived from the earliest colonial militias—still possible. It allows individuals to balance their military commitments with civilian employment, while also allowing the military to rapidly expand its capabilities in times of crisis.

30. For a full analysis of the need for robust defense spending, see Jack Spencer, "Defending Defense: Budgeting for an Unpredictable Future," Heritage Foundation *Executive Memorandum* No. 918, April 1, 2004, at *www.heritage.org/Research/ NationalSecurity/em918.cfm.*

31. See Jack Spencer, "Guidelines for a Successful BRAC," Heritage Foundation *Backgrounder* No. 1716, January 6, 2004, at *www.heritage.org/Research/NationalSecurity/ bg1716.cfm.*

32. The debate about the meaning of transformation is described in Ian Roxborough, "From Revolution to Transformation: The State of the Field," *Joint Force Quarterly*, Autumn 2002, pp. 68–75.

33. The least compelling argument is that the number of troops required to support post-conflict operations in Iraq is the problem. Initial projections for occupation troops were between 75,000 and 100,000. See Scott Feil, Testimony before the Committee on Foreign Relations, U.S. Senate, August 1, 2002, at *www.iraqwatch. org/government/US/HearingsPreparedstatements/feil-sfrc-080102.htm* (May 30, 2004). Some skeptics, including the U.S. Army Chief of Staff, suggested that several hundred thousand

would be needed for the occupation. See Vernon Loeb and Thomas E. Rick, "For Army, Fear of Postwar Iraq," *The Washington Post*, March 11, 2003, p. A1. The actual troop levels during the occupation have ranged from about 125,000 to 160,000. Critics have pointed to these lower force levels as a significant contributing factor in the outbreak of violence. Yet, as one pre-war analysis conducted by the U.S. Army War College pointed out, criticizing pre-war projections is unrealistic. The report concluded that any forecasts of actual troop numbers made before the actual postwar situation develops are "highly speculative." Conrad C. Crane and W. Andrew Terrill, *Reconstructing Iraq: Insights, Challenges, and Missions for Military Forces in a Post-Conflict Scenario* (Carlisle, Pa.: Strategic Studies Institute, 2003), p. 33. Indeed, claims that force-structure estimates were based on historical precedents from previous occupations are dubious. Given the diverse conditions and requirements for different operations, drawing useful comparisons appears to be unrealistic. Likewise, recognizing that Iraq is a country the size of California with porous borders awash with arms and a population of about 25 million people (with at least 10 million in eight major cities), it is unclear how numbers alone might have made a difference. Considering the scope of the security challenge, 300,000 troops would likely have had just as much difficulty as 100,000. Clearly, more troops would have helped, but numbers by themselves are not a silver bullet solution.

34. For an alternate view, see James Fallows, "Blind into Baghdad," *The Atlantic Monthly*, January/February, 2004, pp. 53–74.

35. James Jay Carafano, Ph.D., "The U.S. Role in Peace Operations: Past, Perspective, and Prescriptions for the Future," Heritage Foundation *Lecture* No. 795, August 14, 2003, at *heritage.org/Research/NationalSecurity/hl795.cfm*.

36. Gunter Bischof and James Jay Carafano, "Marshall Plan Won't Work in Iraq," Heritage Foundation *Commentary*, October 13, 2003, at *www.heritage.org/Press/Commentary/ed102303f.cfm*.

37. Antuilo J. Echevarria II, *Toward an American Way of War* (Carlisle, Pa.: Strategic Studies Institute, 2004), p. v.

38. U. S. Army, *American Military Government of Occupied Germany, 1918–1920: Report of the Officer in Charge of Civil Affairs, Third Army and American Forces in Germany* (Washington, D.C.: U.S. Government Printing Office, 1943), p. 64.

39. Department of Defense, "Joint Doctrine for Military Operations Other Than War," Joint Pub. 3–07 (June 16, 1995).

40. This doctrine included a general discussion of various kinds of peace actions. The categories included the following: Peace Building—post-conflict actions (predominately diplomatic and economic) that strengthen and rebuild governmental infrastructure and institutions in order to avoid a relapse into conflict; Peace Enforcement—the application of military force, or the threat of its use (normally pursuant to international authorization) to compel compliance with resolutions or sanctions designed to maintain or restore peace and order; Peacekeeping—military operations undertaken with the consent of all major parties to a dispute (designed to monitor and facilitate implementation of an agreement such as a ceasefire, truce, or other such agreement, and to support diplomatic efforts to reach a long-term political

settlement); and Peacemaking—the process of diplomacy, mediation, negotiation, or other forms of peaceful settlements that arrange an end to disputes and resolve issues that led to them. *Ibid.,* pp. III–12 to III–13.

41. For a discussion on the nature of various peace operations, see Carafano, "The U.S. Role in Peace Operations."

42. Joint doctrine for operations other than war also included military support to civil authorities. These tasks include providing support in the wake of natural and technological (man-made) disasters and terrorist acts. Department of Defense, "Joint Doctrine for Military Operations Other Than War," p. I–1.

43. See John T. Fishel, *The Fog of Peace: Planning and Executing the Restoration of Panama* (Carlisle, Pa.: Strategic Studies Institute, 1992), and *Liberation, Occupation, and Rescue: War Termination and Desert Storm* (Carlisle, Pa.: Strategic Studies Institute, 1992).

44. *In the Wake of the Storm: Gulf War Commanders Discuss Desert Storm* (Wheaton, Ill.: Cantigny First Division Foundation, 2000), p. 25.

45. Joseph McMillan, "Building an Iraqi Defense Force," *Strategic Forum,* No. 198, June 2003, at *www.ndu.edu/inss/strforum/SF198/sf198.htm* (May 10, 2004), and James Jay Carafano, "Swords into Plowshares: Postconflict Arms Management," *Military Review,* Vol. 77 (November/December 1977), pp. 22–29. Likewise, difficulties were experienced in Iraq until the United States revised its methods of operations. See United States Institute of Peace, "Establishing the Rule of Law in Afghanistan," *Special Report* No. 117, March 2004, p. 4.

46. U.S. Constabulary, Historical Subsection, G3, "The Establishment and the Operations of the United States Constabulary 3 Oct. 1945–30 June 1947," Halley G. Maddox Papers, Military History Institute, 1947.

47. Described in Lewis Sorley, *A Better War: The Unexamined Victories and the Final Tragedy of America's Last Years in Vietnam* (New York: Harcourt, 1999).

48. For detailed recommendations, see James Jay Carafano, "Citizen-Soldiers and Homeland Security: A Strategic Assessment," The Lexington Institute, March 2004, pp. 20–21, at *www.lexingtoninstitute.org/defense/CitizenSoldiers.pdf* (September 13, 2004).

49. This notion dovetailed well with contemporaneous administrative theory, which envisioned a clear delineation between the civilian and military functions of government. James Stever, "The Glass Firewall Between Military and Civil Administration," *Administration and Society,* No. 31(March 1999), pp. 28–49.

50. James Jay Carafano, *Waltzing into the Cold War: The Struggle for Occupied Austria* (College Station: Texas A&M University Press, 2002), pp. 19–20. For a narrative of the debates about post-war policy between the Department of Defense and the Departments of State and Treasury, see Michael R. Beschloss, *The Conquerors: Roosevelt, Truman and the Destruction of Hitler's Germany, 1941–1945* (New York: Simon and Schuster, 2002), *passim.*

51. See, for example, Larry Wentz, ed., *Lessons from Bosnia: The IFOR Experience* (Washington, D.C.: National Defense University, 1998), pp. 119–138, and George A. Joulwan and Christopher C. Shoemaker, *Civilian–Military Cooperation in the Prevention of Deadly Conflict: Implementing Agreements in Bosnia and*

Beyond (Washington, D.C.: Carnegie Endowment for International Peace, 1998), pp. 26–48.

52. See Richard L. Greene, testimony before the Subcommittee on National Security, Emerging Threats, and International Relations, Committee on Government Reform, U.S. House of Representatives, May 31, 2003, at *reform.house.gov/UploadedFiles/ 051303%20RG%20ts.pdf* (May 10, 2004).

53. See, for example, Melinda Hofstetter, "Battling Storms—Interagency Response to Hurricane Mitch," *Joint Force Quarterly*, Vol. 26 (Autumn 2000), pp. 75–81.

54. Clark A. Murdock *et al.*, *Beyond Goldwater-Nichols: Defense Reform for a New Strategic Era* (Washington, D.C.: Center for Strategic and International Studies, 2004), pp. 60–63.

55. David Jablonsky, "Eisenhower and the Origins of Unified Command," *Joint Force Quarterly*, Vol. 23 (Autumn/Winter 1999–2000), pp. 24–31.

56. This argument is made in Dana Priest, *The Mission: Waging War and Peace with America's Military* (New York: Norton, 2003).

57. W. Spencer Johnson, "New Challenges for the Unified Command Plan," *Joint Force Quarterly*, Summer 2002, p. 63.

58. James Jay Carafano, Ph.D., "9/11 Commission: More Hits than Misses," Heritage Foundation *WebMemo* No. 545, July 22, 2004, at *www.heritage.org/Research/ HomelandDefense/wm545.cfm*.

Chapter 2
Protecting the Homeland

1. Steven L. Reardon, "Reassessing the Gaither Report's Role," *Diplomatic History*, Vol. 25, No. 1 (Winter 2001), p. 153.

2. May, *American Cold War Strategy*, p. 105.

3. John Newhouse, *The Nuclear Age: From Hiroshima to Star Wars* (London: Michael Joseph, 1989), p. 89.

4. Walter Isaacson and Evan Thomas, *The Wise Men: Six Friends and the World They Made* (New York: Simon & Schuster, 1986), p. 485.

5. The writing and reception of the Gaither Report are described in David L. Snead, *The Gaither Committee, Eisenhower, and the Cold War* (Columbus: Ohio State University Press, 1999).

6. Paul Dickson, *Sputnik: The Shock of the Century* (New York: Walker and Company, 2001), p. 122.

7. May, *American Cold War Strategy*, p. 116.

8. Richard A. Falkenrath, "The Problems of Preparedness: Challenges Facing the U.S. Domestic Preparedness Program," Executive Session on Domestic Preparedness Discussion Paper, John F. Kennedy School of Government, Harvard University, 2000, p. 1.

9. Presidential Decision Directive 39, "U.S. Policy on Counterterrorism," June 21, 1995.

10. Laura K. Donohue, "In the Name of National Security: U.S. Counterterrorist Measures, 1960–2000," Belfer Center for Science and International Affairs Discussion

Paper 20001–6, John F. Kennedy School of Government, Harvard University, August 2001, p. 4, at *bcsia.ksg.harvard.edu/BCSIA_content/documents/In_the_Name_of_National_Security.pdf* (September 14, 2004).

11. White House, *National Strategy for Homeland Security*, 2002, pp. 63–65, at *www.whitehouse.gov/homeland/book/* (September 14, 2004).

12. White House, *The National Strategy for the Physical Protection of Critical Infrastructur and Key Assets*, February 2003, pp. 63–65, at *www.whitehouse.gov/pcipb/physical_strategy.pdf* (September 14, 2004).

13. Amanda Ripley, "How the U.S. Got Homeland Security," *Time*, Vol. 163, No. 13 (March 29, 2004).

14. Judi Hasson, "Making His Mark: Profile: For Rep. Christopher Cox, His Diplomacy Will Come in Handy on Homeland Issues," *Federal Computer Week*, March 31, 2003, at *www.fcw.com/fcw/articles/2003/0331/mgt-cox-03-31-03.asp* (September 14, 2004).

15. In addition, 28 countries are part of the U.S. Visa Waiver Program. This program allows citizens of participating countries to enter the U.S. for a period of 90 days without a visa. For a list of countries and program details, see U.S. Department of State, Bureau of Consular Affairs, "Visa Waiver Program (VWP)," at *travel.state.gov/visa/tempvisitors_novisa_waiver.html* (October 16, 2003).

16. U.S. General Accounting Office, *Border Security: Visa Process Should Be Strengthened as an Antiterrorism Tool*, GAO–03–132NI, October 2002, p. 6.

17. Steven A. Camarote, *The Open Door: How Militant Terrorists Entered and Remained in the United States, 1993–2001* (Washington, D.C.: Center for Immigration Studies, 2001), p. 19.

18. U.S. General Accounting Office, *Identity Theft: Prevalence and Links to Alien Illegal Activity*, GAO–02–830T, June 25, 2002, p. 7.

19. U.S. Department of Justice, "The Potential for Fraud and INS's Efforts to Reduce the Risks of the Visa Waiver Program," Inspection Report I–99–10, March 1999.

20. James Jay Carafano and Ha Nguyen, "Better Intelligence Sharing for Visa Issuance and Monitoring: An Imperative for Homeland Security," Heritage Foundation *Backgrounder* No. 1699, October 27, 2003, at *www.heritage.org/Research/HomelandDefense/BG1699.cfm*.

21. John Brennan, "Information Sharing and Coordination for Visa Issuance: Our First Line of Defense for Homeland Security," testimony before the Committee on the Judiciary, U.S. Senate, September 23, 2003, at *www.usdoj.gov/oig/inspection/INS/9910/i9910results.htm#Terrorists* (September 14, 2004).

22. Ambassador Francis X. Taylor, testimony to the Joint Congressional Intelligence Committee Inquiry, Select Committee on Intelligence, U.S. Senate, and Permanent Select Committee on Intelligence, U.S. House of Representatives, October 1, 2002, at *www.state.gov/s/ct/rls/rm/13891.htm* (August 30, 2004).

23. U.S. Commission on National Security, "Road Map for National Security: Imperative for Change," *The Phase III Report of the U.S. Commission on National Security*, February 15, 2001, p. viii, at *www.nssg.gov/phaseiiifr.pdf* (September 14, 2004).

24. NBC News, *Meet the Press*, June 29, 2003, transcript at *www.jamiemetzl.com/meetthepress.html* (September 14, 2004).

25. The study determined that effectively meeting all of the nation's emergency response needs could total over $98.4 billion. However, the report underestimated costs because the task force was unable to obtain reliable data on the additional requirements of state and local law enforcement agencies. In addition, the council report examined only one (disaster preparedness and response) of the six critical functions established by the National Strategy for Homeland Security. See Council on Foreign Relations, *Emergency Responders: Dangerously Underfunded, Drastically Unprepared: Report of an Independent Task Force Sponsored by the Council on Foreign Relations* (New York: June 2003), at *www.cfr.org/pdf/Responders_TF.pdf* (September 14, 2004).

26. From FY 2001 to the Bush Administration's FY 2005 budget request, over $14 billion in grants will have been made available. According the Department of Homeland Security Inspector General, as of February 10, 2004, most of the grants allocated in FY 2002 and FY 2003 had not been drawn down. Department of Homeland Security, Office of the Inspector General, "Review of the Status of Department of Homeland Security Efforts to Address its Major Management Challenges," OIG–04–21, March 2004, p. 10. Due to a lack of national standards, clear prioritization, and performance measures, much of the money that has been spent has been used inefficiently. James Jay Carafano, "Homeland Security Dollars and Sense #1: Current Spending Formulas Waste Aid to States," Heritage Foundation *WebMemo* No. 508, May 28, 2004, at *www.heritage.org/Research/HomelandDefense/wm508.cfm.*

27. Advisory Panel to Assess Domestic Response Capabilities for Terrorism Involving Weapons of Mass Destruction, *Forging America's New Normalcy: Securing Our Homeland, Protecting Our Liberty*, Vol. V, p. iv, December 15, 2003, at *www.rand.org/nsrd/terrpanel* (June 3, 2004).

Chapter 3
Between Liberty and Order

1. William Rehnquist, *All the Laws But One: Civil Liberties in Wartime* (New York: Knopf, 1998), p. 222.

2. Allen Weinstein and Alexander Vassiliev, *The Haunted Woods: Soviet Espionage in America—The Stalin Era* (New York: Random House, 1999), passim.

3. Ted Morgan, *Reds: McCarthyism in Twentieth-Century America*, (New York: Random House, 2003), p. xiii.

4. James C. Hagerty, diary entry, February 25, 1954, Eisenhower Presidential Library.

5. Hagerty, diary entry, March 11, 1955.

6. L. Arthur Minnich, notes concerning "McCarthyism," June 21, 1955, Eisenhower Presidential Library.

7. See Uniting and Strengthening America by Providing Appropriate Tools Required to Intercept and Obstruct Terrorism Act of 2001 (USA Patriot Act), Pub. L. 107–56, 115 Stat. 272, (October 26, 2001).

8. Typical of public criticism was the recent National League of Cities resolution calling for repeal of various portions of the Patriot Act. See Audrey Hudson, "Cities in

Revolt Over Patriot Act," *The Washington Times,* January 5, 2004, p. A1. A number of cities and municipalities have passed similar resolutions. See Jessica Garrison, "L.A. Takes Stand Against Patriot Act," *Los Angeles Times*, January 22, 2004, p. B4. Responding to these criticisms, President Bush has called for reauthorization of the Patriot Act. See George W. Bush, State of the Union Address, January 20, 2004 ("The terrorist threat will not expire on [a] schedule. Our law enforcement needs [the Patriot Act] to protect our citizens.").

9. Kim Zetter, "The Patriot Act Is Your Friend," *Wired News,* February 4, 2004, at *www.wired.com/news/politics/0,1283,62388,00.html* (September 16, 2004).

10. See MoveOn.org, "The Administration Is Using Fear as a Political Tool," *The New York Times,* November 25, 2003, p. A1. This Web site offers a full-page ad reprinting excerpts of speeches by former Vice President Al Gore. It is no coincidence that many Democratic presidential aspirants garnered great applause with the "novel" suggestion that, if elected, they would fire Attorney General John Ashcroft. See Carl Matzelle, "Gephardt Talks the Talk Steelworkers Want to Hear," *Cleveland Plain Dealer*, December 7, 2003, p. A24 (promise to fire Ashcroft "within first five seconds" of new administration), and Greg Pierce, "Inside Politics," *The Washington Times*, September 23, 2003, p. A6 (noting the "frenzy" of "Ashcroft bashing"). To the extent that criticism of the Patriot Act and related activities is purely political, the debate about these truly difficult questions is diminished. Thoughtful criticism recognizes both the new realities of the post-9/11 world and the potential for benefit *and* abuse in governmental activity.

11. See Office of the Inspector General, U.S. Department of Justice, "Report to Congress on Implementation of Section 1001 of the USA Patriot Act," January 27, 2004, at *www.usdoj.gov/oig/special/0401a/index.htm* (September 15, 2004), and Associated Press, "Report Finds No Abuses of Patriot Act," *The Washington Post*, January 28, 2004, p. A2. This is consistent with the conclusions of others. For example, at a Senate Judiciary Committee hearing about the Patriot Act, Senator Joseph Biden (D–DE) said that "some measure of the criticism [of the Patriot Act] is both misinformed and overblown." His colleague Senator Dianne Feinstein (D–CA) said: "I have never had a single abuse of the Patriot Act reported to me. My staff. . .asked [the ACLU] for instances of actual abuses. They. . .said they had none." Even the lone Senator to vote against the Patriot Act, Russ Feingold (D–WI), said that he "supported 90 percent of the Patriot Act" and that there is "too much confusion and misinformation" about the Act. See "Efforts to Prevent Terrorism in the United States," hearing before the Committee on Foreign Relations, U.S. Senate, October 21, 2003, at *Feingold.senate.gov/ ~feingold/statement/ 03/10/2003A22748.html* (September 15, 2004). These views, from Senators outside of the Bush Administration and from an internal watchdog, are at odds with the fears often expressed by the public.

12. This summary of the history is substantially derived from a lecture Professor Geoffrey Stone of the University of Chicago recently gave to the Supreme Court Historical Society. See Geoffrey Stone, "Civil Liberties in Wartime," *Journal of Supreme Court History*, Vol. 28, No. 3 (November 2003), pp. 215–251. This article provides a far more detailed summary and understanding of these historical events, and is the

source of much of the historical information summarized in this chapter (although it reaches different conclusions regarding the lessons to be drawn from that history). See also Paul Rosenzweig, "Securing Freedom and the Nation: Collecting Intelligence Under the Law," testimony before the Permanent Select Committee on Intelligence, U.S. House of Representatives, April 9, 2003.

13. See An Act Concerning Aliens, 5th Cong., 2d Sess, 1 Stat 570–72; An Act Concerning Enemy Aliens, 5th Cong., 2d Sess., 1 Stat 577–78 (the Alien Acts); An Act for the Punishment of Certain Crimes Against the United States, 5th Cong., 2d Sess., 1 Stat. 596–97 (the Sedition Act).

14. Roy P. Balser *et al.*, eds., *The Collected Works of Abraham Lincoln* (New Brunswick, N. J.: Rutgers University Press, 1953–55), pp. 436–437.

15. Mark E. Neely, Jr., *The Fate of Liberty: Abraham Lincoln and Civil Liberties* (Oxford University Press, 1991), pp. 113–138. See also Rehnquist, *All the Laws But One*, pp. 49–50 (estimating the number at 13,000).

16. *Ex Parte Milligan*, 71 U.S. 2 (1866).

17. Act of June 15, 1917, ch. 30, tit. I, §3, 40 Stat. 219.

18. For example, see *Schenck v. U.S.*, 249 U.S. 47 (1919); and *Debs v. U.S.*, 249 U.S. 211 (1919).

19. For example, see *Brandenburg v. Ohio*, 395 U.S. 444 (1969).

20. 7 Fed. Reg. 1407 (1942).

21. *Korematsu v. United States*, 323 U.S. 214 (1944).

22. Civil Liberties Act of 1988, 102 Stat. 903, Pub. L. 100-383 (August 10, 1988).

23. Stone, "Civil Liberties in Wartime," p. 215.

24. *Kennedy v. Mendoza-Martinez*, 372 U.S. 144, 160 (1963). Justice Goldberg was quoting Justice Robert Jackson, who made the same observation in *Terminnelo v. Chicago*, 337 US. 1, 37 (1949). To wit: "The choice is not between order and liberty—it is between liberty with order and anarchy without either. There is a danger that, if the court does not temper its doctrinaire logic with a little practical wisdom, it will convert the Bill of Rights into a suicide pact."

25. For example, see Harry V. Jaffa, *A New Birth of Freedom: Abraham Lincoln and the Coming of the Civil War* (Lanham, Md.: Rowman & Littlefield Publishers Inc., 2000) p. 364; William Rehnquist, "Civil Liberty and the Civil War," National Legal Center for the Public Interest, 1997, at *www.nlcpi.org/search/VolInfo. CFM?VolID=13&BookID=43* (September 16, 2004) ("Not every historian today would credit it [i.e., the suspension of habeas corpus] with saving Maryland for the Union, but that conclusion became almost a truism in Lincoln's day."); and Rehnquist, "All the Laws But One," interview with *Online Newshour*, November 11, 1998, at *www.pbs.org/newshour/gergen/november98/gergen_11-11.html* (September 15, 2004) (Lincoln's suspension protected troop movements and Washington, D.C.).

26. Lincoln made the argument in a special address to Congress on July 4, 1861. See Don Fehrenbacher, ed., *Abraham Lincoln: Speeches and Writings 1859–1865* (New York: Library of America, 1989), pp. 246–262.

27. The draft riots have been called the greatest instance of domestic violence in U.S. history. See James G. Randall and David Donald, *The Civil War and Reconstruction*

(Boston: D.C. Heath and Co., 1961), p. 361. They were no trivial threat to the Union's ability to wage war successfully.

28. Neely, *The Fate of Liberty*, pp. 69–70.

29. An Act relating to Habeas Corpus, and regulating Judicial Proceedings in Certain Cases, ch. 81, §1, 12 Stat. 755, 755 (1863).

30. The relevant text of the proclamation (issued on September 15, 1863), which suspended the writ nationwide in cases involving draftees and deserters, is reprinted in Neely, *The Fate of Liberty*, p. 72.

31. See Michael Chertoff, "Law, Loyalty, and Terror," *The Weekly Standard*, December 1, 2003, pp. 15–16 (In response to September 11, "the government quite self-consciously avoided the kinds of harsh measures common in previous wars.").

32. Rehnquist, *All the Laws But One*, pp. 224–225. Or, as Jeffrey Rosen has written: "[N]one of the legal excesses that followed 9/11 could compare to those that followed World War I." Jeffrey Rosen, *The Naked Crowd: Reclaiming Security and Freedom in an Anxious Age* (New York: Random House, 2004), p. 131.

33. Akhil Reed Amar, "Scholars and Scribes Review the Rulings: The Supreme Court's 2001–2002 Term," remarks given at The Heritage Foundation, July 9, 2002, at *www.heritage.org/Press/MediaCenter/mediaevents.cfm*. Compare Cass Sunstein, "A Hand in the Matter," *Legal Affairs*, March/April 2003, p. 27 (noting that the Rehnquist Court has struck down 26 Acts of Congress since 1995).

34. The Supreme Court has yet to accept any cases directly arising from the Patriot Act. However, the Court's recent decision to hear both the "enemy combatants cases." See *Hamdi v. Rumsfeld*, 337 F.3d 335 (4th Cir. 2003), *cert. granted*, 124 S. Ct. 981 (2004); and *Padilla v. Rumsfeld*, 352 F.3d 695 (2d Cir. 2003), *cert. granted*, 124 S. Ct. 1353 (2004); and the "Guantanamo detainees case" (See *Al Odah v. U.S.*, 321 F.3d 1134 (D.C. Cir. 2003), *cert. granted*, 124 S. Ct. 534 (2003) (consolidated with *Rasul v. Bush*) reflects this activism and the involvement of the Court at a very early stage of the war—far earlier than in past conflicts. For example, see *Ex parte Milligan*, (decision rendered one year after hostilities ended in the Civil War).

35. See Michael Kinsley, "An Incipient Loss of Freedom," *The Washington Post*, June 15, 2003, p. B07 ("The American Civil Liberties Union is alarmed, but the ACLU's function, which I admire and support, is to be alarmed before I am, like the canary down the mineshaft.").

36. Dennis Bailey, *The Open Society Paradox: Why the Twenty-First Century Calls for More Openness—Not Less* (Dulles, Va.: Brassey's, Inc., 2004), passim. See David Brin, *The Transparent Society: Will Technology Force Us to Choose Between Privacy and Freedom?* (Reading, Mass.: Addison-Wesley, 1998).

37. Survey evidence supports the instinct that the public is reacting cautiously. Immediately after 9/11, 60 percent agreed that the average citizen would have to give up civil liberties to fight terrorism. By June 2002, that number had fallen to 46 percent. See Amatai Etzioni and Deidre Mead, "The State of Society—A Rush to Pre-9/11," at *www.gwu.edu/~ccps/The_State_of_Society.html* (September 15, 2004). One suspects the number has fallen still further in the subsequent months.

38. U.S. Constitution, Article I, §8.
39. For example, see Paul Rosenzweig and Michael Scardaville, "The Need to Protect Civil Liberties While Combating Terrorism: Legal Principles and the Total Information Awareness Program," Heritage Foundation *Legal Memorandum* No. 6, February 6, 2003, at *www.heritage.org/Research/HomelandDefense/lm6.cfm*, pp. 12–13, and Paul Rosenzweig, "Anti-Terrorism Investigations and the Fourth Amendment After September 11: Where and When Can the Government Go to Prevent Terrorist Attacks?" testimony before the Subcommittee on the Constitution, Committee on the Judiciary, U.S. House of Representatives, May 20, 2003, at *www.heritage.org/ Research/HomelandDefense/test052103b.cfm*.
40. *Katz v. U.S.*, 389 U.S. 347 (1967).
41. *U.S. v. White*, 401 U.S. 745 (1971). A few states have consent laws that restrict the ability of state law enforcement officials to conduct taping of telephone conversations without consent.
42. *U.S. v. Karo*, 468 U.S. 705 (1984).
43. *Florida v. Riley*, 488 U.S. 445 (1989) (plurality opinion).
44. *California v. Greenwood*, 486 U.S. 35 (1988).
45. The same is true of the physical characteristics that one exposes to the public every day. Many have ridiculed a research proposal to develop a means of identifying people from their physical characteristics, deriding it as the "Ministry of Silly Walks." Others fear such a capacity. Yet the government already has the authority and the capacity to identify an individual by surveillance photographs whenever he or she walks out the front door. (They may not, however, use technology to penetrate that door. *Kyllo v. U.S.*, 533 U.S. 27 [2001]). From a legal perspective, the "better telephoto lens" proposed is not off limits.
46. *S.E.C. v. O'Brien*, 467 U.S. 735, 743 (1984). According to the Court, the lack of entitlement to notice flows from the individual's abandonment of a claim of privacy arising from conveying the information to a third party.
47. See James X. Dempsey, "Communications Privacy in the Digital Age: Revitalizing the Federal Wiretap Laws to Enhance Privacy," *Albany Law Journal of Science & Technology*, Vol. 8 (1997), p.65.
48. See 12 U.S.C. §§ 3402, 3403 (bank disclosure) and § 3407 (subpoenas to bank).
49. See 13 U.S.C. §§ 8, 9 (prohibition on disclosure of Census data), and § 214 (penalties for disclosure). Recent reports claiming that Census data have been used to test the new CAPPS II algorithm have been categorically denied by the Census Bureau. See Drew Clark, "The Outcry Over Airline Passenger Records," *National Journal of Technology Daily*, January 26, 2004, at *www.drewclark.com/issueoftheweek.htm* (September 15, 2004).
50. This discussion is taken from Rosenzweig and Scardaville, "The Need to Protect Civil Liberties," pp. 5–6.
51. Eric Lichtblau, "Administration Creates Center for Master Terror 'Watch List'," *The New York Times*, September 17, 2003, p. A1.
52. During an interview on NBC's *Meet the Press*, U.S. Senator Bob Graham (D–FL) was quoted as saying that "al-Qaeda has trained between 70,000 and 120,000 persons in

the skills and arts of terrorism." Bob Graham, *Meet the Press* television broadcast, July 13, 2003.

53. Terence Hunt, "Bush Shows Resolve by Visiting Bali," *Chicago Sun–Times*, October 22, 2003, p. 36.

54. Bill Gertz, "5,000 in U.S. Suspected of Ties to al-Qaeda," *The Washington Times*, July 11, 2002, p. A1.

55. White House, "Securing America's Borders Fact Sheet," January 25, 2002, at *www.whitehouse.gov* (January 14, 2003).

56. U.S. Department of Commerce, Office of Travel and Tourism Industries, "Inbound Travel to the U.S.," U.S. Dept. of Commerce, at *tinet.ita.doc.gov/outreachpages/inbound. general_information.inbound_overview.html?ti_cart_ cookie=20030127.125013.04230* (September 15, 2004).

57. White House, "Securing America's Borders."

58. Michelle Malkin, *Invasion: How America Still Welcomes Terrorists, Criminals, and Other Foreign Menaces to Our Shore* (Washington, D.C.:Regnery Publishing Inc., 2002), p. 8.

59. Office of Travel and Tourism Industries, "Inbound Travel."

60. Malkin, *Invasion: How America Still Welcomes Terrorists.*

61. Institute of International Education, "International Student Enrollment Growth Slows in 2002/2003, Large Gains from Leading Countries Offset Numerous Decreases," November 3, 2003, at *opendoors.iienetwork.org.* (September 15, 2004).

62. See Dana Dillon, "War on Terrorism in Southeast Asia: Developing Law Enforcement," Heritage Foundation *Backgrounder* No. 1720, January 22, 2004, at *www. heritage.org/Research/AsiaandthePacific/BG1720.cfm.*

63. Peter Slevin, "U.S. Pledges Not to Torture Terror Suspects," *The Washington Post*, June 27, 2003, p. A01.

64. Francis Taylor, "Transcript: State Dept Official Says War Against Terrorism Continues," June 9, 2003, at *usembassy.state.gov/tokyo/wwwh20030611a6.html.*

65. *Furman v. Georgia*, 408 U.S. 238, 367 n.158 (1972).

66. "In a criminal case...we do not view the social disutility of convicting an innocent man as equivalent to the disutility of acquitting someone who is guilty....[T]he reasonable doubt standard is bottomed on a fundamental value determination of our society that it is far worse to convict an innocent man than to let a guilty man go free." *In re Winship*, 397 U.S. 357, 372 (1970).

67. The closely related point, of course, is that we must guard against "mission creep." Because the justification for altering the traditional assessment of comparative risks is based in part upon the altered nature of the terrorist threat, we cannot alter that assessment and then apply it in the traditional contexts. See Rosenzweig and Scardaville, "The Need to Protect Civil Liberties," pp. 10–11 (arguing for use of new technology only to combat terrorism), and William Stuntz, "Local Policing After the Terror," *Yale Law Journal*, Vol. 111 (2002), pp. 2183–2184 (arguing for use of information sharing only to combat most serious offenses).

68. See Phillip Kurland, "The Private I," *University of Chicago Magazine*, Autumn 1976, p. 8 (characterizing three facets of privacy, broadly characterized as anonymity, secrecy, and autonomy).

69. For example, see 26 U.S.C. § 7213 (prohibiting disclosure of tax information except as authorized for criminal or civil investigations).

70. But compare *Lawrence v. Texas*, 123 S. Ct. 2472 (2003) (recognizing that certain intrusions into individual privacy are beyond governmental power).

71. Thomas Powers, "Can We Be Secure and Free?" *The Public Interest*, Spring 2003, at *www.thepublicinterest.com/archives/2003spring/article1.html*.

72. James Madison, speech to the Virginia Ratifying Convention, June 16, 1788, in Matthew Spalding, ed., *The Founders' Almanac* (Washington, D.C.: The Heritage Foundation, 2002), p. 133.

Chapter 4
After the Patriot Act

1. Nathan Miller, *Spying for America* (New York: Dell Publishing, 1989), pp. 232–234.

2. Douglas M. Charles, "Informing FDR: FBI Political Surveillance and the Isolationist-Interventionist Foreign Policy Debate," *Diplomatic History*, Vol. 24, No. 2 (Spring 2000), p. 215.

3. *In re Sealed Case*, 310 F.3d 717, 743 (FISCR 2002).

4. See memorandum from Jamie S. Gorelick, Deputy Attorney General, *Instructions on Separation of Certain Foreign Counterintelligence and Criminal Investigations* (1995).

5. Sandip Roy, "'Freedom's Attendant': Patriot Act Drafter Defends His Vision," January 27, 2003, at *www.imdiversity.com/villages/asian/politics_law/roy_freedoms_attendant_patriot_act.asp* (September 7, 2004).

6. Report, *Joint Inquiry Into Intelligence Community Activities Before and After the Terrorist Attacks of September 11, 2001*, Senate Select Committee on Intelligence, U.S. Senate, and Permanent Select Committee on Intelligence, U.S. House of Representatives, 107th Cong., 2nd Sess., S. Rept. No. 107–351 and H. Rep. No. 107–792, December 2002, Finding 9, at xvii, at *www.fas.org/irp/congress/2002_rpt/911rept.pdf* (September 7, 2004); see also *id.*, Finding 1, at xv (concluding that both the intelligence community and the FBI were not well organized to address the domestic terrorism threat).

7. *In re Sealed Case* at 742.

8. See *Dalia v. U.S.*, 441 U.S. 238 (1979).

9. See *Katz v. U.S.*, 389 U.S. 347 (1967).

10. See Access to Business Records and Other Items Under the Foreign Intelligence Surveillance Act, USA Patriot Act, Pub. Law 107–56, § 215, October 26, 2001, at *news.findlaw.com/hdocs/docs/terrorism/patriotact.pdf* (September 22, 2004).

11. *Ibid.*

12. *Ibid.*

13. *Ibid.*

14. See *U.S. v. R. Enterprises Inc.*, 498 U.S. 292 (1991).

15. See James P. Sensenbrenner, statement before the Committee on the Judiciary, U.S. House of Representatives, October 17, 2002, at *www.house.gov/judiciary/news101702.htm* (September 22, 2004).

16. 18 U.S.C. § 2339B.
17. These guidelines were, as the text makes clear, of purely executive character, reversing earlier executive orders originally promulgated in the 1970s. (The most recent reissuance prior to 2001 was in November of 1995.) See "Advice to FBI Regarding Domestic Security/Terrorism Investigations and Preliminary Inquiries," November 21, 1995. As executive orders, they have no formal relationship to the Patriot Act. Yet concern about the "FBI invading mosques" is one of the perpetual criticisms of the Patriot Act—reflecting the public's broader conception of the act rather than the reality of its parameters. As such, it seems appropriate to address the issue in this chapter, which deals with the broad context of civil liberty and the necessities of anti-terrorism investigations.
18. See Attorney General John Ashcroft, "Attorney General's Guidelines on General Crimes, Racketeering Enterprise and Terrorism Enterprise Investigations," May 30, 2002, at *www.usdoj.gov/olp/generalcrimes2.pdf* (September 7, 2004).
19. See *Handschu v. Special Servs. Div.*, 605 F. Supp. 1384 (S.D.N.Y. 1985), *aff'd*, 787 F.2d 828 (2d Cir. 1985).
20. Data mining involves identifying patterns and anomalies from the observation of vast datasets. Both government and industry have spent millions of dollars developing these technologies. Data mining, for example, has been used by both commercial and government agencies to combat fraud and money laundering. Usama Fayyad *et al.*, "From Data Mining to Knowledge Discovery in Databases," *Artificial Intelligence*, Fall 1996, p. 2. It has been widely proposed that data mining systems be applied to homeland security for a host of purposes.
21. Biometrics are methods of identifying a person based on physiological or behavioral characteristics, including the person's face, fingerprints, hand geometry, handwriting, iris, retina, vein, and voice. Michael D. Kirkpatrick, statement in *Hearing on How New Technologies (Biometrics) Can Be Used to Prevent Terrorism*, Subcommittee on Technology, Terrorism, and Government Information, Committee on the Judiciary, U.S. Senate, November 14, 2001, at *www.fbi.gov/congress/congress01/kp111401.htm* (September 8, 2004). See also U.S. General Accounting Office, *Technology Assessment: Using Biometrics for Border Security*, GA0–03–174, November 2002, pp. 4–5. For an introduction to these capabilities, see the Web site of the Biometric Consortium (which serves as the U.S. government's focal point for research, development, test, evaluation, and application of biometric-based personal identification/verification technology) at *www. biometrics.org*. Also see Paul Skokowski, "Can Biometrics Defeat Terror?" paper presented to the Conference on Technology for Preventing Terrorism, Hoover Institution, Stanford University, Palo Alto, California, March 12–13, 2002, pp. 1–12.
22. See *The 9/11 Commission Report: Final Report of the National Commission on Terrorist Attacks Upon the United States*, § 13.1, 2004 (calling for unity of effort across the foreign-domestic divide of responsibility); *id.* § 13.3 (unity of effort in sharing information); and *Ibid.* at § 13.5 (integration of the FBI into the national intelligence structure). The USA Patriot Act eliminated many of these systematic problems. For a brief discussion of the emerging consensus as to the utility of the Patriot

Act, see James Jay Carafano and Paul Rosenzweig, "A Patriotic Day: 9/11 Commission Recognizes Importance of Patriot Act," Heritage Foundation *WebMemo* No. 480, April 15, 2004, at *www.heritage.org/Research/HomelandDefense/wm480.cfm*. For an in-depth treatment of various aspects of the Patriot Act, including the information sharing provisions, see Paul Rosenzweig, "Civil Liberties and Terrorism," *Duquesne Law Review*, Vol. 42 (2004), pp. 663–723.

23. The Classified Information Procedures Act (CIPA) is codified at 18 U.S.C., App. II. CIPA is a procedural statute; it neither adds to nor detracts from the substantive rights of the defendant or the discovery obligations of the government. Rather, the procedure for making these determinations is different in that it balances the right of a criminal defendant with the right of the sovereign to advance knowledge of a potential threat from a criminal prosecution to its national security. See, e.g., *United States v. Anderson*, 872 F.2d 1508, 1514 (11th Cir.), *cert. denied*, 493 U.S. 1004 (1989); *United States v. Collins*, 720 F.2d 1195, 1197 (11th Cir. 1983); and *United States v. Lopez-Lima*, 738 F. Supp. 1404, 1407 (S.D.Fla. 1990). Each of CIPA's provisions is designed to achieve those dual goals—preventing unnecessary or inadvertent disclosures of classified information and advising the government of the national security "cost" of going forward.

24. See *CIA v. Sims*, 471 U.S. 159, 176 (1985) (noting potential for harm if identity of a source is revealed).

25. According to Anthony Blinken, an NSC official now at the Center for Strategic and International Studies (CSIS), the disclosure of bin Laden's use of cell phones "ended that channel of information." Tony Raum, "U.S. Stingy on Bin Laden Evidence," Associated Press, October 30, 2001.

26. *United States v. Moussaoui*, 365 F.3d 292 (4th Cir. 2004).

27. See Federal Rules of Evidence, No. 801 (defining hearsay), and No. 802 (prohibiting hearsay as evidence except in limited circumstances). Also see *Crawford v. Washington*, 124 S.Ct. 1354 (2004) (prohibiting admission of testimonial hearsay, even if otherwise reliable).

28. *Moussaoui*, 365 F.2d at 306.

29. David Ignatius, "Small Comfort" *The Washington Post*, June 15, 2004, p. A23.

30. See 18 U.S.C. § 3144.

31. E.g., *In re Bacon*, 449 F.2d 933 (9th Cir. 191).

32. *United States v. Awadallah*, 202 F.Supp.2d 55, 202 F.Supp.2d 82 (S.D.N.Y. 2002), *rev'd* 349 F.3d 42 (2d Cir. 2003).

33. *United States v. Awadallah*, at 349.

34. See Office of the Inspector General, U.S. Department of Justice, "The September 11 Detainees: A Review of the Treatment of Aliens Held on Immigration Charges in Connection with the Investigation of the September 11 Attacks," April 2003, p. 34.

35. *Ibid.* at 37. The report also identified 84 instances of abuse at the Metropolitan Detention Center in Brooklyn. *Id.* at 118.

36. *Ibid.* at 70.

37. *Ibid.* at 15 and n. 22.

38. See U.S. Department of Justice, "Summary of Jose Padilla's Activities with al-Qaeda," May 28, 2004 (transmitted to Congress June 1, 2004).

39. See *Hamdi v. Rumsfeld*, 124 S.Ct. 2633 (2004). Although Padilla's petition was dismissed on jurisdictional grounds (see *Rumsfeld v. Padilla*, 124 S.Ct. 2711 [2004]), there is little doubt that Padilla's detention will be subject to standards similar to those applied to Hamdi.

40. See *Hamdi*, 124 S.Ct. 2646–52; also see John Yoo, "The Supreme Court Goes to War," *The Wall Street Journal*, June 30, 2004.

41. Ignatius, "Small Comfort."

42. Some of our thinking in this area has benefited from discussions with our colleague, Robert Levy of the Cato Institute.

43. Pretrial detention is authorized by 18 U.S.C. §3142.

44. See, for example, Benjamin Wittes, "Enemy Americans," *The Atlantic Monthly*, July/August 2004, and Stuart Taylor, "The Fragility of Our Freedoms in a Time of Terror," *National Journal*, May 5, 2004, at *www.theatlantic.com/politics/nj/taylor2004-05-05.htm* (September 7, 2004).

45. Michael Chertoff, "Law, Loyalty, and Terror," *The Weekly Standard*, December 1, 2003, pp. 15–17.

46. John Locke, *Two Treatises of Government* (Cambridge: Cambridge University Press, 1988), p. 305.

Chapter 5
Guns and Butter

1. Aaron L. Friedberg, *In the Shadow of the Garrison State: America's Anti-Statism and Its Cold War Grand Strategy* (Princeton, N.J.: Princeton University Press, 2000), p. 126.

2. Robert H. Ferrell, ed., *The Eisenhower Diaries* (New York: W.W. Norton, 1981), p. 153. See also Raymond J. Saulnier, *Constructive Years: The U.S. Economy Under Eisenhower* (Lanham, Md.: University Press of America, 1991).

3. U.S. Department of State, *Foreign Relations of the United States, 1955–1957* (Washington, D.C.: U.S. Government Printing Office), pp. 638–661.

4. *Ibid.*, p. 632.

5. Chris Suellentrop, "Glenn Hubbard: First-Rate Economist, Tax-Cut Champion, Presidential Yes Man," *Slate*, January 22, 2003, at *slate.msn.com/1d/2077330* (September 17, 2004).

6. Russell Roberts, "An Interview with R. Glenn Hubbard on the Fundamentals of Tax Reform," February 3, 2003, at *www.econlib.org/library/Columns/y2003/Hubbardtaxes.html* (September 17, 2004).

7. Congress could fund new spending by printing new money ("money by fiat"), which would only create inflation.

8. This argument was heavily influenced by Robert Bartley, "Thinking Things Over: Does Spending Stimulate? Do Deficits?" *The Wall Street Journal*, February 4, 2002, p. A17.

9. This three-category breakdown of the side effects of government spending is from James Gwartney, Robert Lawson, and Randall Holcombe, "The Size and Functions of Government and Economic Growth," Joint Economic Committee, U.S.Congress, April 1998, at *www.house.gov/jec/growth/function/function.htm* (September 17, 2004).

10. Milton Friedman, winner of the Nobel Prize in economics, has argued persuasively that individuals, because they are spending their own money and not someone else's, have better incentives to spend efficiently than do governments. Consequently, allowing families to spend their own money on items such as education and health care will be more effective than having governments tax these families in order to purchase the services for them.

11. Harvard economist Robert Barro has published groundbreaking work showing the minor interest rate effects of budget deficits. See Robert Barro, "Have No Fear: Bush Tax Plan Won't Jack Up Interest Rates," *Business Week*, May 5, 2003, p. 24.

12. Unless otherwise noted, all statistics in this chapter come from Office of Management and Budget, *Budget of the U.S. Government, Fiscal Year 2005* (Washington, D.C.: U.S. Government Printing Office, 2004).

13. Mandatory programs are those for which annual spending totals are not set annually, such as Social Security, Medicaid, and most welfare programs. Policymakers decide who is eligible for a program and what the benefit formula will be. For the next several years, total spending is determined by how many eligible individuals enroll in the program and where they fit in the benefit formula. Because these programs run on autopilot, their costs are generally considered "uncontrollable." Entitlements are the fastest growing part of the federal budget.

14. Congressional Budget Office, "Historical Budget Data," from *The Budget and Economic Outlook for Fiscal Years 2005–2014*, January 26, 2004, at *www.cbo.gov/showdoc. cfm?index=1821&sequence=0* (May 19, 2004).

15. These percentages were calculated from the dollar figures provided in Congressional Budget Office, "Historical Budget Data."

16. Congressional Budget Office, "Historical Budget Data."

17. *Ibid.*

18. *Ibid.*

19. *Ibid.*

20. Office of Management and Budget, *Budget of the U.S. Government,* p. 370.

21. Heritage Foundation calculations based on data from the Office and Management and Budget and the Congressional Budget Office.

22. Brian M. Riedl, "Most New Spending Since 2001 Unrelated to the War on Terrorism," Heritage Foundation *Backgrounder* No. 1703, November 13, 2003, at *www. heritage.org/Research/Budget/BG1703.cfm.*

23. *Ibid.*

24. *Ibid.*

25. Office of Management and Budget, *Budget of the United States Government, Fiscal Year 2005: Analytical Perspectives* (Washington, D.C.: U.S. Government Printing Office, 2004), at *www.whitehouse.gov/omb/budget/fy2005/pdf/spec.pdf* (September 23, 2004).

26. Brian M. Riedl, "Another Omnibus Spending Bill Loaded with Pork," Heritage Foundation *WebMemo* No. 377, December 2, 2003, at *www.heritage.org/Research/Budget/wm377.cfm.*

27. For these and more examples of waste, see Brian M. Riedl, "How to Get Federal Spending Under Control" Heritage Foundation *Backgrounder* No. 1733, March 10, 2004, at *http://www.heritage.org/Research/Budget/bg1733.cfm.*

28. Brian M. Riedl, "$20,000 per Household: The Highest Level of Federal Spending Since World War II," Heritage Foundation *Backgrounder* No. 1710, December 3, 2003, at *www.heritage.org/Research/Budget/BG1710.cfm.*

29. Heritage Foundation calculations based on Congressional Budget Office, "Long-Term Budget Outlook," December 2003, at *www.cbo.gov/showdoc.cfm?index=4916&sequence=0* (September 23, 2004).

Chapter 6
Trade in a Challenging World

1. Justus D. Doenecke, "William Appleman Williams and the Anti-Interventionist Tradition," *Diplomatic History*, Vol. 25, No. 2 (Spring 2001), p. 284.

2. *Ibid.,* p.290.

3. Progressive Review, "Free Speech: Words about Freedom and Democracy," at *prorev.com/quotefree.htm* (September 17, 2004).

4. International Monetary Fund, *World Economic Outlook*, September 2002, p. 132, at *www.imf.org/external/pubs/ft/weo/2002/02/index.htm* (September 14, 2004).

5. U.S. Department of Commerce, "Manufacturing in America," January 2004, p.25, at *www.hongkong.usconsulate.gov/usinfo/2004/doc_mfg_report.pdf* (September 14, 2004).

6. Ana Isabel Eiras, "Why America Needs to Support Free Trade," Heritage Foundation *Backgrounder* No. 1761, May 24, 2004, at *www.heritage.org/Research/TradeandForeignAid/bg1761.cfm.*

7. U.S. Department of Commerce, "Manufacturing in America," p. 28.

8. See U.S. Trade Representative, "NAFTA at 10: A Success Story," September 12, 2003, at *www.ustr.gov/Document_Library/Fact_Sheets/2003/NAFTA_at_10_A_Success_Story.html* (September 17, 2004).

9. World Trade Organization, "10 Benefits of the WTO Trading System," April 2003, pp. 10–11, at *www.wto.org/english/thewto_e/whatis_e/10ben_e/10b07_e.htm* (September 14, 2004).

10. U.S. Trade Representative, "NAFTA at 10."

11. U.S. Trade Representative, "U.S. Pork Industry and Trade," *Trade Facts*, June 6, 2003, at *www.thepigsite.com/FeaturedArticle/Default.asp?AREA=Markets&Display=893* (September 17, 2004).

12. Prime Minister Paul Martin, transcript of speech at Sun Valley 2004 Conference, Sun Valley, Idaho, July 7, 2004.

13. Gary Clyde Hufbauer, "NAFTA in a Skeptical Age: The Way Forward," Institute for International Economics, July 2000, at *www.iie.com/publications/papers/hufbauer0700.htm* (September 14, 2004).

14. Gerald P. O'Driscoll, Jr., Kim R. Holmes, and Melanie Kirkpatrick, *2000 Index of Economic Freedom* (Washington, D.C.: The Heritage Foundation and Dow Jones & Company, Inc., 2000), p. 5.

15. Marc A. Miles, Edwin J. Feulner, Jr., and Mary Anastasia O'Grady, *2004 Index of Economic Freedom* (Washington, D.C.: The Heritage Foundation and Dow Jones & Company Inc., 2004), p. 355.

16. Miles, Feulner, and O'Grady, *2004 Index of Economic Freedom*, pp. 121–122.

17. Mike Moore, *A World Without Walls*: *Freedom, Development, Free Trade and Global Governance* (Cambridge, N.Y.: Cambridge University Press, 2003), p. 89.

18. Michael J. Ferrantino, "International Trade, Environmental Quality and Public Policy," *The World Economy*, Vol. 20, No. 1 (January 1997), p.43.

19. Aaron Schavey, "Raising Labor Standards Through Trade," Heritage Foundation *Executive Memorandum* No. 785, October 19, 2001, at *www.heritage.org/Research/TradeandForeignAid/EM785.cfm*.

20. President George W. Bush, "Ignite a New Era of Global Economic Growth Through Free Markets and Free Trade," Part VI in *National Security Strategy*, September 17, 2002, p. 17, at *www.whitehouse.gov/nsc/nssall.html* (September 14, 2004).

21. Robert B. Zoellick, U.S. Trade Representative, testimony before the Committee on Finance, U.S. Senate, March 9, 2004. World Bank research echoes this sentiment, stating that "the evidence from individual cases and from cross-country analysis supports the view that globalization leads to faster growth and poverty reduction in poor countries." See David Dollar and Aart Kraay, "Trade, Growth, and Poverty," World Bank, Development Research Group, June 2001, at *www.imf.org/external/pubs/ft/fandd/2001/09/dollar.htm* (September 14, 2004).

22. Trade Promotion Authority (TPA) gives the President the authority to negotiate free trade agreements and then present them to Congress for an up or down vote. As long as the President has TPA, Congress may not amend an agreement.

23. Robert Zoellick, "The President's Trade Policy Agenda," *2004 Trade Policy Agenda and 2003 Annual Report*, p. 1, at *www.ustr.gov/Document_Library/Reports_Publications/2004/2004_Trade_Policy_Agenda/Section_Index.html* (September 17, 2004).

24. Murray Hiebert, "The Perils of Bilateral Deals," *Far Eastern Economic Review*, December 25, 2003–January 1, 2004.

25. World Trade Organization, Ministerial Declaration, adopted on November 14, 2001, at *www.wto.org/english/thewto_e/minist_e/min01_e/mindecl_e.pdf* (September 14, 2004).

26. Organisation for Economic Co-operation and Development, Directorate for Science, Technology and Industry, Maritime Transport Committee, "Security in Maritime Transport: Risk Factors and Economic Impact," July 2003, p.18, at *www.oecd.org/dataoecd/19/61/18521672.pdf* (September 14, 2004).

27. California Country, "Long Beach Port Keeps California Farm Goods Moving," 2004, at *www.cacountry.tv/2004/2026_1.asp* (September 14, 2004).

28. Port of Miami, "Cargo Facts," Miami–Dade County, at *www.miamidade.gov /portofmiami/cargo_facts.asp* (September 14, 2004).

29. U.S. Department of Homeland Security, remarks given by Asa Hutchinson at the Economic Development Administration's Annual Conference, May 7, 2003, at *www.dhs. gov/dhspublic/display?theme=44&content=626&print=true* (September 14, 2004).

30. "Maritime Will Wrestle With Anti-Terror Regs," *Journal of Commerce Online*, January 7, 2004, at *www.rsicopyright.com/ics/prc_main/select_usertype.html?prc=3.5560.2630140* (September 23, 2004).

31. *Ibid.*

32. Neil Q. Miller, "Special Report: Maritime Emergencies," *Lloyd's List*, December 10, 2003, at *folk.uio.no/erikro/WWW/HNS/press/Neil.pdf* (September 20, 2004).

33. United Nations Conference on Trade and Development, "Efficient Transport and Trade Facilitation to Improve Participation by Developing Countries in International Trade," note by the UNCTAD secretariat, TD/B/COM.3.60, October 3, 2003, p. 11, at *www.unctad.org/en/docs//c3d60_en.pdf* (September 8, 2004). Issued as Item 4 of the provisional agenda for Trade and Development Board, Commission on Enterprise, Business Facilitation and Development, 8th session, Geneva, December 8–12, 2003.

34. Maritime Transport Committee, Directorate of Science, Technology, and Industry, "Security in Maritime Transport: Risk Factors and Economic Impact," July 2003, p. 39, at *www.oecd.org/dataoecd/19/61/18521672.pdf* (September 8, 2004).

35. U.S. Agency for International Development, *U.S. Overseas Loans and Grants and Assistance from International Organizations: Obligations and Loan Authorizations*, July 1, 1945–September 30, 2001, CONG–R–0105, at *www.dec.org/pdf_docs/ PNACR900.pdf* (June 28, 2004).

36. World Bank, *World Development Indicators Online*, 2004, at *www.worldbank.org/data* (September 14, 2004), and U.S. Agency for International Development, "U.S. Overseas Loans and Grants and Assistance from International Organizations."

37. U.S. Agency for International Development, "U.S. Contributions to Trade Capacity Building: Improving Lives Through Trade & Aid," September 2003, p. 2, at *usembassy.state.gov/guatemala/wwwftcbcontributionseng.pdf* (September 14, 2004).

38. *Ibid.*

39. *Ibid.*, p. 5.

40. For instance, the United States helped Nepal join the WTO by identifying "changes to laws, regulations, policies, and procedures necessary to complete negotiations on the terms of WTO membership." See *Ibid.*, p. 10.

41. "Bermuda Based Accenture Wins Department of Homeland Security Contract," CNN, *Lou Dobbs Tonight*, June 1, 2004, at *cnnstudentnews.cnn.com/ TRANSCRIPTS/0406/01/ldt.00.html* (July 2, 2004).

42. U.S. Department of Labor, Bureau of Labor Statistics, "The Employment Situation, June 2004," USDL 04–1170, July 2, 2004, at *www.bls.gov/news.release/empsit. nr0.htm* (July 2, 2004).

43. U.S. Department of Labor, Bureau of Labor Statistics, "Extended Mass Layoffs Associated with Domestic and Overseas Relocations, First Quarter 2004," June 10, 2004, at *bls.gov/news.release/reloc.nr0.htm* (June 29, 2004).

44. Organization for International Investment, "The Facts About Insourcing," at *www.ofii.org/insourcing* (April 27, 2004).

45. Robert Perlman, "U.S. International Tax Reform," testimony before the Committee on Finance, U.S. Senate, March 11, 1999, at *finance.senate.gov/3-11perl.htm* (June 6, 2004).

46. KPMG, "Corporate Tax Rates Survey," January 2004, p. 17, at *www.kpmg.com/Rut2000_prod/Documents/9/2004ctrs.pdf* (June 29, 2004).

47. *Ibid.*, p. 1.

48. Japan has the highest corporate tax burden. *Ibid.*, p. 3.

49. Miles, Feulner, and O'Grady, *2004 Index of Economic Freedom*, p. 231.

50. These principles are similar to those laid out by the declaration of principles that Senator John McCain (R–AZ) included in his amendment (S.Amdt. 3461) to the National Defense Authorization Act for Fiscal Year 2005 (S. 2400).

Chapter 7
The War of Ideas

1. Colin L. Powell, "Remarks on the Occasion of George Kennan's Centenary Birthday," February 4, 2004, at *www.state.gov/secretary/rm/29683.htm* (September 20, 2004).

2. *Ibid.*

3. Andrew C. McCarthy, "The War That Dares Not Speak Its Name," *National Review* online, May 13, 2004, at *www.nationalreview.com/mccarthy/mccarthy200405130837.asp* (September 20, 2004). McCarthy led the prosecution in the case against Sheikh Omar Abdel Rahman, who was accused of masterminding the World Trade Center bombing in 1993.

4. Angelo M. Codevilla, "Heresy and History," *The American Spectator*, May 14, 2004, at *www.spectator.org/dsp_article.asp?art_id=6564* (September 20, 2004).

5. For information regarding Wahhabi Islam, see Stephen Schwartz, *The Two Faces of Islam: Saudi Fundamentalism and Its Role in Terrorism* (New York: Anchor Books, 2003), pp. 101–136. It is particularly relevant that the Wahhabi Kingdom of Saudi Arabia and the Muslim Brotherhood were established during the same decade that saw the official dismantlement of the Caliphate (which represented the religious dimension of the Ottoman Empire) by Atatürk, Turkey's great national leader. Atatürk saw the next step for Turkey as the creation of a strong secular state.

6. See Edward Said, "Orientalism: A Brief Definition," taken from Edward Said, *Orientalism* (New York: Vintage, 1979), at *www.65.107.211.206/post/poldiscourse/pol11.html* (September 20, 2004). See also "Orientalism," at *www.emory.edu/ENGLISH/Bahri/Orientalism.html* (September 20, 2004).

7. Ariel Cohen, "Targeted Killings," *The Washington Times*, March 26, 2004, at *www.washingtontimes.com/commentary/20040325-091452-7923r.htm* (September 20, 2004). These were prescriptions promoted by European Union President Romano Prodi, former French Foreign Minister Dominique de Villepin, German Foreign Minister Joschka Fischer, and French President Jacques Chirac.

8. Karen Armstrong, *Islam: A Short History*, (New York: The Modern Library, 2002), pp. 35–47, 87.

9. Campus Program.com, "Ali bin Abu Talib," at *www.campusprogram.com/reference/en/wikipedia/a/al/ali_ben_abu_talib.html* (September 20, 2004).

10. Codevilla, "Heresy and History," quoting Dore Gold, *Hatred's Kingdom* (Washington, D.C.: Regnery Publishers, 2003).

11. Schwartz, *The Two Faces of Islam*, pp. 96–121, 172–195; and Codevilla, "Heresy and History," pp. 4–5.

12. Michael Dobbs, "A Few Loyal Men Direct bin Laden's Sprawling Network," *The Washington Post*, September 27, 2001, p. A1.

13. For the full list of terrorist organizations, see U.S. Department of State, Office of the Coordinator for Counterterrorism, *2001 Report on Foreign Terrorist Organizations*, October 5, 2001, at *www.state.gov/s/ct/rls/rpt/fto/2001/index.cfm?docid=5258* (September 20, 2004).

14. Timothy Appelby, "Jihad: Not Just a Word for War," *The Globe and Mail* (Toronto), September 20, 2001, *www.theglobeandmail.com/special/attack/pages/other_0920_a8_5.html* (September 20, 2004).

15. Interestingly, Stephen Schwartz noted that in Khomeini's revolutionary struggle against the Shah, the Ayatollah himself never declared a jihad, and in the Bosnian defensive war against the Serbs, no jihad was declared.

16. John Dawson, "The Bali Bombers: What Motivates Death Worship?" *Capitalism Magazine*, October 19, 2003, at *capmag.com/article.asp?ID=3000* (September 20, 2004).

17. Lawrence Auster, "The Clintons, Abdurahman Alamoudi, and the Myth of 'Moderate' Islam," *NewsMax.com*, at *www.newsmax.com/archives/articles/2000/11/6/170946.shtml* (September 20, 2004).

18. "Hardline Cleric in London Rejects 'Terrorist Mastermind' Charge," *The Guardian*, August 10, 1999, at *www.guardian.co.uk/yemen/Story/0,2763,202941,00.html* (September 20, 2004). This was confirmed in a personal interview conducted by the author with a House of Lords staff member who requested anonymity, Washington, D.C., November 21, 2001.

19. Reuters, "Muslims Doubt Arabs Mounted September 11 Attacks," February 27, 2002, at *www.serve.com/Lincolnheritage2/Articles/The_Address__Article_Search/Address_Articles_since_1997/Address__1997___National_Secur/Muslims_doubt_Arabs_mounted_Se/muslims_doubt_arabs_mounted_se.html* (September 20, 2004).

20. White House, *The National Security Strategy of the United States of America*, September 20, 2002, p. 6, at *www.whitehouse.gov/nsc/nss.pdf* (September 20, 2004).

21. Jeff Gerth and Judith Miller, "Philanthropist, or Fount of Funds for Terrorists," *The New York Times*, October 13, 2001, p. B3.

22. Dave Eberhart, "Hamas Touts Untouchable 'Secret' Funding Sources," *NewsMax.com*, December 5, 2001, at *www.newsmax.com/archives/articles/2001/12/4/175008.shtml* (September 20, 2004). See also John K. Cooley, "Islamic Terrorists: Creature of the U.S. Taxpayer?" March 13, 1996, at *www.webcom.com/hrin/magazine/july96/hamas.html* (September 20, 2004).

23. Stephen Schwartz, "Wahhabism and Islam in the U.S.," testimony before the Sub-committee on Terrorism, Technology and Homeland Security, Committee on the Judiciary, U.S. Senate, June 30, 2003, at *www.defenddemocracy.org/in_the_media/ in_the_media_show.htm?doc_id=180218* (September 20, 2004).

24. See United Nations Development Programme, *Arab Human Development Report 2002*, at *www.undp.org/rbas/ahdr/english2002.html* (September 20, 2004) and *Arab Human Development Report 2003*, at *www.undp.org/rbas/ahdr/english2003.html* (September 20, 2004).

25. Middle East Media Research Institute, "Terror in America (4)," *Special Dispatch Series* No. 270, September 20, 2001, at *www.memri.org/bin/articles. cgi?Area=jordan&ID=SP27001* (September 20, 2004).

26. Adnan Malik, "Gunmen Kill At Least Six at Saudi Oil Facility," Associated Press, May 1, 2004.

27. CBS, "Al-Qaeda Claims Saudi Strike," June 13, 2004, at *www.cbsnews.com/sto-ries/2004/05/29/terror/main620280.shtml* (September 20, 2004).

28. The Middle East Media Research Institute, "Terror in America (4)."

29. *Ibid.*

30. *Ibid.*

31. Middle East Media Research Institute, "Terror in America (28)," *Special Dispatch Series* No. 303, November 27, 2001, at *www.memri.org/bin/articles. cgi?Area=middleeast&ID=SP30301* (September 20, 2004).

32. Middle East Media Research Institute, "Terror in America (24)," *Special Dispatch Series* No. 297, November 7, 2001, at *www.memri.org/bin/articles. cgi?Area=jihad&ID=SP29701* (September 20, 2004).

33. For more about culture clash in Muslim education in the United States, see Valerie Strauss and Emily Wax, "Where the Two Worlds Collide: Muslim Schools Face Tension of Islamic, U.S. Views," *The Washington Post*, February 25, 2002, p. A1.

34. Republican Policy Committee, "The Need for U.S.–Saudi Cooperation to Win the War on Terrorism," June 2, 2003, pp. 7–12.

35. The reported pro-American sentiments among the less religious, middle-class Iran-ian urban youth can be seen as a protest against the ruling clerics and do not con-tradict the phenomenon elsewhere.

36. Arnaud de Borchgrave, "Holy Warriors of Pakistan," United Press International, December 28, 2001.

37. *Ibid.*

38. Barry Shlichter, "Inside Islamic Seminaries, Where the Taliban Was Born," *The Philadelphia Inquirer*, November 25, 2001, p. A23.

39. Rick Bragg, "Nurturing Young Islamic Hearts and Hatreds," *The New York Times*, October 13, 2001, p. A1.

40. Glenn R. Simpson, "Diplomatic Visas of Saudis Revoked for Preaching Wahhabism at Virginia Schools," *The Wall Street Journal*, January 30, 2004, p. A4.

41. Frank Gaffney, "Preaching Terror," Center for Security Policy, *Decision Brief* No. 03–D39, October 10, 2003, at *www.centerforsecuritypolicy.org/index. jsp?section=papers&code=03-D_39* (September 20, 2004). Captain James Yee, a

military chaplain at Guantanamo, accused by the U.S. military of major security violations and later acquitted on a technicality, was trained in one of these institutions, as well as in Syria.

42. Daniel McGrory, "Militants Outside Control of Mosques Target Teenagers," *The Times of London*, December 28, 2001, at *www.thetimes.co.uk/article/0,,2001570018-2001602324,00.html* (September 20, 2004).

43. Author interviews with members of the United Kingdom's House of Lords who requested anonymity, January 2003.

44. J. Michael Waller, "A Resounding Voice in Traditional Islam: Sheik Muhammad Hisham Kabbani" *Insight Magazine*, October 1, 2002, at *www.iwp.edu/news/newsID.93/news_detail.asp* (September 20, 2004).

45. Sheikh Abdul Hadi Palazzi, "Radical Islamists Have Perverted the Traditions of Islam," October 10, 2001, at *members.xoom.virgilio.it/amislam/kabbani2.htm* (September 20, 2004).

46. Ted Thornton, "History of the Middle East Database," at *www.nmhschool.org/tthornton/mehistorydatabase/fatima_mernissi.htm* (September 20, 2004).

47. Irshad Manji, *The Trouble With Islam, A Muslim's Call for Reform in Her Faith* (New York: St. Martin's Press, 2003), chapters 1 and 6. See also Muslim-Refusenik.com, "The Official Site of Irshad Manji," at *www.muslim-refusenik.com/* (September 20, 2004).

48. Ibn Warraq, *Leaving Islam* (New York: Prometheus Books, 2003).

49. Muqtedar Khan, "Muslims Condemn Israel But Ignore Their Own Crimes," *The Daily Telegraph*, November 17, 2001, at *www.portal.telegraph.co.uk/news/main.jhtml?xml=%2Fnews%2F2001%2F11%2F17%2Fwkhan17.xml* (September 20, 2004).

50. The Middle East Media Research Institute, "The Fight Against Terrorism Must Begin With Curricular, Educational, and Media Reform in the Arab World," *Special Dispatch Series* No. 307, December 4, 2001, at *www.memri.org/bin/articles/cgi?Area=persiangulf&ID=SP30701* (September 20, 2004).

51. Robert Satloff, "Devising a Public Diplomacy Campaign Toward the Middle East," Washington Institute for Near East Policy, *Policy Watch* No. 579, October 30, 2001, at *www.washingtoninstitute.org/watch/Policywatch/policywatch2001/579.htm* (September 20, 2004).

52. Adrian Karatnycky, "Essay: The 2001–2002 Freedom House Survey of Freedom: The Democracy Gap," at *www.freedomhouse.org/research/freeworld/2002/akessay.pdf* (September 23, 2004).

53. Miles, Feulner, and O'Grady, *2004 Index of Economic Freedom*, passim.

54. Satloff, "Devising a Public Diplomacy Campaign Toward the Middle East."

55. Alexandra Starr, "Charlotte Beers' Toughest Sell," *BusinessWeek www.businessweek.com/@@*f5NQYQQo6iUuAsA/magazine/content/01_51/b3762098.htm* (September 23, 2004).

56. Interviews by author with Voice of America personnel, January–February 2002.

57. Colin L. Powell, "The Marshall Plan: The Vision of a Family of Nations," July 13, 2004, at *www.state.gov/secretary/rm/34374.htm* (September 20, 2004).

Appendix 1

1. See George Kennan, "The Long Telegram," at *www.gwu.edu/~nsarchiv/coldwar/ documents/episode-1/kennan.htm* (September 20, 2004).

Appendix 2

1. For the full text of this report, see National Security Council, "NSC 68: United States Objectives and Programs for National Security," April 14, 1950, at *www. fas.org/irp/offdocs/nsc-hst/nsc-68.htm* (September 20, 2004).

Appendix 4

1. This appendix is excerpted from The White House, *The National Security Strategy of the United States of America*, September 2002, at *www.whitehouse. gov/nsc/nss.pdf* (September 24, 2004).

Appendix 6

1. See L. Arthur Minnich, notes concerning the McCarthy hearings, May 17, 1954, at *www.eisenhower.archives.gov/dl/McCarthy/Minnich51754reMccarthypg1. pdf* and *www.eisenhower.archives.gov/dl/McCarthy/Minnich51754reMccarthypg2. pdf* (September 24, 2004).

Appendix 7

1. Text can be found online at *teachingamericanhistory.org/library/index. asp?document=425* (September 24, 2004).

Appendix 8

1. For more information about the Church Committee reports and for the complete text of selected documents, see "COINTELPRO," at *www.icdc.com/~paulwolf/ cointelpro/cointel.htm* (September 24, 2004).
2. The text of this appendix was taken from "Supplemental Detailed Staff Reports on Intelligence Activities and the Rights of Americans," Select Committee to Study Governmental Operations, U.S. Senate, Report No. 94–755 (April 23, 1976), at *www.gulfwarvets.com/cointelpro.htm* (September 29, 2004).

Appendix 9

1. For the full text of the USA Patriot Act, see *frwebgate.access.gpo.gov/cgi-bin/getdoc. cgi?dbname=107_cong_public_laws&docid=f:publ056.107* (September 24, 2004).

Appendix 16

1. See Federation of American Scientists, at *www.fas.org/irp/world/para/docs/ 980223-fatwa.htm* (September 24, 2004).

Index

Contributors

Dr. James Jay Carafano, Senior Research Fellow on Defense and Homeland Security at the Kathryn and Shelby Cullom Davis Institute for International Studies at The Heritage Foundation, is a principal contributor to this book and the author of Chapters One and Two, *Taking the Offensive* and *Protecting the Homeland*. A graduate of West Point and the U.S. Army War College, Dr. Carafano earned his Ph.D. from Georgetown University and now researches national security relative to the long-term interests of the United States. Before joining Heritage, he spent 25 years in the U.S. Army, where he served as the head speechwriter for the Army Chief of Staff and executive editor of *Joint Force Quarterly*, the Defense Department's premier professional military journal. He is the author of two books, *Waltzing Into the Cold War* and *After D-Day*.

Dr. Ariel Cohen is the principal author of Chapter Seven, *The War of Ideas*. Dr. Cohen is a Research Fellow at the Kathryn and Shelby Cullom Davis Institute for International Studies at The Heritage Foundation, where he studies the former Soviet republics, the global war on terrorism, and the continuing conflict in the Middle East. He is also a member of the Council on Foreign Relations, the International Institute for Strategic Studies in London, and the American Association for the Advancement of Slavic Studies. He is the author of *Russian Imperialism: Development and Crisis*. Dr. Cohen received his Ph.D. at the Fletcher School of Law and Diplomacy at Tufts University and has served as a consultant to both the executive branch and the private sector about policy toward Russia, Eastern and Central Europe, the Caucasus, and Central Asia. He was also an audience researcher for Radio Liberty–Radio Free Europe's Media and Opinion Research.

Sara F. Cooper, formerly a trade policy analyst at The Heritage Foundation in the Center for International Trade and Economics, contributed to Chapter Six, *Trade in a Challenging World*. Mrs. Cooper graduated from George Mason University with a master's degree in international commerce and policy. Before joining Heritage she served at Americans for Tax Reform, a Washington-based watchdog group.

Dr. Daniel Mitchell, contributor to Chapter Five, *Guns and Butter*, holds a Ph.D. in Economics from George Mason University. Dr. Mitchell is the McKenna Senior Fellow in Political Economy at The Heritage Foundation's Thomas A. Roe Institute for Economic Policy Studies, where he is also the chief expert on tax policy and the economy. Before joining Heritage Dr. Mitchell was an economist for Senator Bob Packwood (R–OR) and the Senate Finance Committee and served on the 1988 Bush/Quayle transition team.

Brian Riedl, Hermann Fellow in Federal Budgetary Affairs at the Thomas A. Roe Institute for Economic Policy Studies at The Heritage Foundation, contributed to Chapter Five, *Guns and Butter*. Mr. Riedl is the lead budget analyst at The Heritage Foundation and holds a master's degree in public affairs from Princeton University. Before coming to Heritage, Mr. Riedl worked for Representative Mark Green (R–WI) and as a policy analyst for former Wisconsin Governor Tommy Thompson.

Paul Rosenzweig, Senior Legal Research Fellow at The Heritage Foundation's Center for Legal and Judicial Studies, is a principal contributor to this book and author of Chapters Three and Four, *Between Liberty and Order* and *After the Patriot Act*. Mr. Rosenzweig is a *cum laude* graduate of the University of Chicago School of Law and has served as Senior Litigation Counsel in the Office of the Independent Counsel. His current work at the Center for Legal and Judicial Studies includes research on issues of civil liberties and national security, criminal law, law enforcement, and legal ethics.

Baker Spring, contributor to Chapter Five, *Guns and Butter*, is the F.M. Kirby Research Fellow in National Security Policy at The Heritage Foundation's Kathryn and Shelby Cullom Davis Institute for International Studies. In this capacity, he focuses on U.S. national security studies. Before coming to Heritage, Mr. Spring served as a defense and foreign policy expert in the offices of two U.S. senators. A graduate of Washington and Lee University, Mr. Spring received his M.A. in national security studies from Georgetown University.

Acknowledgments

Thanks to Edwin Meese III and Larry Wortzel for their support and guidance in bringing this project to fruition. Thanks also to Todd Gaziano, Rachel Brand, Dan Gallington, K.A. Taipale, and Jim Dempsey for their contributions to the understanding of civil liberties and domestic counterterrorism issues. Likewise, thanks to Marc Miles, Ana Eiras, and Anthony Kim for their insights about international trade and development issues, as well as to Jack Spencer and Michael Scardaville for giving their views on defense and homeland security.

A special thank you to former Governor James Gilmore of Virginia who generously shared his time and views with Heritage scholars, helping us to think through the tough challenges of protecting the nation and the rights and liberties of its citizens. Thank you as well to Alison Fraser for her superb efforts in organizing the contributions to Chapter Five on the domestic economy. Special thanks to Ha Nguyen and Alane Kochems, brilliant researchers who made the production of this book possible, as well as to our intern, Rebekah Robblee, for all of her hard work.

Most of all, our most heartfelt thanks to our editor, Marla Graves, and the watchful eye and peerless wisdom of Richard Odermatt, The Heritage Foundation's Senior Editor. Senior Copy Editor William Poole; Publishing Services Director Jonathan Larsen and his associates Therese Pennefather, Elizabeth Brewer, and Alex Adrianson; Jim Peters; and Khristine Bershers were also invaluable resources during the editing, design, production, and distribution of this book. Thanks also to Rena Cohen, who did additional editing and proofreading on Chapter Seven. We are grateful to *The Duquesne Law Review* for allowing us to reprint portions of Chapters Three and Four from Paul Rosenzweig's article, "Civil Liberties and Terrorism."

Finally, thank you to the many contributors and supporters of The Heritage Foundation, whose generous support makes our work possible.